The Zone of Indifference

"SURVIVAL *in competition depends on the ability to maintain* RELATIVE *competitive strength at a level which permits the existence of a boundary of indifference . . ."*

Kenneth E. Boulding,
PROFESSOR OF ECONOMICS,
UNIVERSITY OF MICHIGAN

Also by Robert Strausz-Hupé

AXIS AMERICA

GEOPOLITICS

THE BALANCE OF TOMORROW

INTERNATIONAL RELATIONS
  (With Stefan T. Possony)

THE ZONE OF INDIFFERENCE

Robert Strausz-Hupé

G. P. PUTNAM'S SONS NEW YORK

ACKNOWLEDGMENT

My greatest debt is owed to my wife whose judicious comments and perceptive eye for the heart of the matter are responsible for clearing the dialectic underbrush in which I incline to stray.

My thanks go to Mary Francis Harvey and Stefan T. Possony who read the manuscript and contributed valuable insights to the sociological analysis which prefaces this book. Their critique was all the more valuable because it hardened my convictions. I am beholden to Helen Thorington and Jonathan King for thoughtful editorial suggestions and the painstaking preparation of the manuscript for the press.

ROBERT STRAUSZ-HUPÉ

Newtown Square, Pa.

CONTENTS

AND UPON THE EARTH DISTRESS
OF NATIONS, WITH PERPLEXITY

(ST. LUKE 21:25)

I
The Critical Issue

THE DEBATED GROUND

IF IT is at all possible to reduce the historic developments of the last fifty years to one fact it is this: the close of the European Age. Europe, only a generation ago the center of world power, is now the debated ground upon which powers more powerful than any European nation contest the part Europe is to play in the world order. If American intervention in two world wars that began in Europe has one meaning it is this: to redress the balance of the Old World and thus to act out Canning's rhetoric challenge of a hundred years ago. If recent American foreign policy has held, despite vacillations and contradictions, to one purpose it is this: to raise Europe from the ruins of her former might, forge a Western alliance, and erect the political and military framework of a new and larger structure, the Western Community. It is within the broad context of this policy that we must view American relationships to Europe, to individual European states, and to the globe.

American foreign policy is determined by a choice between alternatives. The United States chose Europe as the principal target of its initiative. That choice has been made and is irreversible. The preservation of the Western Community and hence the defense of Europe have precedence over all other commitments of the United States in world politics. If it is not this decision that oriented American foreign policy then its meaning is indeed that of a child's tale told by an idiot. That the struggle for Europe is being fought out in many places along the arching rim of Eurasia, indeed upon the entire globe, does not belie the fact that its stakes are Europe.

3

The second world war, too, was fought upon every ocean and every continent; its stakes were Europe. Nothing has given rise to as much confusion in American public debate as the geographical ubiquity of a conflict that has but one principal issue: the control of Europe. American foreign policy has been directed toward the settlement of this principal issue. Communist doctrine supplies a challenging reminder that there can be no other choice: Lenin and Stalin viewed Communist conquest of Asia as a vast flanking maneuver depriving Europe of colonial markets and sources of cheap raw materials and thus setting the stage for proletarian revolution in Europe.* Lenin's ultimate goal was European revolution, not Asian conquest. If the United States, mistaking the place where the issue was met for the place over which it arose, should abandon the primacy of Europe to the expediency of Asiatic strategy, it will play the game of Soviet strategy. The objective of Soviet strategy is the control of the industrial regions of Europe.

The United States, by its deliberate choice, faces a dilemma. The defense of Europe is its first concern; yet Europe cannot be defended without Europe's own concerted effort—and Europe is weak. Europe is weak because in the second world war there were no European victors, only categories of the defeated. Europe is weak because it is divided at its geo-

* "... Precisely as a result of the first imperialist war, the East has been definitely drawn into the revolutionary movement, into the general maelstrom of the world revolutionary movement..." (Lenin, *Selected Works*, Vol. IX, p. 399).

"Leninism has proved, and the imperialist war and the revolution in Russia have confirmed, that the national problem can be solved only in connection with and on the basis of the proletarian revolution, and that the road to victory of the revolution in the West lies through the revolutionary alliance with the liberation movement of the colonies and dependent countries against imperialism. The national problem is a part of the general problem...."
(Stalin, *Problems of Leninism*. Foreign Languages Publishing House, Moscow, 1941. The above quotations are from a reprint, in this book, of a lecture delivered by Stalin at Sverdlov University, April 1924, on "Foundations of Leninism.")

graphical center. Europe is weak because its most ancient nations are rent by internecine conflict. Europe is weak because it doubts itself.

The United States set out to tackle the "European Problem" in the characteristic fashion of a banker appointed by the court to reorganize a string of bankrupt undertakings. The "problem" was to raise new working capital, to consolidate balance sheets, and to restore Europe's national economies as working concerns. This solution, it was expected, would take care of the social problems. The latter, it was assumed, derived from the economic distress of the European masses. Communism was equated with a low average standard of living, for did not Communism thrive where men were barred, for one reason or another, from the enjoyment of the good things in life, which good things were theirs by right under the dispensation of bountiful technology? To be sure, this was not the one and only assumption underlying American policies in Europe which culminated in the Marshall Plan. However, the equation, Communism = low standard of living, was indisputably the major one. It was so understood by the American public. That the United States proceeded to apply the social philosophy of Marxianism to the "European Problem" while the Soviet Union mainly confined itself, in its attempt to check American policies, to the bourgeois pursuit of power politics and manipulation of ideas, is only a seeming paradox. Each side fought the battle with what it had and had enough of to spare for the account of international politics: the United States, a surplus of goods; the Soviet Union, a surplus of troops and slogans. Both sides succeeded halfway: the United States managed to put the national economies of Europe back in working order and thus to stave off what might have turned from an economic into a political and revolutionary crisis; the Soviet Union managed to force the United States to shift the base of its foreign policy, to extend the scope and cost of American economic aid, and to retain its ideological levers on the minds of large masses of Europeans. American foreign policy now emphasized the military defense of Europe and led in the development of those complex arrangements which were to consolidate the political alliance of the United States and the states of Western Europe into a joint military organization, to facilitate the rearmament of Western Europe, and to ease the inclusion of Germany into the American-European defensive system. These endeavors were carried forth under an official terminology which stressed the common stake of the contracting parties in the purpose of the alliance and minimized the claims to national sovereignty which might have obstructed—and in fact, continued to obstruct—the co-operation of the treaty partners. Such official designations as, for example, North Atlantic Pact, North Atlantic Treaty Organization, European Defense Community, and Council of Europe, and the increasing usage by statesmen and publicists of such terms as Atlantic Community and Western Community infer the existence of an overarching community of interests, joining the peoples of Western Europe among themselves and Europe and America to each other.

The avowed purpose of these co-operative arrangements is the common defense not only against Communist Russia's military aggression but also against Soviet ideology as the negation of the political and moral ideals of the West. Thus these political and moral ideals must be taken as true factors of Western power: vital forces nourishing the common will to resist and to co-operate in peace and war. That they are indeed so taken by the common consent of governments and the most influential segments of public opinion is attested by ubiquitous and emphatic references to the "Battle for the Mind of Man," in which psychological or spiritual forces are pitted against the onslaught of Stalinism in its diverse ideological and philosophical guises. Obviously, if it were not for these political and moral ideals, then there would be no

reason for most Europeans to choose the Atlantic Community in preference to the Soviet-Satellite Community, except,
perhaps, because of the benefits they derive from the greater
efficiency and productivity of American technology. Not even
the most convinced advocate of American economic intervention, as a means to "raise average standards of living" or
forge lethal instruments and thus to combat Communism,
will care to bank on American "know-how" and plant capacity
as the sole attractions which will keep the European peoples
wedded to the democratic way of life. If it is ideals that matter
—be they vital forces or merely powerful illusions—then the
question must be asked: What are the ideals which the West
holds in common and how strong a bond is the spiritual and
intellectual communion that joins Europe and the United
States?

Once this question is conceded as being relevant and
urgent, the political, economic, and military problems of the
Western Community, its organization and defense against the
Soviet Union must be viewed as pertaining to a wider, en-
compassing context. The striving for unity and strength
through unity presupposes the existence of a community of
devotion, a culture. If Western culture were a meaningless
concept or if it were not worth defending, then the vast
mobilization of ingenuity and hardware in which the Atlantic
nations now employ their most precious resources would
serve no other end but the brutish power interests of individual states and their rulers. That Western culture *is* meaningless and not worth defending and that the West has no
vision beyond the preservation of its naked power is what
Soviet propaganda keeps on saying. Thus the question of the
life and meaning of Western culture is much too serious a
question to be relegated to the mere periphery of the statesman's concern. *It is the question of the survival of the West,
political, economic, intellectual, and spiritual.*

The underlying hypothesis of this study is simple: if Western culture shall endure it must remain whole. Even if, upon the falling apart of Western culture, its fragments were to subsist, then it is unlikely that the schism could be ever healed. The cut would run through the culture's heart. Even if one accepts, as this writer does not, the optimistic assumption that the culture of the West will meet that of the East halfway and blend into a new universal culture, it would be necessary, albeit probably not sufficient, that Western culture enter this marriage as a sentient, living whole. Prior dismemberment will not induce nuptial bliss.

If Western culture is to remain whole, cultural developments in Europe and the United States must converge rather than diverge. So banal is this statement that one is tempted to search for a more subtle definition. Common roots notwithstanding, America has shaped her distinctive cultural environment, and the culture of Europe is a congeries of lively subcultures. Thus far, however, the accommodation of unity and diversity has kept pace with growth. The sum of the affinities that link the centers of Western culture to each other is larger than the sum of affinities that link them singly to non-Western cultures. These plus and minus signs still satisfy the estimate that the Western peoples make of themselves and, equally important, the estimate that other peoples make of the West. Evidently, the lines have been crossed at innumerable places; the edges of all the great historic cultures are fuzzy. The paraphernalia of Western culture are spread over Asia and Africa: the lingua franca of India is English, and Oxford- and Sorbonne-educated Africans administer justice, in their native lands, on the basis of the legal codes of Europe. There is, there always has been, interpenetration of cultures at their peripheries. But Western culture is still a discrete whole. Western culture has not become *the* world culture; nor have the cultures of Africa and Asia yielded their profoundly felt, emphatically stated and restated otherness to the expansive sweep of Western culture.*

How European is American culture? The influence of American and European cultural developments upon each other and of different geographical environments upon each gave rise to cultural differentiations which, as early as the beginning of the nineteenth century, called for a revision of terms: The concept of European culture no longer encompassed the physical as well as spiritual dimensions of the American scene nor, for that matter, the new dimensions of European settlement in other continents. Where there had been, up until the end of the eighteenth century, one center of gravity whence radiated the influences of material power and of culture, there were now several. What had been a one-way motion was now being replaced by reciprocity. The geographical extension of European culture now generated countervailing movements which modified European culture itself. By the end of the nineteenth century, European culture, which from the time of the subsidence of the Islamic wave and the decline of the Byzantine Empire had preserved a vigorous autonomy, was no longer European. The concept of Western culture, a literary concept, gained currency toward the end of the nineteenth century, and served as the

* The achievement of this or that aesthetical synthesis is as much an argument against, as it is an argument for, the blending of two cultures: the use of African tribal motives of design and sculpture by Pablo Picasso in his easel paintings, an art form that has never called forth the African's creative genius, does not signify the "Africanization" of Western art. Nor does it spell a relapse of Western culture into some sort of primitivism—because neither Picasso nor the African artists who inspired him were "primitive." Art is never "primitive." The discussion would be hardly worth the candle were not the market flooded by superficial generalizations on the "internationalism" of art and the "meeting" of cultures. The melting-pot concept of culture is not more absurd than the claim of this or that race or nation to superlative creativeness: its principal contribution to the cause of beauty and truth has been, thus far, the tepid camaraderie of high-brow rotarians. The discovery of the common language of all creative endeavor is as startling as was the discovery of Molière's cultural *arriviste* that he had been speaking prose all the time.

collective term gathering up related, yet discrete, entities. It anticipated changes in demographic and economic relationships and in the distribution of political power long before the peoples of Europe and Europe's settlements overseas had grasped the fact that the epoch of Europe's hegemony had closed. The European Age had come to an end. The Bolshevik revolution, isolating Russia and accelerating the shift of Russia's march toward Asia, and the dissolution of the British Empire, mark the culmination of the process—negatively. Negatively, because both the withdrawal of Russia and the decline of Britain as a world power must be taken for what they are: defeats of the West. There was, indeed, only one compensatory development, the rise of the United States to the status of a world power. European predominance had ended; the succession had passed to the nearest of kin. Western culture is Europe-in-decline and the United States-in-ascendant. And the dynamics of growth that characterize the parts pose the principal problem of the whole.

Ideally, both entities should draw nourishment from the common culture; the more individual features sharpen, the more common characteristics re-enforce the whole. But just as the amoeba must separate so that the parent body shall not perish, so a limit is set to the capacity of culture to contain the divers growth tendencies of its parts. Such a limit was reached by the culture of the Roman world when the division into an Eastern and a Western empire occurred. No contemporary records show that, at the time of separation, anyone faintly suspected either the growth of two distinct cultures, or an ultimate antagonism so vehement as to entail the extinction of one culture and protracted, mortal peril to the other. Rome was to call upon the barbarians of the north, Byzantium upon those of Asia. The strange tides swept over both.

The phenomenon cannot be explained by a theory of geographical optimum size. The Roman Empire managed to dominate and administer for several centuries territories that considerably exceeded its size at the time of the division. The renewal of Asiatic pressure from without the Empire, coinciding with the increase of tensions within it, hastened the crisis of the Mediterranean world. But the cultural conflict which wrenched the old gods from their pedestals and drained the new faith into tortuous schisms, prevented what now seems to us so logical a step: reconciliation in the face of a common threat. For the increasing irrationality of the Hellenistic world, rent by ideological antagonism, is analogous to the battle of reason which is being waged in this century. Not only did the awareness of irrational forces, beating upon the serene edifice of classic civilization, pervade the thought of Stoics and Neoplatonists; their method, concerned as it was with shoring up rational systems and ethical absolutes against the anarchy of words and terms, is none other than that of modern semantics.

The suggestion, nay, the allusion, that Western culture could succumb to fatal schisms as did the ancient world may provoke most varied and vehement objections, if not amusement and derision. Western history, up until our own times, is the clash of nations, but it is also a universal, a common quest. There is a vertical history of national rivalries; there is a horizontal history of the West. It is the latter history which sets forth the common unity of events in which all Western peoples participate. Since sociology addresses itself to the community of events shared by individuals, we may speak of sociological history as the study and interpretation of the universe of historic formations.

The historic landscape is instantly transformed. The antagonism of nations is then but the whirlpool of the historic stream. The Spain of the Catholic kings, the France of Louis XI, and the England of Henry VII were locked in innumerable rivalries and conflicts; yet they developed together the system of kingship as a focal point of central power pitted against feudal anarchy. It was this concentration of political power which engendered the growth of national administrative systems, the expansion of commerce, and the accumulation of national treasuries. It is these developments which provided, in turn, the resources and organization of the greatest European undertaking: the great discoveries. In this vast enterprise all European peoples shared: Portugal, Spain, Holland, England, Scandinavia, Russia, and, in the persons of their astronomers, cartographers, navigators, soldiers, and mere adventurers, the peoples of Italy and the Germanies. There is a close conjunction in time: when Spain, Holland, and England founded their maritime empires Russia began her eastward march which pushed back the Turco-Mongols and reached the Pacific.*

To this day, the West pays greater homage to its national heroes, the heroes of its internecine strife, than to the heroes of its common undertakings. As we contemplate the latter through the eyes of, let us say, Asia, the perspectives change: Napoleon becomes a minor Ghengis Khan, Louis XIV is dwarfed by Shah Jehan, and such celebrated makers of national unity as Bismarck and Cavour appear, as regards quantitative achievement, skill and wisdom, as mere tyros compared with a long line of Chinese statesmen engaged in the same organizational task. But the exploits of Cortes, Pizarro, Clive, Stanley, Bugeaud, Lyautey, Rhodes, Muraviëv were conquests on an Asiatic scale. So were the deeds of casual, half-forgotten conquerors of the American plainslands and the Western Pacific, half-forgotten because they *were* conquerors and because the conqueror-colonizer is not admitted to the American pantheon, reserved for lawgivers, emancipators, crusaders for causes, and the generals who captained the crusaders' causes.

The bulk of Western historiography insists on magnifying

---

* Emmanuel Berl, *Histoire de l'Europe*, Paris, Gallimard, 1945, Vol. I, p. 14.

the rivalries of nations and the reputations of the national protagonists of these rivalries (who, more often than not, left their respective nations poorer than they were before their heroic performances). To an Asiatic the meaning of Western history is contained in its common achievements.

It has become the fashion among Western scholars to stress the dog-eat-dog practices of Western imperialisms and thus to acknowledge, explicitly or implicitly, the validity of the Marxist-Leninist thesis of the projection of the class struggle into world politics. That learned men keep on teaching this one-sided version of the triumphal march of Western culture reflects the wide acceptance of "tough" Darwinism, to which Marxism emotionally owes more than to its own economic theory. What is remarkable about Western imperialisms is not that the "fittest" survived but that the "fit" and the less fit struck a remarkable balance of accommodation and that Western culture offered the non-Western, "conquered" peoples an immeasurably richer variety of forms, as rich as the variety of its national expressions, than any other expansive culture of history.*

If the egoistic, nation-centric drives of Western man had been in truth the dominant ones of his social and political behavior, if the spread of Western culture was merely an accidental consequence of imperialist struggles "for survival," then the universality of Western culture and its irresistible drawing power vis-à-vis non-Western peoples are inexplicable mysteries—then logically Western culture should not exist. If, therefore, we propose as a serious hypothesis the deepening schism of Western culture we do not do so on the basis of evidence derived from the history of imperialist rivalries—

---

* Just as biologically the co-operative forces, the group centered drives, are as vital as, and perhaps more important than, natural selection, so the dominant principle of social and cultural life is coeval with life itself. See M. F. Ashley Montagu, "The Origin and Nature of Social Life and the Biological Basis of Co-operation," *Horizon*, Vol. 19, No. 119; pp. 388-90.

or even of war. The best than can be said about the theory of war as the destroyer of culture is that it is inconclusive. It is probably no theory at all but a tautology. War is not the "originator of all things," including progress; neither is war the specific disease of Western culture.* Tensions lead to war and are generated by what men think, say, and do; the nature of war is determined by the nature of the tensions which war releases and by what men think, say, and do about war. The wars of the eighteenth century were "limited"— and, by our standards, incredibly humane—not because the issues then were less sharply drawn than today or because the civilization was incapable of producing instruments as effective as ours for destroying culture (the cultures of Bactria, Samarkand, and Persia were literally annihilated by bow and arrow, sword, and torch), but because the co-operative drives of eighteenth-century society checked and outpaced disruptive trends.

War may or may not put the final touches upon the dismemberment of Western culture *after* it has accomplished its own disintegration. The process of disintegration takes place, like all social processes, in the realm of the Social Mind.

Man, it has been said, is a "social animal." What does this trite epigram reveal about the nature of man? What else than that his body and soul matter to society only in so far as they determine his nature as a social being? Wherein does man differ from other beings, such as ants, bees, and partridges who lead "social" lives? Three characteristics are peculiarly combined in the nature of man and form the basis of *human* society. Man is a living being because he is possessed of body and soul. Man is an associative being because he lives, as do other species, in groups and shares in the life and activities of the group with a certain part of his powers. Society can only be envisaged as coexistence, co-operation, and conflict

---

* Toynbee's theory—war the destroyer—puts an idealist cart before a materialist horse. See his *Civilization on Trial,* New York, Oxford, 1948.

of groups. Since there are only individuals in society it is they, and they alone, who are the factors of social life. However, human life is associative life. Man is ever in the company of fellow men. Association is a process, not a static condition, a "fact." It is a "procession of activities, a come and go of action, interaction, re-action and counter-action." * This activity is partly haphazard and idle; it is partly purposeful and creative.

What distinguishes *human* society from all other groups and forms of life is its mental context. By the power of his mind man is capable of lifting himself above general causal relationships and the processes of nature. The sorting out of particular causal relationships and the development of self-awareness are accomplished by the objectivation of mental processes and their expression through signs and symbols which are "meaningful" and "significant." These signs and symbols can be communicated to others. The principal means of communication is speech. Mind links men to each other.

Men are linked to each other through meaning and purpose. This is true also of the beehive and the anthill. However, it is mental reality that joins the members of human association, holds them together, and orients their conduct. This overarching mental reality humanizes the herd and transforms it into human society.

The human mind can thus be conceived as composed of three related, yet discrete parts: the personal, the interpersonal, and the social. The personal component is the realm of dreams, mystical experience, anxiety. The interpersonal component comprises one's relationships to others, love, friendship and kinship, and corresponding deprivations. The social component encompasses one's relationships to others as groups and organizations and to "objective" ideas. It is only this component which is "social" in the proper sense. Within

* Harry Alpert, *Emile Durkheim and His Sociology*, New York, Columbia University Press, 1939; p. 155.

it—the Social Mind—hold sway the great political and religious ideologies, supplying the interpretation of correct and faulty thinking and right and wrong conduct, and Utopian ideals and aspirations, supplying the interpretation of "what ought to be." The social universe is hence composed not only of ideas and motives which lead men toward each other, join them, and induce them to act jointly, but also of the products of human thought which issue from co-operation and sustain society. These products of human thought, issuing from the junction of many minds and minds of generations and sustaining society, are bodied forth in such distinct shapes as community, church, and state. Men have conceived community, church, and state as concrete realities and, often, as manifestations of supernatural power.

"Social facts" have no meaning outside the social mental component, the Social Mind. Institutions, modes of association, tools of production and products, as well as ideologies and utopias, strongly or weakly held values, and the making of choices between values; all these are social realities. Social reality includes "what ought to be" and the differences of opinion to which differing interpretations of "what ought to be" give rise. These differences revolve around the nature and form of power; the social organization of association and the limits of organization; what association should or should *not* be organized; the hierarchy of values; and, finally, the validity of existing institutions, their maintenance or modification or destruction.

Constitutions, statute books, and moral codes are social realities because they express the attitudes of society. If they no longer express these attitudes they are still "facts," to wit, historical or legal or anthropological data. They are no longer part of associative life. They have lost their social meaning. The Crown is invested by the thoughts and sentiments of the British people with a power which cannot be defined legally or constitutionally or even politically; yet this power is "real" because it is felt as "real" by British society. The Constitution is enshrined in the thoughts and feelings of the American people. It is a social "fact" above and impervious to the "facts" of jurisprudence. The Constitution "lives." The Soviet Constitution probably is, by the rote of organic law making, a "good" constitution. It is likely that not a few Russians are willing to give their lives for Stalin or the proletarian revolution or the kolkhoz; it is certain that no Russian, Stalin included, is prepared to do and die for the Soviet Constitution.

The Social Mind orders the facts which it perceives along a scale of values. This system of graded relationships is called "value system." "Value systems" play a crucial role in the social process. A value system may be the response to a material deficiency; changing valuations may give rise to changes in material reality, and valuations that remain constant may concretize in a different manner in a different situation. There is, indeed, a relationship between material facts—reality—and values, but this relationship is worked out in, and ordered by, the Social Mind. Only thus does it become socially meaningful. The Social process is a mental process.

"Reality" is a concept embracing the present. That which is real is simply that "which *is*." Reality is defined as "actual existence as opposed to the fictitious or imaginary." Material reality may be ascertained directly by the senses and measured: certain physical properties can be weighed, certain mechanical or chemical reactions can be predicted. This "reality" includes the physical existence of man which can be measured by counting heads. The extent to which certain predictable human wants may be satisfied can be deduced from available information about the present productive capacity of agriculture or manufacturing. But the physical existence of man is accompanied by mental processes which evolve many varied wants and different means of satisfying them. Man's whole "actual existence" thus draws into "reality" all of man's "objectives" which necessarily include his imagination and his speculation as to the "prospect of the future." The historical or present existence of man has no "reality" without reference to objectives. The "reality" of Waterloo is in the attainment of an objective, the defeat of Napoleon. Had the allies not wanted his defeat and had they not looked forward to their victory with some certainty, they would not have offered battle. Their experience in estimating correctly their own strength gave them some foundation in the world of measurable "reality" for their expectations, but the element of chance could not be completely omitted from the outcome, nor could the unpredictable "imagination" of Napoleon.

In the sense that reality refers to what *is* in the present, while "expectations" refer to what will be in the future, there is no equation between the two other than the "actual existence" of man who acts in the present on what he has experienced in the past and what he expects in the future. The physical "reality" which exists today is continually being changed by man's efforts as well as nature's and may be predicted to exist in the future only within broad limits.

An expectation is a "prospect of the future to which one looks forward with some certainty." That which an individual expects out of life is intimately associated with what he wants from life and does about it, especially his political choices. When man evolves a want or need, his activities are focused toward its satisfaction. To the extent that this focusing of activities is conscious we say that man has an aim or an objective: he sees a relationship between his present and future condition. "Expectations" are, rationally or overtly, speculations on the possibilities of achieving future objectives. Their full mental content, however, is less specifically "rational": one may take for granted a future development without consciously perceiving a relationship or formulating an "objective." Habits, good or bad, are in part the result of an attempt to satisfy a need, in part the result of a consciously applied method for reaching a desired objective.

What we want to know is how man's expectations in the present are being affected by other developments in the present "reality." The way to ascertain this is to determine how that part of present "reality" which may be measured is affecting his objectives and, therefore, his speculations about the attainment of his objectives, i.e., his expectations. Difficulty arises since no two people are exactly alike in their capacity for evolving and satisfying wants. Some individuals have within their own power greater control over the satisfaction of their wants or attainment of their objectives than others. This power may depend on individual intelligence or strong motivation, which are difficult to "measure," or upon such incidentals as bank accounts, the effect of which is more easily predictable. However, let us take "average" expectations in society relative to fairly common objectives. Most individuals want to support themselves in some specific manner, to marry and raise families. They see others about them achieve these ends and "expect" to do so themselves. But external forces may reshape these expectations.

For example, a young man expects to attend college, become an engineer, and marry the girl next door. He has saved sufficient money and set a wedding date. Then a war breaks out and he is inducted into the service. College opens without him and his girl marries someone else. The outcome of such an individual problem depends almost as much upon the individual's own power to perceive relationships with his condition in "reality" as they do on external forces.

In the first place, he may go through life hunting for the unlikely replica of his first love. He may renounce the desire to attend college, feeling himself too old to do so. He may drift from the army to inconsequential jobs, consider himself a failure, blame it on the war and, like Miniver Cheevy, acknowledge himself a victim of the times.

Or he may attempt to pursue his education in the service. But the top sergeant may not release him for other duties because he is useful filing reports, or he may be ordered to an Asian battle front. He may work toward a career in the army and achieve it. Or he may, upon release from the army, seek a career in business, feeling himself too old for returning to the classroom. If there is a "depression" he is unlikely to find a new opening and may drift on as in the previous example.

A more zealous young man may go off to war, employ his moments of rest and brief days of leave in boning up on college subjects, save his money and, upon discharge from the army, go to school. By the age of thirty he obtains his academic degree, enters the profession of his choice, finds a suitable wife, and considers himself a contented, "self-made" man.

But an equally zealous individual may doff his uniform only to find that inflation has reduced his savings and that he must therefore work in order to continue his education. He falls in love. He marries, and family cares—"reality"— are heavily upon him. He meets the situation by taking an irksome menial job or by escaping into a nervous breakdown or by doing both.

With the exception of the zealous "self-made" man, such a run of adverse circumstances is likely to diminish the individual's attachment to the ideals or values of his society. Besides breaking the ties of the individual to his community, which is likely to reduce the effectiveness of that unit of society, there is also the individual's lessened "expectations" toward life objectives. When these objectives grow dimmer the groundwork is laid for the advance of philosophies alien to the value system which previously governed his pursuit of objectives. The politician (it is who you know that counts), Hitler (democracies are decadent), and Mussolini (how to live like a lion), are all examples of individuals who preach doctrines stressing the helplessness of man to shape his own life and offering a new external set of forces to help him shape it more satisfactorily. Extremes of alienation are likely to develop because the system of successful living once advocated in society is still upheld by those groups within society, usually the most influential, who have lived successfully through periods of stress because of greater resources, human or material, with which they may pursue objectives.

The problem is one of showing new relationships to the larger group of "average" individuals whose expectations in living have diminished, but whose social and political power —by weight of numbers alone—has not diminished. In some cases these individuals may miscalculate the attainability of objectives and fail to act where action might have been fruitful. In other cases they may rightly estimate their reduced possibilities and may or may not find satisfactory alternatives. To deal with current social "realities" is to calculate the number of persons affected by a given social development and to calculate the probable effect of this development upon their objectives.

Let us take, for example, the problem of scientific advance in relationship to Christian values. Prescientific man's objective in living was to prepare himself for eternity. But as the material blessings of life on earth increased, he concentrated less upon this objective and more upon material objectives. Those who continued to concentrate on the Beyond "expected" it either with diminished certainty or diluted their expectations by this-worldly notions. Modern science, especially the notion of scientific progress, seemed to invalidate theological doctrine upon which belief in the ultimate attainment of the objective of eternity was based. Rightly or wrongly, so far as that doctrine itself was concerned, man expected that a good life of prayer and devotion to the values propounded by the Church insured protection *on earth* from punishments which were the due of the sinful. When widespread disasters subjected the pious and goodly to misfortunes, belief in spiritual values weakened. The attachment of the individual to "his" society was diminished as no "new relationships" between values and material reality were evolved to his satisfaction. But just as "objectives" are conditioned by experience, so each new relationship perceived contributes to the formulation of new relationships.

The cohesiveness of a society hence depends on the degree to which felt and expressed wants are satisfied. It depends also on the intensity of the sense of "belonging together"— *because* or *despite* differences in status and satisfaction of wants. It depends, finally, on the conviction with which the assumption is commonly held that problems *can* be solved within the existing or slightly modified social framework and that, whatever the nature of these problems, society is a "going concern."

It is perfectly true that the "moral crisis" of our times arose from the religious crisis, the widespread alienation from the spiritual values of Christianity. But this explanation begs the question as to why the real problem, namely the "showing of new relationships," has not been solved. The real problem arises from a crisis of reason. On the one hand, those whose participation and political decisions determined the social process and upon whom the "showing of new relationships" devolved were either untrained in methodical thinking or altogether unaware of the nature of the given problems. On the other hand, an unbalance of the value system resulted in the inflation of some values and the atrophy of others. "Values" are interdependent, and this interdependence can be analyzed logically. Thus, for example, peace and well-being are high "values," yet military defeat as the result of the preference given to butter rather than cannon may destroy well-being forever.

The disintegration of Western culture has been induced by *real* forces which can be grasped rationally and can be analyzed and dealt with logically. It has not been wrought by occult powers. There is nothing transcendental about it. It has not been "caused" by technological change. There is no economic law that has made it inevitable or that determines the issue of this crisis. Western man need not contemplate helplessly the dissolution of his order. The process of disintegration was set in motion by lack of cohesion in adversity, the lagging productivity of cultural goods, the flagging will to sacrifice and do "great things together," the fixation of expectancies upon one "value," namely, economic welfare in terms of consumption; the intellectual degradation of leadership; and the consequent inability to reorganize institutions in accordance with new requirements. It is these distortions of cultural development which are the bare bones of the moral-logical crisis of our age. They are, all and sundry, susceptible to logical analysis; they can be remedied by purposeful action.

In sum, the Social Mind does not correspond directly or wholly to palpable realities, such as towns, town councils, hospitals, unemployment insurance, churches, gambling casinos, law courts, fashions, and sundry "working" institutions of society-in-being. The Social Mind invests the social realities with expectations, normative oughts and ought nots, as well as mere "sentiments" which, however, are not identical with these realities themselves. This transcendence, which can be plotted along the axis of time dimension, negates all social symmetry and, consequently, the notion of social equilibrium. It projects social phenomena into the realm of imagination, the working of the mind, outside of which these phenomena have no existence. The Social Mind should thus be understood as twice derived: society is not a biological aggregate, it is derived from the biological "reality"; the Social Mind is not the aggregate of social phenomena, it is derived from the social reality and transcends it. Within this generous frame of reference, Pareto's * "residues" and "derivations" do indeed explain the social process, though they may fall short of supplying a field theory of social dynamics. Within it, too, Northrop's † major thesis, namely that culture is based upon ideological assumptions concerning man's relationship to the universe, shrinks to the unassuming size of a working hypothesis, more serviceable because less metaphysical. Society is not what it is because of environmental or historical necessity, but because philosophical, political, and social theories engaged the minds of men and persuaded them to build society to the scale of theory, rather than the scale of a priori conditions or of man himself. What is important about both explanations of the social process is not their respective contrary premises but what they have in common: the interposition of a mental construct between statistical facts—social realities—and purposive development, the ceaselessly projected, the Good Society. Evidently this point of view lacks the massive simplicity of Marxian sociology; it does not profess to distinguish between the material facts of society and the ideological superstructure. If it claims anything categorically it is that material facts and an ideological superstructure (if, for the sake of argument, these terms are conceded to have meaning) are neither directly related nor sufficient to account for the social process. An "advanced" agrarian society need not be feudal, it can be capitalist or socialist (some agrarian societies, to confuse the Marxists, manage to be both); a highly industrialized society may secure the comfort of its toilers by retaining the political and social institutions of its "primitive" agrarian past (Switzerland).

If the life processes of society are determined by the work-

---

* Vilfredo Pareto, *The Mind and Society,* New York, Harcourt Brace, 1934. See especially Vol. 3, "Theory of Derivations."

† F. S. C. Northrop, *The Meeting of East and West,* New York, Macmillan 1947.

ings of the Social Mind, the crucible of facts perceived and images projected, rather than by material necessity—environment, techniques, etc.—or essences and ideas—freewheeling ideologies—then we must turn for the diagnosis of cultural crisis to the pathology of the Social Mind. A schism of Western culture, its likelihood or irremediability, cannot be deduced from its environment, the tensions of world politics or the incidence of war, or the impact of technological change upon social institutions. The key to the problem lies in the concept of *alienation* from common devotion, the slackening of co-operative drives, and the ascendancy of disruptive forces.

Did "material necessity" compel the break-up of the ancient world? It did not. The Roman Empire, on the eve of dissolution, probably possessed better tools, roads, ships, and a better administrative system than it did, let us say, two hundred years earlier. The external pressures, wars and threats of war, were no greater than they had been several times in Rome's history. Did "material necessity" block the reconciliation of East and West? "Material necessity" should have forced the Western heirs of Rome, the Pope and the princes, and the Byzantine emperors, to coalesce into a common defense against the barbarians and Islam. And this is precisely what "material necessity" failed to do. As for the power of theories, ideas, and ideologies, the Romans, a remarkably unideological, pragmatic race, had managed successfully for centuries to absorb the most diverse philosophies and cults without damage to their political institutions. Even the rise of Christianity to the rank of state religion did not weaken Roman political institutions and the unity of the Empire. However, the irreparable schism within the Christian Church signified the incapacity of the ancient world to do what it had done so superbly for hundreds of years: to grow with changing situations, to adjust and accommodate to "realities"; in brief, to draw from force of change the strength nourishing its own development. This incapacity is the very characteristic of the alienation of the Social Mind. The rending of the ancient world was irreparable not because the people of the West no longer understood each other; they understood each other only too well. They had become estranged within that realm where once they had communed so intimately in a common devotion.

The Byzantine people bethought themselves of their Greek heritage; they felt themselves to be Greeks and no longer Romans. The spread of Monophysitism among the common peoples was, first and foremost, the expression of the popular protest against Rome. The theological controversy obscured, rather than illuminated, the origins of the schism in the revulsion against Rome and the Romanized barbarians that swept the Byzantine masses. So deep was this revulsion that the onslaught of Islam, though it was met valiantly by the new Greek nationalism of Byzantium, did not arouse the Byzantine people to do battle for the common cause of the West. The Byzantine Empire fell to the Islamic conquerors, yet its people had long before surrendered their soul to the East. Radical monotheistic Islam was less alien to the Monophysitic Greek than the dogmatic anarchy of the West where emperor and pope so ferociously fought each other, where holy crusades so easily turned into looting expeditions, and where the Church so supinely yielded its dogma to crude compromise with the pre-Christian folkways of half-tamed barbarians.* Before its fall, Constantinople bequeathed its heritage to Russia, of which heritage Greco-Byzantine culture, as well as the revulsion against Western anarchy, were intrinsic parts. The ambiguity of modern Russia, from Peter the Great to Stalin, always reaching out for the West and

---

* See Edward Gibbon, *The History of the Decline and Fall of the Roman Empire*, Vol. VI, ch. 60. See, on the theological disputes between Greeks and Latins, Charles Diehl, *Byzance, Grandeur et Décadence*, Paris, Flammarion, 1919; pp. 246-47 and p. 275 *passim*.

always rejecting it, is contained in the Byzantine bequest. Russia bears more heavily than any other European country the burden of the alienation of the Roman-Hellenistic world.

Historical analogies are like the wings of butterflies: firmly grasped they crumble into particles which may be of interest to a biochemist but no longer evoke the marvelous whole of functional and aesthetical perfection. It is not here proposed to examine minutely the fragmentary records of the Roman-Hellenistic world for their relevancy to the contemporary problem. We are concerned with a phenomenon which we have called somewhat cumbrously for the sake of better definition: alienation of the Social Mind.

History repeats a timeless score, but not itself. The score remains, the musicians change, no note is played exactly the same way, and the score is subjected to more or less revolutionary orchestral rearrangements. Eleven hundred years elapsed between the establishment of Constantinople as capital of Eastern Rome and its conquest by the Turks. It will forever be a controversial question: precisely when did the schism of Western Christendom become irreparable? Precisely which generation marks the fatal crisis of the culture of the ancient world? Only to ask this question is to provoke other questions which are just as unanswerable: when did the Mediterranean Age end and when did the Age of Europe begin? That any intelligent schoolboy can formulate these questions does not mean that they lack profundity. They go to the heart of the problem of history and of culture. Suffice it that historical analogies have to be handled with care and cannot be pressed too far. If historic analogy can evoke across the centuries a sense of poignant, uncanny familiarity with certain landmarks along a road which we travel for the first time, if they permit us to behold our own particular dilemma in historic situations that we recognize instantly as kin to ours, then indeed they have served their purpose: mirrors of the human condition.

The ancient world wrote the case history of its disease into its own record of religious schisms, of failure to unite politically against Asia, and of final physical disintegration. The intelligent Roman and Greek as well as assimilated barbarians understood perfectly what ailed their culture and why it was breaking up. We, too, are conversant with the ills of our own culture: two world wars in one generation, the Russian revolution, the partition of Europe, and the disintegration of the British Empire—among other symptoms—are not signs of good health. This lucidity paired with paralysis of will, of the will to co-operate and restore the unity of devotion, is characteristic of the pathological condition which we call alienation.

THE IMMENSE REPUBLIC

THE RAVAGES of alienation are cumulative: schisms beget schisms until all beliefs are dissolved into the despair of nothingness and society is driven into the narrow corner where man no longer contemplates his relation to the universe, culture, state, and community, but his solitary confinement in his own condition. That man may wrest from this brutish state a new dignity and that he may descend to dark catacombs in quest of new symbols is possible. That he can and should is the message of the philosophies of desperation which became fashionable in the wake of the last major disaster. But this message is a negative one: it takes the final dissolution of Western culture for granted. Yet what is lacking in the approach to that denouement of Western crisis is one step, and that step is not inevitable if Western man does not make it so: the estrangement of America and Europe. Were this event to occur then the worst dramatic hack could write a Sophoclean last act to the drama of the West. The event need not occur; it may occur precisely because the great mass of educated persons in America and Europe deem it unlikely while being, at the same time, perfectly aware of the growing mass of evidence pointing to growing tensions. Here, too, we are confronted by an ominous incapacity to relate the particular to the whole. If this were merely a matter of "understanding" then more "understanding" would be the best remedy. We have noted: Greek and Roman understood each other only too well. Yet it is upon "understanding" more "understanding" that the bulk of emphasis in public discussion and expert analysis of "communications" has come to rest. Certainly, Americans "know" more today about Europe, Europeans more about America than they have ever "known" before. But if ever such trite sayings—more of a truism than trite—as "a little knowledge is dangerous" and "the reason why Englishmen and Americans do not understand each other is that they both speak English" were apposite, they are most certainly so now.

The confusion of "knowledge," "understanding," with kinship, love, in brief, the emotive forces motivating common devotion, stems from the vulgar degradation of rational philosophy at the hands of the public-relations counsel and his helpmates, eager academics prepared to shift their specialty, psychology, sociology, anthropology, and so forth, lock, stock, and barrel to the international scene. Their teamwork has produced, together with a mass of pompous irrelevancies, a singular devaluation of statesmanship.

Any practicing statesman knows, for example, that understandings or misunderstandings have next to no bearing upon tensions and war, that intimacy of contact on any or all levels of society is no measure of friendship or hostility, that "friendship," "hostility," "frustration," "aggression," and "co-operation" are highly volatile notions, and that war and peace have meaning only in relation to each other and are not absolutes. But no successful statesman nowadays publishes what he knows, for a successful statesman in a democracy cannot do so and a successful statesman in a dictatorship will not do so. In a democracy, a successful statesman either holds office or seeks office—be it that he has not reached the extremes of dotage—when his memoirs are written for him. He owes his success in international diplomacy in no small measure to his sensitivity to public opinion. Yet public opinion in a democratic country is notoriously averse to discussing power politics. It is even more reluctant to admit that democratic countries engage in power politics. This is so not only because religious and pacifist

groups are free to express their views but because sublimation of the struggle for political power by debate and ballot
box is democracy's particular answer to the threat of violence,
the demon of all civilized government. Democratic public
opinion is thus inclined to project the proprieties of democratic conduct and its own idealized version of domestic reason-
ableness into the international arena. No democratic statesman, caring to retain broad domestic backing, can affront
these cherished preconceptions which, however inapplicable
to international affairs they may be, are the core of democratic beliefs. If he inclines to follow the line of least resistance he will blame the manifest presence upon the international scene of violence or threats of violence on the
cussedness of this or that nation, but not upon the nature
of the business in which he engages. If he has an inordinate
bent for braving the tide, he will engage in cautious circum-
locutions, hedging the bare facts of power politics with value
judgments and oblique references to "national interest."

Moreover, the statesman is rare who does not become the
victim of his own propaganda. When he writes his memoirs
he tends to diminish the distance between his deeds and the
interpretation put upon these deeds by his own propagandists.
Since a celebrated statesman, especially in the Anglo-American democracies, writes for a large audience, his reminiscences
may attain a cash value of several million dollars. The publisher's investment can be made to pay only by sales running
into millions of copies. Considerable pains are taken to ensure publicity—but not in the sense the scientist understands
the term, namely, publicity of method and disclosure of all
relevant facts. The larger the audience, the less inclined is
the illustrious autobiographer to unburden himself of the
intimate details and tricks of the trade.

Though illustrious statesmen are not barred from the
possession of sundry virtues, the chaste courage of Lady
Godiva is certainly not among them. And then, there are the

secrets of state, some being secrets in the proper sense, information the disclosure of which would endanger the safety of
the state or of certain persons; some being secrets for no
other reason than that their disclosure would damage not
so much the state but the reputation of the reminiscing
statesman. And then, there are secrets of state or merely facts
of public knowledge which the statesman in question knows
nothing about and which, therefore, may account for blind
spots in his historic vision. But a more important obstacle
still to the endeavor of the statesman, however uninhibited,
of placing the facts before his audience, is the nature of his
craft itself. It is immensely difficult: the materials which it
seeks to shape are painfully complex.

The pretense that foreign policy can be made simple
enough to be understood by all educated men without losing
the authentic flavor of its living realities is crude flattery at
best, dangerous deception at worst. Yet this is the pretense
the statesman, writing for millions of readers, must make,
though no one knows better than he that the understanding
of relatively simple problems in world politics requires considerable elementary knowledge, as considerable and as hard
to come by as differential calculus for solving relatively
simple mathematical problems.

It is unlikely that, under now prevailing conditions,
Machiavelli's *Prince* could be written or that, could any
practitioner muster the courage and intellectual discipline
to set forth so scientific a statement of his calling, it would
be published or bought. Modern political scientists are prone
to wrinkle their noses at Machiavelli's exposé and terminology, so distressingly clear and unprofessional. However,
it is a fact that we have no contemporary statement that
closely approximates the forthrightness and vigor of the
analysis of a Machiavelli, a Comines, a Talleyrand, writing
with a supreme disregard for the layman's susceptibilities
and the royalties' account. Today, the most instructive

teachers are some of the statesmen that failed, the men
under a cloud, the leaders of defeated nations. But their
writings, though perhaps less diluted by the expectation of
vast commercial returns and hopes for important office,
suffer from the compulsive twist that distorts most apologies.
Moreover, their audience in the democratic countries, especially the United States, is infinitesimally small. Nothing
succeeds like the publishing success of a successful statesman.

If the general public can learn little from the public
effusions of our important men, it can learn even less from
the publications by the hand of the dictators. The latter
writings are couched in the language of an alien ideology
and, not infrequently—like Stalin's *Problems of Leninism*—
both in the overt language of an ideology *and* in the hermetic
language of a secret conspiracy. This contrapuntal arrangement is incomprehensible, if not repellent, to the average
educated reader of the West. The semantic difficulty deprives
the published words of Western democracy's ideological foes
of their "educational" value. Hitler's *Mein Kampf* attained,
on the Western reading list, the rank of an atrocious oddity
(which, among other things, it is); it did not teach the West
what the West could have learned from it, and should have
learned for its own safety, about the spiritual state and the
concrete aims of post-Versailles Germany.

At no time in the world's history has the citizenry of any
country been exposed to so great a mass of information—
books, pamphlets, speeches, and pictorial reports—on the
world-without as are the people of the United States since
World War II. Similarly, the peoples of the rest of the
world possess today a greater store of information on the
United States than they ever possessed on any other country.
The peoples of Western Europe, in particular, consume vast
quantities of "facts" about the United States together with
a growing quantity of American products. Thus the belief
that increase of information is being distilled into increased

knowledge appears to rest on solid, at least quantitatively solid, foundations. Alas, we need only ask the questions: what does each people know about itself? How large a part of the population is agreed as to the validity of the knowledge claimed by this or that group? And, last but not least, what is knowledge for? to find our reassurance rudely shaken. The most casual tourist to, let us say, France, cannot help but note the disagreement that divides the French people on fundamental questions. He will be struck not only by what Frenchmen wish to know about the United States, but by the fact that what Frenchmen wish to know is largely determined by what they think they already know about the United States and by preoccupation with their own problems.

Knowledge, it appears, is hard to come by. Though we may admit, for the sake of avoiding a strenuous philosophical argument, that the mathematician and, perhaps, the natural scientist, can attain to pure knowledge, we do insist that knowledge about social and political phenomena is never pure.

Knowledge about human society is based upon a consensus, ethical or ideological, and that consensus orders the known "facts" along a scale of values, ethical or ideological. What an American and a European can know about each other depends upon what they think themselves to be, what each "knows" about himself, what each thinks the other ought to be, and what both assume to be the "knowledge"—the knowledge that is consensus—which they hold in common. In brief, no one knows where the boundary runs between what men can know about society and their beliefs. Once we hold this to be true, national prejudice can no longer be disposed of as mass ignorance. To the contrary, more often than not it is rooted in prolonged, intimate contact. To say that, for example, the aversion to yellow-skinned Asiatics, so strongly felt by many members of the white race, is a matter of ignorance, is to confess an amazing ignorance of history:

Europe fought, for thousands of years, a desperate battle against Hun, Mongols, and Turks. That aversion, far from ignorance, is the conditioned reflex of long and intimate experience. Forty European generations have known the Asiatic, his habits in peace and war, and, more important still, the meaning of the meeting of East and West—upon the soil of Europe. This hostility should not be confused with the racial snobbery of the "White Man's Burden," the racist phantasies of a Gobineau, and the orgiastic hallucinations of Hitler. It was amply justified by the concreteness of the Asiatic threat to Europe. If Europe had not fought that threat ferociously St. Peter's would be a mosque and the dons of Oxford would expound the Koran instead of the doctrines of the Fabians.

Perhaps no two peoples in Europe have known each other more intimately than Frenchmen and Germans; perhaps no two peoples have fought each other in more murderous wars than have Frenchmen and Germans. They did so not because of ignorance or misunderstandings but because of political, economic, and other highly rational considerations each of which can be shown to be internally consistent. Conversely, the United States and China, knowing and, at least as far as the mass of their respective populations is concerned, caring next to nothing about each other's cultures and mores, could boast, until not too many years ago, of a long, untroubled record of friendship. The deterioration of that relationship coincided with the growth of mutual intimacy and knowledge of each other. These facts are so plain that one wonders exactly where the advocates of "education for world citizenship" have been looking for the evidence that sustains their pleasing thesis: peace-by-knowledge, peace-by-getting-acquainted. One wonders even more if one examines the histories of those countries where public opinion most sincerely holds that peace is the fruit of enlightenment. For it can be shown that their own conduct in world affairs is at least as irrational as that of educationally more backward nations and that even in their domestic politics the voice of reason is stilled not infrequently by the most brazenly ill-informed, though vigorous, arguments. If literacy, education, information, and hordes of tourists, exchange professors and students were guarantees for peace, then not one shot should have been fired in anger for these last thirty years.

Though it should go without saying, this discussion is not meant to supply an argument in defense of obscuratism. The humanist ideal, the ideal of education that frees the minds of men, is the vital link between the ancient and the Western culture; it is *the* Western cultural ideal. But the amassing of skills in manipulation of letters, words, and mechanical gadgets, made up of shiny metal or shiny slogans, should not be mistaken for education. Nor does the melee of scholars, delegates of chambers of commerce, and experts in group living, met in international conferences, transform itself automatically into a Socratic World Academy. Writing in the eighteenth century, Montesquieu could reasonably anticipate the emergence of a world-wide "immense republic of cultivated minds." Though actually means of travel did not allow annual get-togethers and few men of letters, artists, scientists, and even statesmen met in the flesh their confreres in other lands, the "immense republic" was then not a mere figure of speech. The correspondence between educated men of all countries, their diary notations and, more striking still, their accomplishments bespeak easy familiarity, nay, intimate communion with each others' points of view. Content of communication does not increase proportionately with the increase in ease of communication. The comparison of the contemporary situation with that obtaining two hundred years ago rather suggests an inverse relationship.

The massive evidence of persisting tensions in the face of progress in literacy, communications, and formal organization of peace—League of Nations, United Nations—cannot be explained away by the argument that bigger doses of the same medicine will effect an improvement. The glaring discrepancy between fact and fancy has been noted by not a few of the newcomers to the field of international relations, psychologists, psychiatrists, sociologists, and anthropologists prepared to introduce the statesman to the field of science. Some of the older theories—as, for example, that nationalism and sovereignty foster aggressiveness, that certain forms of governments predispose to peace while others are conducive to war—failed patently to explain such disturbing phenomena as civil and ideological wars and the emergence of today's aggressors from the ranks of yesterday's peace-loving nations.

Disenchantment and deepening anxieties suggested re-examination of some of the most cherished assumptions concerning man's ability to cope with the demon of violence and, consequently, concerning the nature of man himself. Thus far, the search of academic specialists has yielded a large number of learned studies and theoretical disagreements which are as sharp as are the practical disagreements dividing the international community. What distinguishes this new, this scientific approach to the problem of international conflict from the rationalism of older social philosophies is a more skeptical attitude not only toward the role of reason in human conduct but also toward the role of concrete issues of power politics. As a matter of fact, some adepts of this new approach ignore the latter issues altogether. Territorial, economic, and even ideological issues which heretofore were considered by statesmen and historians as causes of conflict, are now viewed as manifestations of neurosis, maladjustment, and culture traits. In this sense, these issues as such do not exist. Could men be made (by psychoanalysis or psychiatric interview or education) to understand their particular neurosis, or could proper treatment free them of their emotional insecurity, then these issues could be seen and dealt with for what they are: states of mind that can be modified by discussion, adaptation, and compromise. These are the kind of routine problems which any society has to solve all the time in order to remain an integrated whole, namely, problems such as those arising from attitudes toward racial and religious minorities and groups demanding a greater share in economic and social rewards. By proper argument, each side can be made to see the limits of tolerance, the advantages of co-operation over strife, and the precedence of the whole over the particular. Whosoever rejects the argument is psychologically unfit for group living, to be rehabilitated or, in the last resort, to be isolated from society. Sanctions against the psychologically unfit are sublimated into institutions of social defense against the disquiet of the mind. These sanctions are extremely drastic ones even in the avowedly most tolerant societies, and intolerance of intolerance tends not always nor necessarily in the direction of toleration. This is not to cavil at the beneficial role of sanctions. The felt presence of power and the power to impose sanctions, however sublimated, is as much a prerequisite of social order as are co-operative drives. However, the concentration on psychological phenomena and psychological explanations is onesided and relativistic. It does not, it cannot account fully for the broad issues of Western society.

While concrete issues, such as tensions arising out of desire for political power, for higher wages, social equality, can, within a national society, be sublimated into the relatively simple problem of how to control aggressive instincts, tensions between nations and within the existing frame of social consensus, a multinational culture, resist "sublimation," arguments, and psychopolitical sanction. It is difficult enough to follow the psychologists' bold leap from the psychology of the individual to that of the group, or, more ambitious still, to the state. It is barely possible, though not likely, that contemporary psychological techniques can deal with the national society. The latter supplies, however, social and legal norms of which perhaps not all psychologists are aware, but which all psychologists can tacitly or expressly assume as conditioning the individual's expectancies and behavior. Thus the psychologist or psychiatrist, attacking the problem of intragroup and intergroup conflict, finds his task greatly eased by that concept called sovereignty of the state, though he may deplore it as a tribal atavism. All parties to the conflict, no matter how rational or irrational their motives, know the rules, no matter how rational or irrational they hold the rules to be. As a psychiatrist, speaking from the bosom of an organization dedicated to the easing of international tension by education and mental hygiene, UNESCO, put it: ". . . the processes of sovereignty are a manifestation of inherent human potentialities and of their realization through the course of events in historic time." *

Now, it can be argued that the international society, also, recognizes norms and sanctions. But these norms and sanctions are derived from those of national society. Even the most internationally minded American projects *his* national ethos into the future, better world purged of national sovereignties. This new world-without-sovereignty will be democratic, will observe human rights and will, in sum, be modeled in the images of the Bill of Rights, the Preamble, and the Gettysburg Address. That projection will not accord too well with that of the most internationally minded Russian who projects *his* national ethos into the same future, better world. *His* new world-without-sovereignty will be the ultimate state of social reorganization. The basic political and human rights, so dear to the internationally minded American, are relegated by the like-minded Russian to the limbo of class society: a classless international society will

---

* Henry Stack Sullivan, "Tensions Personal and International," *Tensions That Cause Wars*, H. Cantril, ed., Urbana, University of Illinois Press, 1950, p. 128.

enjoy these rights *and* universal peace as a matter of course.

It is unnecessary here to examine in detail the all too obvious limits of internationally recognized norms and sanctions. Suffice it that the psychologist's and the psychiatrist's attitude to international tensions is conditioned by his national milieu, that his techniques are tried and tested against the actualities of his own national society, and that his generalizations on nations and groups of nations derived from the observation of individuals or very small groups are at best sweeping.

We do not know much about the relations of individual psychology to political group behavior, except for unrelated political data and impressionistic suggestions. If, for example, psychologists call war "collective regression to mass infantilism," or totalitarianism, if they happen to be prodemocratic, a "mass neurosis," then they talk shop but tell us nothing meaningful about history or politics. The moral standards of good and evil in society are simply dropped in favor of psychiatric standards of healthy and diseased, though there is no proof that one has much to do with the other. We might speak of a regression of the social psychiatrist to the primitivism of the Middle Ages when, in reverse, disease was equated with evil. Psychologism, rigorously indifferent toward the standards of good and evil, is itself a symptom of the moral crisis. The *Neurotic Personality of Our Time* is an expression for a problem that psychologism seeks to remove from the realm of ethics—where it belongs—into the realm of science where it is meaningless, scientifically *and* morally.

Thus the syndrome of cultural crisis defies diagnosis by the techniques of psychology and psychiatry, and the remedies proposed by psychologists and psychiatrists, in so far as they perceive the phenomenon at all, are addressed to the symptoms rather than the disease. This does not mean that individual psychologists and psychiatrists did not discern the nature of the problem, but they did so by virtue of insights other than those vouchsafed by their craft.

If one then notes that the explorations of sound clinical methods have run lately into serious snags—as, for example, the extreme improbability of retrospective accounts of childhood experience—then psychologists and psychiatrists cannot be expected to contribute decisively to the solution of the problem which we have called the alienation of the Social Mind, and which we pose as *the* problem of Western culture.

Needless to say, the very concept, alienation of the Social Mind, is fraught with psychological connotations. However, the crisis of our time is a moral crisis. The pathology of the Social Mind, a phenomenon *sui generis* without adequate analogies in the pathology of the individual mind, is concerned with ills that afflict a whole society, its politics, economics, arts, and science. The causes of these ills cannot be found in areas of activity they afflict. They can be found only in the realm of vital beliefs whence society draws its cohesive strength and its sense of direction. The erosion of these vital beliefs leaves the apparatus intact; society keeps on going; and the cultural momentum simulates organic growth. Men go on building temples long after the gods have departed. If any society is in danger of mistaking the apparatus for the motive power, it is ours. This circumstance, result of the fantastic harvest reaped by technology from the furrows of Western science, suggested the distinction Oswald Spengler drew between culture and civilization. This distinction corresponds to that between the motive forces that channel the powers of the mind toward the quest of the unknowable, and "understanding," "information," "facts," and like serialized vehicles of the known, senseless, and insensate. Cultured man knows because he believes, and believes because he is humble in his knowledge;

civilized man knows everything except the limits of knowledge, and believes nothing.

It is perhaps this common confusion of culture with
civilization, sedulously fostered by the utilitarian appeals of
industrialism and the promises of the great mass ideologies,
which blocks most effectively men's vision from the reality
of cultural crisis. The fireworks of "know-how" of science
that has "conquered time and space" and of a civilization
that has "banished fear and want" blind the eyes of the de-
lighted spectators against the storm cloud in the darkened
sky. By the same token, what Europe and America might
have to say to each other about their respective cultures and
about the culture they hold in common is drowned in a
cacophony of mixed signals. Mutual recriminations of "materialism" are addressed largely to the grotesque images both
Europe and America behold in the mirror of each other's
civilization. On this, the lowest level of American-European
intercourse, it is as true as it is unpleasant to say that Europe
spurns what it cannot have but wants, the gadgets of machine
civilization, and that America taunts Europe for feigning
contempt toward all those wonderful things that men need
to be happy. Innumerable are the statements, whether
couched in the sublime language of cultural snobbery or of
less refined invective, that can be reduced to common preoccupation with the debris of culture: the civilization of things
divorced from the purpose of life. Were we to hold that this
is indeed the issue of American-European relationships—
a "new, progressive," civilization and an "old" one that has
gotten out of step with its more proficient kin—then we
could rest our case and need not look further. This is *not*
the issue, because what seems like a novel feature in American-European relationships is in fact a familiar characteristic
of Western history, antedating the discovery of America: the
introversion of the West. The West is painfully aware of

its internal differences, strangely indifferent to its image in the eyes of the world. This introversion blinds both Americans and Europeans to how much they have in common, to how small are the differences of their respective "standards of living," and how immeasurably higher is the lowest of these "standards" in comparison with that of the great mass of mankind. Secondly, these differences fade into insignificance before the true crisis that encompasses both Europe and America, and threatens their common culture as well as their material civilization which is an outgrowth of that culture, though not that culture itself. Were it not for that cultural crisis the West could handle its civilization of things and need not fear that the machines of its own devising will grind it down into dust.

The West has always experimented with gadgets. The idea of "labor-saving" devices nagged Western minds long before the Industrial Revolution. The quest for the control of nature and the struggle against drudgery are as intrinsic to Western culture as are Chartres Cathedral and Leonardo's "Last Supper." Gadgets are good: the water closet, the dentist's drill, electric power that turns the dentist's drill, have raised life not only above its brutish shortness in other ages, but also its dignity. That Keats was killed, at the age of twenty-five, by the state of hygiene and medicine of his times, most decidedly did not enrich Western culture: in our times, his life expectancy would have been about the same as the Western average, and his productive expectancy perhaps no less than that of George Bernard Shaw. That large numbers of men can now gather together even in tropical summers to listen to a Beethoven symphony without suffocating by their own stench is most decidedly not the refutation of culture by gadgetry. America's gadgets are not the last, but, here and now, the best hope of mankind—the appalling nonsense that is being written about the machine-made threat to culture notwithstanding.* Our gadgets are not killing our culture; no culture ever succumbed to its utilitarian tools. It is our loss of a cultural sense of direction that makes it seem as if the gadgets were endowed with a malevolent dynamism of their own.

To accept the thesis that man-made machine civilization is dragging us to our cultural grave is to accept another, perhaps even the most pernicious doctrine of historic inevitability: man's irreversible descent onto the scrap heap. That this doctrine engages the minds of clever men in Europe and, perhaps, even more obsessively, in America, is a striking case of misplaced concreteness in arguing about man, culture, and things: a drunken driver is no criterion for determining what is better for the soul, a dogcart, or a Buick. In its nastiest form this doctrine is a doctrine of reaction: the great mass of men should be denied the benefits they derive and can still derive from technical ingenuity—especially American—and thus be kept at the proper distance from the purlieus of the select. The reasonings supporting this doctrine are most varied. In Europe, it owes its appeal in no small measure to such dismal facts as that automotive transportation and widely advertised household conveniences have created a ubiquitous servant problem and that workmen now ride motorcycles whereas formerly the select few could take to the highway in expensive Rolls-Royces without having to share it with anyone but their peers in Daimlers.

Our gadgets are innocent. Though culture is not the same thing as civilization, culture and civilization are not opposites. There never has been a vital culture that did not develop techniques for coping with man's insecurity before the elements. Ours has been the most successful to date; in this respect only does it differ from the utilitarian achievements of other cultures. The escape into the cultures of Asia,

* See Bertrand Russell, "The Political and Cultural Influence," *The Impact of America on European Culture*, New York, Beacon Press, 1951, p. 16.

as a protest against Western materialism, may be the earnest quest for a spirituality Western culture is about to lose or may have lost. But if the anguished Western seeker has turned his back upon his native culture because it is gadget ridden and gadgets bar the road to his salvation, then he will not find the answer in the East. For if the great wisdom of the East has something to teach—and Eastern wisdom is intensely realist—it is that man must learn to live with this world, including its gadgets. How he chooses to use them and what he uses them for, this is a question of moral choice to which the East can indeed give meaningful answers. As for the average man of contemporary Asia, his enthusiasm for Western gadgets is alarmingly unbounded: when his traditional wisdom fails to unravel the mystery of combustion it is the West who can teach him not only how gadgets work but how to use them as, for example, not to drive Buicks on rice wine or on an empty belly.

The measure of a culture's wholeness is the balance between that culture and its derivative civilization. When this balance is upset, then a cultural crisis ensues: when a man uses a standard blade of rustless steel to cut his throat we do not blame mass production. We infer that man's hold on life has slipped but not the blade.

It is the increasing schisms of Western culture—schisms that cut across the realm of ideas, aesthetical, moral, and philosophical, and sap the will which man applies to their realization in life—which are the root causes of cultural crisis.

Little can be gained by seeking to determine what is cause and effect of the unbalance: is it the cultural crisis that engenders distortions and breakdowns of the civilization, or is it the weight of the civilization that crushes the culture? Since both are complementary, it is logical that the civilization acts upon the culture from which it derives. It is in this sense, and only in this sense, that the terms "materialism," "mechanization," "mass civilization," "reification," and others defining the ascendancy of man-made things at the expense of man, must be understood in the context of this discussion. We would not ride the steed so hard were it not that we propose to complete our exploration in daylight. The minutiae of definition are always boring, nearly always indispensable. Because America and Europe talk so very nearly the same language, the opportunities for misunderstanding are unlimited. The stereotypes of a venerable, highly personal, and slightly other-worldly Europe and of a brash, practical, materialist America are examples in point. The residual truth in both is what makes them so misleading.

The survival of Western culture is no more certain than the unity of the West is secure. Western culture lives by the vital beliefs America and Europe hold in common, and alienation of the Social Mind, estrangement from common devotions, is the mortal threat to the whole and to its parts. If cultural unity is the critical issue of American-European relationships, what then, is "Western culture" and the heritage that all the peoples of the West hold in common, marking them off against peoples of other cultures?

II
The Four Legacies

Culture is the name for what people are interested in, their thoughts, their models, the books they read and the speeches they hear, their table talk, their gossip controversies, historical sense and scientific training, the values they appreciate, the quality of life they admire. All communities have a culture. It is the climate of their civilization. Without a favorable culture political schemes are mere impositions. They will not work without a people to work them.

—Walter Lippmann

THE IDEA OF CULTURE

THE DEVELOPMENT of Western culture, like that of any great historic culture, was paced by increasing awareness of self. However, Western culture has now attained heights of introspective and retrospective preoccupation with itself never attained by its neighbors in time and space. No other culture has accumulated so vast a treasure of records of its own history and of the history of other cultures. No other culture has been so intently bent upon explaining itself to itself. Not so surprisingly this quest is getting stuck in the foggy bottom of highly specialized controversies. Embattled scholars delight in setting methodological and semantic booby traps, designed chiefly to discommode each other, but which disturb the lay seeker of enlightenment.

The very word culture is fraught with heavy ideological ballast. Spengler's celebrated thesis is that cultures burst into bloom, attain the splendor of maturity, and then harden into sclerotic senility battening on the past creativeness of their respective golden ages. The generalization of this thesis into *the* organic law of all culture development has engendered probably more printed pages in defense and in rebuttal than any other philosophy of history. Hardly anything worthwhile has been said or written about culture since the *Untergang des Abendlandes* appeared in print, that, knowingly or unknowingly, does not carry the burden of Spenglerian thought. In this sense, contemporary discussion of culture resolves itself into a dialogue between the host of disputants—and Spengler. No one, possessed of ordinary sensitivity to the influence of ideas, can fail to notice how deeply Spengler's formulations have stirred contemporary philosophies of culture, especially those who tacitly acknowledge their impact.

Spengler was a German. Though his value judgments on "Caesarism"—totalitarianism by any other name—cannot be easily confounded with an apology for the institution, Spengler, like Marx, deemed what *had* to be as requiring no moral approval or disapproval. He steadfastly refused, up until his death, to place the highly prized endorsement of his philosophy upon national-socialist ideology. Yet Spengler has been listed—or rather, black-listed—as a spiritual harbinger of the Nazi myth. Leaving aside again the question as to whether this verdict was justified (the genealogy of Hitlerian ideology is probably more polyglot, more international, than that of any major modern ideology), we can safely say that the debate over what Spengler said, that is, the intrinsic merit of his central thesis and his findings in general, has gotten inextricably enmeshed with the debate over his ideological and political sympathies, that is, his alleged fascist bias. If we recall that the bulk of his *Decline of the West* was completed before World War I, this confusion appears slightly ludicrous. The accuracy of his forecasts ranks him as the major seer of our times, though his predictions may owe less to his systematic projections than to his innate historic tact, his wonderful ability to see the whole where more academically inhibited minds could only see the parts. How sweeping was his grasp is now revealed by thirty-eight unhappy years of Western history. However, his scholarship has suffered a decline in reputation. It is on his scholarly apparatus, on his definitions and his stylistic idiosyncrasies, that his enraged critics have concentrated. The barbs were aimed at the prophet, though ostensibly directed at the scholar. Undoubtedly, a faint odor of phoniness attaches itself to Spengler as it does to all highly eclectic thinkers, especially those who, like

Spengler, are gifted with the power of poetic imagery. Unquestionably, great advances in the last thirty years in archeological and anthropological research have greatly diminished Spengler's stature as a historian and social scientist. Modern scientific theory, postulating the "statistical quality" of certainty and the impossibility of predicting individual events as such with certainty, has been no kinder to Spengler's deterministic pretensions than to those of Marx, Hegel, and other cheerless artificers of "social laws." The result of these deflationary developments has been a gleeful exposure of Spenglerian slips and foibles together with a summary rejection of his most brilliant formulations. Among the latter is his concept of culture. The job was done with thoroughness: both bath water and baby have gone down the drain.

Let us examine what some of the best known contemporary students of culture have to say on what culture *is*. Arnold J. Toynbee's monumental *A Study of History* is, first and foremost, a study of the great cultures. However, Toynbee appears to use the words "society," "civilization," and "culture," though the latter but rarely, as interchangeable terms. His catalogue of contemporary, living societies includes "an Orthodox Christian Society," "an Islamic Society," "a Hindu Society," "a Far Eastern Society," and "Western Christendom." * The latter society is also defined as "Western Society" or "*Civilization*." †

Pursuing his investigation, Toynbee speaks of the "cultural elements" of the "cultural plane" upon which "the lineaments" of civilization can be distinguished. He then proceeds to distinguish between "species of societies" that are commonly called civilizations, and primitive societies which are also "intelligible fields of study" and which form another,

---

* Arnold J. Toynbee, *A Study of History*, Abridgment of Volumes I-VI by D. C. Somervell (New York & London: Oxford University Press, 1947), p. 8.
† *Ibid.*, p. 12.

in fact *the* other, species within this genus.* On the other hand Toynbee quotes an anthropologist's assertion that "Environment . . . is not the total causation of culture-shaping." † Similarly, Mayan civilization is also a "culture." These interchanges occur with enough frequency throughout the *Study of History* that the terms must be taken as being identical in meaning. In addition, Toynbee, speaking of "the great religious organization extant in the world today," draws the distinction between civilization *tout court* and "material civilization," to wit, the *things* of scientific knowledge and technique.‡ He also speaks of "dynamic, growing civilizations" as contrasted with "static" and "arrested" civilizations, of "creative minorities" evoking great new social forces, contrasted with the great mass of "uncreative" majority which, though participating in a growing civilization, is in the same "stagnant quiescent condition as the members of a primitive society." It is, therefore, difficult to see wherein his formulations differ concretely from Spengler's neat distinction between "culture" and "civilization"—except for the greater conciseness of the latter. But now to the thing itself! What is the thing Toynbee calls civilization?

To begin with, civilizations are "not built on bricks," nor even on alphabets or numerals.§ Civilization is the creation of creative personalities. Whereas in primitive society "mimesis" (imitation) is directed by the average man toward dead ancestors and living elders, in civilized society mimesis "is directed toward creative personalities because they are pioneers." Such a society is in dynamic motion along the line of growth. Society is also a "field of action." ¶ In that field operate the creative personalities who "transfigure" their fellow men into

* *Ibid.,* p. 36.
† *Ibid.,* p. 61.
‡ *Ibid.,* p. 214.
§ *Ibid.,* p. 40.
¶ *Ibid.,* p. 213.

fellow creators, re-creating them into their own image. So strongly is Toynbee's definition weighted toward creativeness, creativeness that breaks the "cake of custom," and so emphatically is that definition equated with the great discoveries of ideas in religion and science, that Toynbee's concept of civilization can be said to resolve itself into the presupposition of spiritual forces as the source of cultural life, as that life itself. If we then examine his introduction of mimesis as the binding substance of society, we find that mimesis, or rather the condition it produces, is none other than the "Social Mind," poised in common devotion or split by heresies. It is in this context that Toynbee refers elsewhere to the "alienation of the proletariat from the dominant minority."

For the sake of polarity, let us now examine what we will call the bucket concept of culture. Clyde Kluckhohn, renowned anthropologist, has this to say about culture: "By 'culture' anthropology means the total life way of a people, the social legacy the individual acquires from his group: Or culture can be regarded as that part of the environment that is the creation of man." * To leave no loose ends and scotch allusive thinking, Professor Kluckhohn insists that to the anthropologist the "technical term has a wider meaning than the 'culture' of history and literature," and that, though in certain "cliques" to have culture means to be able to talk about James Joyce and Picasso, "to the anthropologist to be human is to be cultured." "A humble cooking pot is as much a cultural product as is a Beethoven sonata." This is a far cry from Toynbee's creative demiurge who recreates society in his image. We need here not trouble ourselves over the question as to whether Professor Kluckhohn's definition is or is not a useful tool in the workshop of the anthropologist. It has only a remote bearing on the task of defining so complex a thing as Western culture which, together with all kinds of peoples

* Clyde Kluckhohn, *Mirror for Man: The Relation of Anthropology to Modern Life*, New York, Whittlesey House, 1949; p. 17.

and their potsherds, harbors such highly differentiated denizens as Picasso, Joyce, and anthropologists with their ideas about culture. Professor Kluckhohn infers something of this sort when he writes in a later chapter: "There is a unifying philosophy behind the way of life of each society at any given point of its history. The main outlines of the fundamental assumptions and recurrent feelings have exceptionally been created out of the stuff of unique biological heredity and peculiar life experience. They are usually cultural products." * Thus the unifying philosophy—fundamental assumptions and beliefs—behind the way of life of each society—is itself a "cultural product." Which may be interpreted as saying that we arrived back where we started from. For how is that unifying philosophy put into society and how does it become a cultural product? Professor Kluckhohn maintains that there is "organic push" in each man toward certain kinds of acts. But to each biologically given characteristic is imputed a cultural meaning. To say that the same biological characteristic may have different cultural meanings dependent on the environment, part of which man creates to his liking in different ways, is to trace a path of causation that is, shall we say, elliptic. Dr. Kluckhohn's hypothesis resembles the challenge-and-response scheme of Arnold Toynbee in which societies make or fail to make the right kind of adjustment to environment in order to "grow." But, whereas for Toynbee this scheme requires the creative personality or minority for the sake of completeness, the anthropologist foregoes introducing this *deus ex machina*.

Though the anthropologist may proceed more scientifically by hitching his method of observation to the idea of "biological" push that underlies or, rather, translates itself into, the cultural meaning, a correspondence that requires no inter-

* *Ibid.,* pp. 202-03.

vention from outside the system, his hypothesis is not very helpful in solving the riddle of creation, man's leap into the unknown, man's transcendence of himself. To say that the Cathedral of Chartres or Leonardo's "Last Supper," or—for that matter—"unifying philosophies" have issued from the imputation of meaning to biological characteristics, may or may not be an exact scientific statement. But this statement tells us nothing more than that the human animal is capable of amazing tricks, including the trick of imputing meanings to his biological drives. It tells us nothing about the uniqueness of the works of art, religious thought, and great philosophies in which a culture celebrates its fulfillment. What man, though possessed of far finer tools of research than those now available to science, could presume to trace with any degree of accuracy in these high achievements the pattern of "biological characteristics" and their "imputed cultural meaning"? And if he could, would he then have succeeded in doing more than giving us an explanation of the fabulous potentialities of the "human animal" as animal, that is, as a biological phenomenon? Would he have told us anything worth knowing about culture? *

G. D. H. Cole's strictures on Oswald Spengler's method apply fully to what we have called the "bucket concept of culture." Cole wrote: "Social theorists, instead of finding and steadily employing a method and a terminology proper to their subject, have attempted to express the facts and values of society in terms of some other theory and science. On the analogy of physics they have striven to analyze society as a

* Sigmund Freud in his atheist-scientist primer, *The Future of an Illusion*, New York, Liveright, 1949, defined culture as follows: "... All the knowledge and power that men have acquired in order to master the forces of nature and win resources from her for the satisfaction of human needs; and on the other hand ... all the necessary arrangements whereby men's relations from each other, and in particular the distribution of the attainable riches may be regulated." To create and maintain culture men must bring "instinctual sacrifices"; p. 9 and p. 12.

mechanism, on the analogy of biology they have insisted on regarding it as an organism. . . ."

Culture is a phenomenon *sui generis* that cannot be explained as the product of "organic push" and "imputed meaning." To be human is *not*, as a matter of course, to be cultured. The "human animal" is endowed with the ability to use concepts, to frame these concepts in language and transmit learned concepts from generation to generation. This use of concepts stands in a relationship of "complementarity" to inherited instincts. The term, complementarity, was coined by Niels Bohr, the great Danish scientist and philosopher, to describe regularities for which the classical principle of causality cannot account adequately. Because it cannot use concepts, a newborn child can scarcely be reckoned as a human being; yet belonging to the species of man, it has the organic possibilities of receiving through learning a culture and taking its place in it. Is every child born with a predisposition for the adoption of a specific human culture, or can any culture be implanted and thrive in different physical backgrounds? The distinction between genotype and phenotype, so fruitful for the classification of heredity in plants and animals, presupposes the influence of external conditions of life upon the characteristic properties of the species. In the case of the cultural characteristics of human societies, the problem is, however, reversed. The basis for classification here is traditional habits shaped by the histories of these societies *and* natural environment. "Indeed, in characterizing different nations and even different families within a nation, we may to a large extent consider anthropological traits and spiritual traditions as *independent* of each other, and it would even be tempting to reserve the adjective 'human' for just those characteristics *which are not bound to bodily inheritance.*" * It may or may not be proper to view the

---

* Niels Bohr, "Natural Philosophy and Human Cultures," *Nature*, Vol. 143, 1939, p. 271. Italics are mine.

"human animal" as a biological sport; culture is not something superimposed on the biological characteristics of the "human animal." Within the frame of reference of culture, the "human animal" does not exist—except as an internal contradiction.

It is precisely the achievement of Oswald Spengler to have freed the concept of culture from the false analogies of nineteenth-century natural philosophy and thus, incidentally, from the gross superstition of Marxism: culture as the "superstructure" of the material means of production. Now, it can be shown that Spengler's thesis—growth, maturity, death of culture—is itself derived from biological analogy. But his understanding of the meaning of culture is not so derived. It owes nothing to naturalism and everything to Goethe's unitary views on man and nature and Goethe's "unquestioning acceptance of the phenomenon itself." * Spengler wrote:

I distinguish, again, "soul" and "world." *The existence of this opposition is identical with the fact of purely human waking consciousness [Wachsein].* There are degrees of clearness and sharpness in the opposition and therefore grades of the consciousness, of the spirituality, of life. These grades range from the feeling-knowledge that, unalert yet sometimes suffused through and through by an inward light, is characteristic of the primitive and of the child (and also of those moments of religious and artistic inspiration that occur ever less and less often as a Culture grows older) right to the extremity of waking and reasoning sharpness that we find, for instance, in the thought of Kant and Napoleon, for whom soul and world have become subject and object. . . .

Thus, by regarding waking-consciousness structurally as a tension of contraries, and applying to it the notions of becoming and the thing-become, we find for the word *Life*

---

* L. L. Whyte, *The Next Development in Man,* London, 1944, p. 197.

a perfectly definite meaning that is closely allied to that of "becoming."

If, now, we designate the Soul—that is, the Soul as it is felt not as it is reasonably pictured—as the *possible* and the World on the other hand as the *actual* (the meaning of these expressions is unmistakable to man's inner sense), we see life *as the form in which the actualizing of the possible is accomplished.* With respect to the property of Direction, the possible is called the *Future* and the actualized the *Past.* The actualizing itself, the center-of-gravity and the center-of-meaning of life, we call the *Present.* "Soul" is the still-to-be-accomplished, "World" the accomplished, "life" the accomplishing. . . .

The possibilities that we have of possessing an "outer world" that reflects and attests our proper existence are infinitely numerous and exceedingly heterogeneous, and the purely organic and the purely mechanical world-view (in the precise literal sense of that familiar term) are only the extreme members of the series. Primitive man (so far as we can imagine his waking-consciousness) and the child (as we can remember) cannot fully see or grasp these possibilities. One condition of this higher world-consciousness is the possession of *language,* meaning thereby not mere human utterance but a culture-language, and such is non-existent for primitive man and existent but not accessible in the case of the child. In other words, neither possesses any clear and distinct notion of the world. They have an inkling but no real knowledge of history and nature, being too intimately incorporated with the ensemble of these. *They have no culture.*

And therewith that important word is given a positive meaning of the highest significance which henceforward will be assumed in using it. In the same way as we have elected to distinguish the Soul as the possible and the World as the actual, we can now differentiate between *possible* and *actual* culture, i.e., culture as *an idea in the* (general or individual) *existence* and culture as the *body* of that idea as the total of its visible, tangible and comprehensible expressions—acts and opinions, religion and state, arts and sciences, peoples and cities, economic and social forms, speech, laws, customs, characters, facial lines and costumes. *Higher history,* intimately related to life and to becoming, *is the actualizing of possible Culture.* *

Now, with some pains it could easily be shown in which respects the definitions of culture given by Toynbee, Kluckhohn, Bohr, and Spengler differ, each advancing upon its meaning from a different national milieu and a different mode of thought. However, our purpose is to find a meaning for the word "culture" that we may use throughout this discussion without being constantly harried by ambiguities. Hence the important question here is not: in what respects do these definitions differ? but, wherein do they agree? and, is the agreement broad enough to tell us something worth while about our specific topic, the problem of Western culture here and now? It can be instantly seen that English historian, American anthropologist, Danish scientist, and German eclectic are agreed on the presupposition that what we called vital beliefs are the impalpable essence of culture: Toynbee's classification of the Great Societies (or cultures) is based on the criterion of religious organization—Western Christendom, Islamic Society, and so forth—and his very allegory of the creative act, by which the rare individuals "transfigure" their fellow men, is suffused by Christian imagery. Kluckhohn's "unifying philosophy behind the way of life of each society" is the spiritual consensus "behind" as well as above and beneath the aggregate of anthropological and social facts.

---

* Oswald Spengler, *The Decline of the West,* Authorized Translation with Notes by Charles Francis Atkinson, Special Edition (New York: Alfred A. Knopf, 1939) pp. 54-55. Italics are mine.

Bohr's "spiritual traditions" are *the* characteristic of cultural man who is human precisely because he is "not directly bound to inheritance." Spengler's "culture as an idea in the existence and culture as the body of that idea" is what Bohr would call "spiritual traditions" and Spengler, in a later passage, explicitly avows the identity of culture and consensus of belief: "The spiritual in every living culture is religious, has religion whether it be conscious of it or not. That it exists, becomes, fulfills itself, is its religion. It is not open to a spirituality to be irreligious. . . ." The withering away of vital beliefs is, for Spengler, the unmistakable symptom of cultural decline, of culture hardening into civilization, into what-has-become and no longer has the capacity of "becoming," of growth. Spengler quotes Goethe's profound observation, anticipating by more than a hundred years the menace of alienation that now casts its shadow upon Western culture. "The great views of Life were brought into shapes, into Gods; today they are brought into notions. Then the productive force was greater; now the destructive force or art of separation." *

In sum, culture is vital belief. It is not potsherds, not social institutions and cities. Culture is not even sublime works of art or lofty philosophical systems. It is the faith immanent in these things and relating them to each other, binding them, as it were, into a whole. Indeed, faith does move mountains. As long as a society lives by the canons of its faith the artifacts it bodies forth have meaning: tools and forms serve man to attain his purpose on earth, a purpose that is not in these objects themselves nor in their making but in the fulfillment of the cultural mission, in "what life is for." If that sense of mission dulls, if faith flags, then the things of man's devising merely simulate purposes of their own, simulate life and "what life is for." They have become false to their makers. Then society is without guide and direction since men no

* Spengler, *op. cit.,* Vol. II, pp. 411-14.

longer can set their course by the lodestar that had been visible to them, and is now blocked to their vision by the walls they built around themselves. Within these walls men are "safe," safe with their possessions, bent upon devising new means for acquiring more possessions and in securing safety of possession.*

That man is now incapable of reconciling his appetite for things with safety, and that he has lost the security which he found in the strivings of a common faith is the meaning of the phenomenon which sociologists are wont to term social atomization. In the great cultures, men have prayed to gods for knowledge and knew themselves to be part of the divine order. In a civilization of things, ordered by statistical averages, men hurl imprecation at their own anonymity: a headless government, nameless doors of serried tenements, authorless journalism, and public men without faces. There is no answer to their anguished cries for a meaning, an answer to the question of "what life is for?" The voice is mute; and men live their disconsolate lives, marooned on the cliffs of the "standard of living." All modern political ideologies have derived sustenance from the threat of "atomization" which gnaws at the heart of Western man. It is a question of "more" or "less," for the great fear affects all Western peoples. There, where the great fear had its deepest roots, in Central and Southern Europe, mass ideologies exploited that fear most directly.

The history of culture is the history of the beliefs that bridge the dualism of man's nature, "the human animal" and the human being, things and spiritual aspirations, instinct and intellect, living and the purpose of life, individual and society. Western culture must be viewed as the last stage in

* Shelley wrote: "The accumulations of the materials of external life exceed the quantity of power of assimilating them to the internal laws of human nature." Quoted by Lewis Mumford, *The Condition of Man*, New York, Harcourt, Brace, 1944; p. 418.

this age-old quest for reconciliation of man with his fellow man and his divided self. Whence sprang the force that set Western man upon his course and where along the path is he moving now?

Western culture of all historic cultures is the most "open." This is so, if for no other reason, than because of its unprecedented spatial range and retrospective extension into the past. A study of Western culture must thus include that of virtually every known major culture of history, for virtually every major culture can be shown to have impinged upon the development of the West. This sets Western culture apart from such "closed" cultures as the Islamic and Chinese, not to speak of older cultures. True, it can be shown that the Hindu and Chinese cultures were in touch with the Hellenistic world through trade. The impact of these influences is not easily determined and can hardly have been great, for the most sensitive contemporaries did not record them and appear to have ignored them altogether. Western culture is thus unique among cultures. Its roots, old and new, reach into the soil of every culture, past and present. Conversely, it has intruded itself upon every primitive culture still extant—which means that in the true sense there are no primitive cultures left.

When studying cultures other than our own, we are confronted by a problem of observation which closely resembles that besetting modern physics and psychology: the interaction between the object studied and measuring tools, and the inseparability of objective content and observing subject, prevent the application of the methods of knowing suited to accounting for experiences of daily life. This epistemological difficulty has been overcome by physics. However, the concepts which physics had to introduce in order to meet this problem are exceedingly complex and still in the stage of methodological refinement.* The difficulty besetting the com-

* See N. Bohr's concept of "complementarity," *op. cit.,* p. 271.

parative study of cultures is even more formidable than that facing the physicist. For, in observing cultures, there is no equivalent to the isolation of laboratory conditions. The "laboratory" in which cultures must be studied is now as large as the confines of Western culture itself, or the entire earth. The observer of Western culture is confronted by an involvement of objective content and observing subject far more complex and subtle than anything analogous in physics. Spengler argued that a great culture is so poised in itself as to make its inwardness inaccessible to an observer stationed in another culture. Though we need not follow Spengler all the way we must beware of overestimating our ability to slough off our own rooted cultural attitudes and to receive, so to speak, as a reading instrument, the message of the culture under observation. We may immerse ourselves in another culture and thus develop a heightened sensitivity to its characteristic manifestations. However, returning then to our own culture, we will never be the same and may have lost about as much as we have gained in our capacity as "neutral" observer and analyst. The Western scholar who spent many fruitful years of research in, let us say, China, may have gained deep insights into Chinese culture and even into his own. But are his attitudes toward his own culture not then slanted by Chinese perspectives?

These difficulties are greatest in the study of one's own culture. The limitations on the comparative study of cultures impede the development of apt analogies. The snares of introspection, familiar to psychologists, and retrospection, familiar to historians, add to the hazards of exploration. If we then seek to mount toward the sources of Western culture and descend again toward their confluences we must do so aware of how poorly we are equipped. At best, our efforts will yield those impressionistic *aperçus* which are the despair of the social scientist, though they are the best he is apt to come up with having exhausted his more rigorous methods.

THE CONFLUENCES

WESTERN CULTURE and the techniques it bodied forth originated in the Mediterranean orbit of cultures. To Western culture Greece bequeathed her critical spirit and methods of observation and political concepts; Rome her secular laws and principles of organization; and Judaea her concepts of one God, the creator of Man, and of Man as a moral being subject to the commandments of the Law of God. Asia supplied the challenge which compelled Western man to affirm, to live, and to defend his triple heritage against the perennial threat of military invasion and cultural annihilation.

It can be readily seen how much this formulation leaves out. The history of Greece is the struggle for survival against the cyclic irruptions of Asia. However, her culture reached its roots into Asia Minor and Egypt and drew nourishment from the autochthonous cultures of both. The spiritual ferment that brought forth the Judaean-Christian conception of God and Man was leavened by the religious insights of the East, and Christianity was, in turn, to weave into its pattern the threads of earlier beliefs. The tribal folkways, as well as political and military organization, of the Germanic and Mongol invaders who broke into the Mediterranean world, may account for much more in the composite cultural foundations of the emerging West than is conceded by surviving contemporary records compiled nearly in their entirety by those least inclined to acknowledge barbarian contributions. Saracen Islam, though it embodied the mortal threat of Asia to the nascent West, transmitted to Western culture via Spain and

Italy part of the Hellenic heritage which the West had lost in the times of its painful gropings amidst the debris of the Roman Empire. The Arabs were to the West teachers of science. They contributed new scientific concepts which had issued from the marriage of Greek philosophy to the questing and observant outlook of their race. All these influences can be traced with varying degrees of exactness. However, in the consciousness of Western culture these contributions were recorded as negative. They make up the heritage which the West has wished to forget. The West has succeeded so well in pushing back into the nether region of oblivion the debts it owes to barbarians and infidels that it can no longer account for what it received or rejected. The psychologist's categories come readily, all too readily, to hand. Should we not explore Western culture's "subconscious" in search for what it forgot and made itself forget? for what Christendom owes to the Saracens whom it drove from the geometric elegance of the Generalife of Grenada? to the Druids whom it humbled before the cross? to the cult of Mithra and the reforms of Mani, both equally abominable in the eyes of Western Christendom? The result of our labors would be about as significant as those derived from exploits in long-distance psychoanalysis, at best comic relief, at worst tedious platitudes. We are thus confined largely to what Western culture knows about itself, believes about itself, and avows about itself. Western man has not rejected the bequest of Greece, Rome, and Judaea.

Western culture avows itself the heir of Greek thought, Christian religion, and Roman law. The fusion of these three components into one tradition is so complex a process that it is impossible to assess the relative importance of each. We, the latter-day heirs, are apt to assign a specific weight to each, which corresponds to what we conceive to be the need for each in the contemporary situation as we see it. He who views the catastrophes of this century as irruptions of unreason may trace plausibly the calamity to the denial of the Greek ideal.

He who views the sufferings visited upon the West by war and revolution as the external manifestations of spiritual crisis may hold justly that these evils were brought upon Western man by his denial of Christ. He who views the accomplishments of Western society in self-destruction as the result of Western man's failure to impose organizing principles upon the anarchy of his own political and social institutions and of international society at large may ascribe universal disorder to Western man's paralysis of will, the will to govern his conduct by Rome's ideal of a universal society under law.

These three ideals may not have been the ones that shaped most characteristically the life of the societies that bore them. Athens put Socrates to death; the history of the Catholic Church begins with the struggle of its ministers for earthly power; Roman law did not curb the excesses of populace and Caesars. Perhaps Western man attributed a meaning to these ideals which is real only to him and which did not hold for the peoples from whose strivings these ideals arose. There are regions in the depth of Greek thought, of early Christian faith, of Roman sagacity which are closed to us forever. Some attempts to "produce" antiquity in modern dress are downright ludicrous, such as attributing to Plato the parentage of Hegel and—for what could be more obvious—of Marx, Mussolini, Hitler, and Stalin,* or presenting the Romans as organizationally minded practical Americans, complete with their problems of big-city slums, organized sports, and political corruption. This is indeed history as the art of predicting the past. This is Spengler's allusive legerdemain at its worst. The three components of the West's cultural heritage have coalesced into a whole; we cannot help putting into the interpretation of each our awareness of the whole. This and two

---

* For an attempt to "expose" Plato as a "sociologist of decay" see K. R. Popper, *The Open Society and Its Enemies*, London, Routledge, 1945, especially Vol. 1, chaps. 4 and 6.

thousand years of exceedingly complex history, separate us from antiquity's man of thought, man of faith, and man of action. That the three component parts of Western tradition could join to make the whole is probably due, as L. W. Whyte surmised, to the fact that "they correspond to three complementary aspects of the mind: thought, emotion and will." * They did join, and to deny one is to seek to alter the whole beyond recognition. If we deem one to have ceased to matter, then we can speak no longer of Western culture. That culture contains other components. But it is these three major components that were necessary and sufficient for the making of the West.

The development of the Greek intellect first distinguished Europe from Asia. Asia prayed, conjured, compiled, observed, or escaped into the mystical intuition of another world. The Greek mind, too, observed but sought to abstract from observation general laws which inspired the order of nature. In the realm of politics, this turn of mind led the Greek to seek for an intelligible order of political society and to ponder forms of power and authority, hence, to differentiate new forms of authority from the single relation of the ruler and ruled which had circumscribed the relationships of man and state. The Greek innovation of method constituted a decisive forward step which the most advanced Asiatic civilizations, China included, were never able to take. Today, wherever one observes and reasons, one stands upon the ground of Western culture. There the contrast between a social organization cast in the mold of despotism and a society that has become aware of itself as a community, free to make its own laws, marks the dividing line between East and West which twenty-five hundred years have not erased.

The business of the community is the business of every citizen. Man possessed of reason is free, subject only to those

* L. W. Whyte, *op. cit.*, p. 89.

laws which he imposes upon himself. Being endowed with reason, man has the right of subjecting political institutions to reasoned criticism. From this it follows that he has the right to employ his critical faculties without peril to his dignity as man. The law is made so that he is guaranteed the exercise of these rights; wherever these rights are not made into law, there rules tyranny. When the Greeks fought the Persians they fought as free men aware of their freedoms. They fought aware of what they were fighting against: the unlimited power of the single ruler, the master of the horde of ruled. Our idea of political man was conceived then. It was tested in the defense of an integrated community, subject to no rules but those freely agreed upon, against the amorphous might of despotism, subject to no rules but its own whims.

It does not matter greatly whether the West's champions of freedom—French Illuminati, American planters, or English squires steeped in the humanities—endowed in their imagination the warriors of Marathon with sublime virtues which the most recent scholarly investigations show they did not possess; or whether they mistook Greek methods of reasoning for the rationalism of eighteenth-century Europe. The pure and genuine voice of Greece, the affirmation of the dignity of man, echoed in their hearts. Nor is it in our times a mere caprice of intellectual fashion that Greek political thought shines forth with a new luster as it is brought to bear upon the examinations of the state of Western polity. Not only is Plato still read, he is still intensely controversial. There is no major issue in the life of Western democratic peoples—the state's power to levy taxes, how much, and upon whom; or the state's power to ensure the national welfare be it by the most complex social legislation or merely by providing dentures upon demand; or the state's power to abridge in times of public danger individual rights—that cannot be reduced easily to the language of the Platonic dialogue. There is not a single political argument advanced by the parties to these issues, no matter what their technical aspects, that would not have been instantly understood by every literate Athenian. We strongly suspect that it would not have been understood at all by a scholar of Confucius' China.

The Greek *logos* reflected an awareness of relationships and hence proportions. The East lavished its genius upon the gigantic, the monuments that dwarfed man. Greece sought the realization of her ideal in harmonious measure. Knowledge of relationships guides man in pursuing ends that do not exceed his means, and shapes his means so that they will attain reasonable ends. Thus a sense of measure imposes upon man a rule of conduct that, though it is not an ethical imperative, imposes a moral discipline: to distinguish clearly not only the processes of reason but to abide in the search for general laws by the canons of reason, and hence to seek the truth by arguing the proposition from clearly defined and consistent premises. Discipline, intellectual and moral, is the single most powerful instrument of the mind that Greece handed down to the West. It is at once the corner stone of Western science and the *sine qua non* of Western technical prowess. The advances of Western science, especially those discoveries that overthrew the systems of logic and mathematics devised by Greek thought, are unthinkable without the Greek discovery of the process forms of reason. If Western science has rejected some, and profoundly altered most, Greek concepts of man and nature, it could do so only by using the tools of the intellect fashioned by Greece. Moreover, some of the concepts thus rejected or altered may require an intense second look by modern science, physical, medical, psychosomatic, and social.

The genealogy of Western science and Western technology can be traced back to Greece. It is Greek intellectual discovery that blazed the trail for both, and thus for the development of one characteristic of Western culture, efficiency, that has no counterpart in any other culture, except where other cultures borrowed it. Perhaps no other country pays more reverent daily homage to this part of the Greek heritage in Western culture than does America. And perhaps this lesson, too, may have been learned too perfunctorily. For, if Greece taught intellectual rigor, hence discipline and efficiency, she taught in the same sitting that discipline and efficiency must serve attainable ends, and that the worth of the works of man could be ascertained only by one measure: man's own.

The Greek mind, though it conceded reverently a large and colorful region of life to the irrational (or perhaps because of this concession, which, too, was dictated by the Greek's innate sense of measure applied to all things including the power of reason), staked out a province of life in which reason operated independently and acknowledged no other master but itself. This liberation was not complete. The Greek mind did not cast off all the shackles that bound politics and economics to the custom of more primitive society. Free Greeks held men as slaves. It is easy for us to decry Plato's acceptance of slavery. It was five hundred years after Plato that Seneca rejected it on moral grounds. It was more than 2,200 years after Plato laid the basis of the Western political and social science, that the last Western nation abolished slavery because it had become not only an intolerable institution morally but also an obsolescent means of production technically and economically. Greece was a congeries of city-states that also happened to be "class societies." Greek society did not succeed in sloughing off—2,400 years before the popular democracies showed us how they proposed to accomplish this feat—its "class character." Greek culture—perhaps because it could not solve this problem which so far no other culture has solved—lapsed ultimately into sterility. The Byzantine Empire carried Greek culture bedecked by strange trappings and wan in the candlelight of Christendom, into the Western era. But the Greek city-states perished, and living Greek culture with them. They did not perish because they failed to solve problems no one else knew how to solve; they fell because they *were* city-states and could not impose an organizing principle upon their anarchy. Greece did not unite in a state that could have coped with the dangers that arose from the altered geopolitical equilibrium of the ancient world. By this failure Greece taught a lesson, perhaps the most important one at this stage of Western history. No one acknowledged this lesson more freely and knowingly than the makers of the American Constitution. In this respect, as in others, the document bears the authentic stamp of Greece. The same lesson now haunts the chancelleries and parliaments of Western Europe. The challenge to the West, here and now, is to step across the limits of Greek political imagination. That these limits still hold marks today a greater failure in the ambiguous history of human progress than any that can, in measured reason, be attributed specifically to Greece.

The skeptically polytheist Greeks could not develop a passionate devotion to a universal faith. The Greeks had given the irrational a wide berth; within its precincts reigned the dark chthonic powers and gods, so human in their conduct and so feeble in their mastery of the passions. The realm of the irrational was thus left to the rule of anarchy. Greece did not search her emotional wilderness, so intelligently fenced off from the neat fields of reason, for one all pervasive spiritual truth. It could not, therefore, create a religious system. The genius of Judaism centered upon just that: the revelation of one spiritual truth that contained all other truths. The Jews accepted man's separation from nature and interposed between man and nature the mediation of God. Their monotheism personalized God and individualized man. They conceived of the one God in relation to man as a moral being. Separated from nature, man is governed by the truth of the word. The moral law is not a convention of reason but the mandate of divine authority. Christ did not alter the essence of the Jewish concept of the personal God and of man as a moral individual. The tremendous influence of Christianity upon the formation of the West bespeaks the originality of the Jewish conception of man as a receiver of divine revelation, not as a reasoning being. The Greek searched for the orderly processes of reason; the Jew, and, after him, the Christian, searched for the scheme of divine justice of which this world is but a transient manifestation. In the eye of the just God all men of faith are equal. From this revolutionary concept of justice and equality are derived the religious and social protests that rocked Western society, transformed it, and still shake its structure.

The Jew's repudiation of ancient hierarchies set in motion a process of fermentation that kept Christianity from hardening into the mold of orthodoxy, religious and social. It is at the root of the prodigious spiritual and social dynamism of Western culture. That dynamism is more apparent in the Protestant tradition than in the Catholic; it is most forceful in the tradition of Anglo-Saxon Protestantism. The Scriptures are the basic document of religious reform. The Anglo-Saxon peoples drew from the Scriptures a Biblical culture that is alive to this day in their language, poetry, rhetoric, and humanitarian aspirations. Biblical culture is a popular culture. In America it has brought forth a host of sects and a homespun wisdom that, perhaps more than any formal institution, guided the community in settling its conflicts and "doing the right thing." The Scriptures were alive in that passionate sense of justice and that deep compassion which animated America's attitude toward other peoples and not infrequently swept aside that graven idol called the national interest.

The Scriptures are the basic document of social reform, honored and blasphemed. The ardent, dynamic faith of the Hebrew prophets speaks through the great Victorian reformers, the Populists, the New Dealers, and, though phrased in the hieratic language of the Catholic Church, the great Catholic reformers, the author of *Rerum Novarum,* the French, German, and Italian leaders of militant, radical Catholicism. It also speaks through Karl Marx. The *Communist Manifesto* said what others had said before and what some had said more tersely. But it is *how* it *said* it that roused the passion of the masses. The Hebraic demand for justice, the due of the man of faith, reverberated through the political phraseology of the *Manifesto* and sounded a note that evoked the oldest theme of the Faith: justice. Had this not been so, then the appeal of Communism would be indeed what Marx, Lenin, and Stalin said it is: the appeal of a reasoned interpretation of economic process. If it were just that, then the sum total of the world's Communists today could be comfortably housed in the classroom of one of our more prosperous universities. It was the appeal to the deepest, latent emotional forces which nineteenth-century society had allowed to ferment in frustration, which elicited the explosive response to Marxism. Marxism is a blasphemy. But what is the faith that it blasphemes if it is not the faith of the Scriptures? The crushing masses of book learning that have gone into "explaining" Communism are so much informative pulp if their nuggets of insight are not placed in the setting of one illuminating truth: Communism is a religion. It is the religion of antichrist in the most literal sense, precisely because it drew its message from the Scriptures and denied the source upon which it had fed. Not to see this is to fall into the trap historical materialism has set for reason.

The history of Russia is fatefully determined by the alienation of the Byzantine Church from the Church of Rome. It has been pointed out that the relationship of state and church in czarist Russia and the hostility of the Russian masses to Western rationalism and skepticism eased the transformation of Marxism into a religious system. But the phenomenon, though most spectacular in its Russian manifestation, is observable in every land that shared Christianity's history. There is hardly one phase in the history of Communism that has not its counterpart in that of Christianity. The analogy is replete with catacombs, schismatics, heretics, purges, and counterreformation, tedious exegesis, saints, sinners, and the paradise beyond the vale of tears in the present. There is only one concept that is lacking in Communist religiousness: man, a determinate spiritual being, alone with his God. On this distinction revolve all others. It is only armed with this distinction that the West can join the battle for men's souls. This is the real battle, not the one Western propaganda bureaus have called with characteristic circumlocution the Battle-for-the-Mind-of-Man.

Jewry, by interposing God, separated man from nature. Christianity, as it developed, separated the world of the flesh here and now from the world of the spirit hereafter, by promising immortality. To save one's soul one must resist the temptations of the senses and their seductive images. This ascetic imperative demands of the believer in his daily life a moral discipline which, though prompted by different, if not to say, contrary, assumptions, re-enforced the moral discipline imposed by the Greek ideal: both are precepts of self-control. The other-worldliness of Christianity begot its opposite: material success. For the believer, by exercising self-control and by resisting the temptations of today, was paradoxically rewarded by earthly riches. Max Weber showed how the rise of capitalism was facilitated by the strict moral discipline of Protestantism. Long-range planning and efficiency in the execution of well-laid plans require self-control. Asceticism and the cult of efficiency are branches of the same tree. The efficiency of industrial production owes an inestimable debt to dour Calvinist artisans and Presbyterian traders and to the stern discipline of the monastic orders.

The immense contribution to Western culture of Christianity outweighs the price Western man paid for its blessings.

Intellectually the Gospels were a step back on the road blazed by Greek reason. Christianity hardened the dualism of the Western mind. Man was deprived of his part in the whole of nature. Perhaps no Western mind felt so deeply this sense of loss and separation as did Goethe. Goethe's life, even more than his intellectual striving, is the noblest search for the unity which Western man sacrificed on the altar of his faith. There is, however, nothing in the history of the West that holds out the promise of reconciling man to nature. Cultures do not transcend themselves: cultures are at best absorbed by other cultures. It is not difficult to imagine a world culture in which man will regain on a higher plane the capacity of unitary thought which he lost with his innocence. But that culture, whatever its inspirations, will not be Western, just as Western culture is not the mere extension of the cultures that preceded it. The facility with which academic minds project the synthetic shapes of world cultures and call upon the East to rescue the West from its materialist sloth betrays their deep misunderstanding of the uniqueness of historic cultures. Like individual man, cultures have the vices of their virtues and must live with both of them.

Greece lavished her serene genius upon the search for the universal idea; the Jews sought passionately the one God. Rome was concerned with neither. The Roman mind centered upon order, hence upon tradition. The West received from Rome the concept of the political community under law in which every free citizen participated in the making of the law and was equal before it. The Roman was singularly dispassionate. His law and ethics were not anchored in absolutes as were Christianity and Greek rationalism, but in the principle of continuity. If the adjective spontaneous can be applied to the Roman character it fits only its reaction to tradition. Rome's intellectual history is barren of doctrinaires and Utopias. If Greece was alive to thought and Christianity harnessed emotion, Rome cultivated the will to action. Rome applied her stark, practical genius to the integration of individual wills into a rational political system. Rome resolved the conflict between reason and emotion by a compromise: Rome put the requirements of social order above both. The compromise was made this side of our concepts of morality. To the Roman, morality meant continuity, tradition. Roman morality called for the deliberate control of social action and the voluntary subordination of the individual to the requirements of the community. Therein did Roman virtue lie. Because Rome occupied the practical, political middle ground, her achievement could be made to serve the perpetuation of the Greek and Christian ideals. The Roman built the bridge upon which faith and reason walked into the dawn of the Western era. The parallel has been often drawn between the Roman Empire and the British. The Roman, though more often than not bored with intellectual subtleties and embarrassed by an unseemly show of emotion, nonetheless tolerated both. The Roman peace protected the traffic not only of goods and persons but also of ideas. Marx working out, in the British Museum, his theories on the extinction of capitalism was in the best Roman tradition; so were the Irishmen who lampooned the stately indifference of the Victorian era in matters of taste, art, and letters; so was Gandhi. "Just because the Romans and English-speaking peoples do not take thought seriously, they were able to act as its carrier without themselves succumbing to its weaknesses." * The formulation would not have displeased a cultivated senator at Petronius' table. If a new culture, a world culture should arise, Anglo-Saxondom may be the golden bridge across which the old culture will join the new.

Europe was to seek for centuries the restoration of the Roman order. The Limes still mark today the authentic West. Europe's nostalgia for the *Pax Romana* found its most mov-

* L. W. Whyte, *op. cit.*, p. 79.

ing, most paradoxical expression in the Holy Roman Empire which as the cliché says, was neither Holy nor Roman nor Empire. It shed the blood of its warriors, its saints, and its polyglot peoples to be all three things. Perhaps nothing bespeaks as convincingly as this vast and absurd sacrifice the tremendous hold upon the West of Roman tradition, the tradition of continuity. Logically, the Germanic Empire should have sought its "living spaces" to the north and east. It was the miraculous good fortune of the West that the Germanic emperors turned their eyes stubbornly toward the legacy of Roman order and thus to the ancient lands of Mediterranean culture. They thus served the interests of their peoples far more effectively than if they had sought more practical, more realistic ends. Nothing could have been more absurd; nothing failed more abysmally; nothing redounded more prodigiously to the interest of Western culture and of all its members. This strange, inexplicable phenomenon should dampen the ardor of those who propose to tell rulers and peoples what is and is not in their interest.

The West fell heir to three traditions that were complementary and cumulative in their effects. Destiny, purpose, and providence are linguistic symbols of the riddle which lies beyond process. So varied is the landscape of human history and so imperceptible its watersheds that our imaginations can construe innumerable possibilities, the might-have-beens that would have brought forth every conceivable development but the one which has made us what we are. From the confluence of Mediterranean cultures there emerged one epochal discovery that opened a new stage in human history: man the individual. In Western society, man stands in direct relationship to ideas, God, and law.

A thousand years passed from the dissolution of the Roman Empire to the culmination of the Renaissance before the West had become fully aware of itself and had filtered from its varied legacies its unique concept of man and society.

About 1600, that concept emerges so sharply etched that its imprint is still today the indelible mark of Western culture, setting it apart from all other cultures. From it are derived the West's integrating principles of social life, the state, and the laws; the relation to the community of the artist, the scientist, the philosopher, and the man of action; and the community as an association of individuals, each deemed capable of acceding intellectually, ethically, and legally to the universal verities and thus joined in the common venture. With the Renaissance began the West's time of venture and discovery. From the Renaissance leaped fully armed the idea of progress that freed Western culture from the static view of life of the *ancient societies* and from the pessimism and fatalism of the Orient. The Renaissance, in search of classic culture, discovered the joys and vicissitudes of search for its own sake. That passionate search pierced the medieval veil between man and nature. Man now set out to express himself through all his faculties. The new methods of thought— Bacon's, Kepler's, and Galileo's objective observation of na- ture—challenged scholastic dogmatism. Society's focus of attention shifted from religion to politics. Machiavelli investi- gated objectively the anatomy of power. Possessed of new insights, man challenged authority. Man, freed from author- ity, was now alone, the philosopher in the contemplation of nature and society, the artist with the forms of his personal experience, and the navigator with his stars. Yet their dis- coveries, the new insights, and the new universals, were, at least potentially, the common possession of all men.

Though the Renaissance, breaking the "cake of custom," freed man's mind from ancient bondage and launched him upon the path of political and economic emancipation, it opened the fissure of alienation that, in our times, threatens to break apart the wholeness of Western culture. The new freedom of humanism as well as the intellectual and moral tensions of individualism revealed themselves in the most splendid expression of Renaissance man: his creative arts.

The decay of the Roman Empire and Europe's failure to reconstitute the Roman order on the one hand, and the apparent imperviousness to time of Byzantium and the splendor of the Saracenic empires on the other, had magnified the cultural attraction of the East. Though Europe became dimly aware of herself in the Crusades, the main effect of the latter was to make Europe more Oriental than she had ever been. The stained glass of the Gothic cathedral is a transparent mosaic; the Gothic architecture borrowed the filigree of the arabesque; the frescoes of Cimabue were Byzantine in technique as well as hieratic feeling; the animal statuary of Siena's Piazza could have been wrought by the Arabs who sculptured the lions of the Alhambra. The break was sudden: the "David" of Michelangelo, Leonardo's "Gioconda," Botticelli's "Venus" are inconceivable in an Oriental setting. To accomplish their liberation from the Oriental pattern, the artists of the Renaissance had to find a style of their own. They searched, as artists developing a new style always did and still do, the works of other artists for inspiration, for the more creative is the artist the more he feels the need to admire and to affirm, not to negate. When Renaissance man lowered his eyes from the lofty cathedral it was to rejoice in the serene proportions of the Greek temple; when he cast off the heavy folds of Byzantine robes it was to contemplate the clean lines of Attic youth. Most certainly, the Renaissance was not the rebirth of antiquity. Contemporaries of Henry VIII and Calvin could not reincarnate Praxiteles and Virgil. An enormous amount of learned ink has been spilled to prove that they could not, and that the art of the Renaissance issued from the art of the Middle Ages. The amazing thing is not that the artists of the Renaissance engaged upon so absurd a venture as to try to rouse the classic dead but that they never abandoned the quest and that they were more successful than, archeologically speaking, they should have been. The light of Greece bathes the sculpture of Michelangelo and the frescoes of Raphael. Tasso imitated Virgil without sharing with the latter a shred of religious and social awareness. Yet in Tasso's epic the classic ideal is alive in every cadence. Logically, all this should have been impossible, yet the man of the Renaissance made the impossible come true.

The painting and sculpture of the Renaissance yield their meaning only to an observer steeped in classic mythology. A vast part of Italian, French, Spanish, and English Renaissance literature presupposed a thorough acquaintance with Greek myths and Roman biography and historiography. The Renaissance artist performed not only an astonishing feat of aesthetical symbiosis, he also divided the public into two sectors: those, the few, who possessed the learning of classic culture and those, the many, who did not. The cathedral and its shrines were accessible to all men, the classical allegory only to the educated man of taste. Art thus tended to become the realm of the specialist. Renaissance art, despite its fidelity to nature, reduced the number of people to whom it had something to say, and lost part of the ground upon which Gothic art and its public had communed in religion. True, this separation between elite art and vulgar art did not occur abruptly. Gothic architecture flourished up until the end of the seventeenth century and still contends awkwardly with other styles. Folk art perpetuated the style of the chansons and the tales of the Middle Ages long after the bulk of Renaissance literature, imitating the classics, had begun to collect dust. The European romantic reaction against classicism virtually begins with the revival of the latter. Shakespeare is a romantic, so is El Greco. But the Renaissance marks nonetheless the beginning of a disassociation pregnant with social as well as aesthetical conflicts assailing the harmony of Western culture. The Renaissance separated art from the collectivity; it separated art from art itself. It provoked strange execrescences—the bureaucratic classicism of Washington and the steel-girded Grecian temples of Wall Street with columns that support nothing; the statues of civic mediocrities posing as Roman consuls; and the monstrosities of the World Fair style. It cast up myriad artistic cliques; books that resemble other books more than the speech of their authors; paintings that must be "learned" as must the occult language of novels addressed to psychoanalysts and their patients rather than to lay readers of tales; and the tortuous allusiveness of art criticism that is not concerned with any work of art but with the self-revelation of the critic. But the Renaissance also freed the artist as has no other cultural movement. It made him the final, perhaps the only, judge of his own work. It placed in his hand great power and great responsibility. And finally, the artistic creation of the Renaissance has posed the question of alienation more clearly than have politics and science and has anticipated, in one brilliant revelation, the dilemma of Western man. We behold in its mirror the noble, distraught visage of Western culture.

THE FOURTH LEGACY

THE THREE great legacies of the ancient world blended in the new culture of the West. This is easy to see: the heirlooms of Greece, Rome, and Christianity are all around us. What is not so easy to see is that the combination of the three components occurred under pressure and that this pressure in fact represents the fourth legacy. Geography tells us how precarious is the position of the promontories that we call Europe, in relation to the immense hinterland that we call Asia. There is one theme that runs through the histories of the Mediterranean, the European, and the Western culture: the pressure of Asia; the man of the steppe against the man of the sown; the mounted horde against the dwellers of the city; mass against form. There is no dearth of theories purporting to explain the phenomenon. One theory avers that the Asiatic push obeys a cyclic law. Observed variations in the climate of inner Asia account for cyclic changes in temperature and precipitation. In periods of drought the nomadic populations of the steppe regions, in search of new pasture for their domesticated animals, encroached upon the sown rimlands of Asia. Other theories ascribe the "'pulsations" of Asia not to climate but to population dynamics. After a generation or two, populations rose because pastures were good, food was plentiful, and more infants survived to the age of procreation. The second or third generation found that it exceeded available food resources—the Malthusian law operating its geometric progression of population growth over the arithmetic progression of material productivity—and proceeded to transfer, by conquest, its population problem to the lands of neighboring tribes. The process then assumes the nature of the "multiplier." Those who were thus pushed out of the pastures pushed others in turn until entire tribes were set in motion. At such moments, Asia irrupted.

The momentum of the inner Asian push was imparted to the peoples at the margin of the grasslands who themselves moved into the lands of other settled peoples, either bent on conquest for their own account or as captives and auxiliaries of the conquerors from the steppe. The Völkerwanderung, it is believed, was the culmination in Europe of such a climactic general movement generated in the heart of Asia. Still another theory holds that, after certain intervals of quiescence, the latent restlessness of the nomadic peoples was stirred and caught up into a single will by an individual: Attila, Genghis Khan, Tamerlane, Shah Mohammed, Djelaleddin, Baber. The superhuman prowess, endurance, imperviousness to overwhelming odds, unsurpassed generalship, and intransigence in defeat of these conquerors appear to sustain this thesis. Since Asia did not develop a social principle of integration beyond the one-way relationship of ruler and ruled, its formless masses were set in motion not by the spontaneous will of peoples but by the will of rulers. Hence the personalities of the great Asian conquerors appear to tower above the tribes and peoples whom they swept before them in their implacable appetite for conquest for conquest's sake. Napoleon, compared with Genghis or Tamerlane or even the rulers they defeated, appears stunted, a conqueror who talked and wrote too much and was overawed by his own conquests.

We may choose any one of these theories or take from each what seems most plausible, and concoct our own explanation. It is not unlikely that the coincidence of climatic change, population pressure, and the appearance of a leader accounts for the series of Asiatic outbreaks that shook Europe and, alternately or simultaneously, southeast Asia, south Asia, and

China. Conversely, the unfolding and fulfillment of the Mediterranean cultures appear to coincide with periods of Asiatic quiescence; periods of Asiatic resurgence coincide not only with a contraction of the geographic area over which Mediterranean cultures held sway but also with crisis situations in these cultures themselves. The Hunnic invasion (A.D. 451-52) marks the nadir of Christendom. Within the life span of the generation of Aëtius who halted Attila on the Catalaunian Fields, the formal separation of Byzantium from Rome sealed the disintegration of the Empire and the breakup of Rome's European dominions. The Arian schism threatened the unity of Christendom. The arts, the learning, and the institutions which the Empire had transmitted to the peoples of Gaul, Spain, Britain, the Germanies, and the Danubian Basin appeared irretrievably lost in the tide of Barbarian conquest.

Within the lifetime of the generation of German, Hungarian, and Polish knights who, in 1241, went down to defeat before Subotai, Genghis Khan's general, Europe seemed lost to the Mongol furor. The Mongols had come not so much to conquer and rule, but to lay Europe waste in order to secure their western flank. Indeed, had not dynastic complications deflected the heirs of Genghis Khan, the Mongols might, and certainly could, have turned Europe into a wilderness as they had turned Bactria into a desert. That same smitten European generation beheld the first signs of the mortal crisis of Christendom, the decay of papal power that was to culminate in the age of the schismatic popes, and the disastrous failure of the Crusades, culminating in the fall of Jerusalem. Again, night seemed to fall upon the world of the spirit and of the arts. About 1300, the style of Gothic architecture hardens into convention. The work of St. Thomas Aquinas was done and the insights of Scholasticism seemed now lost in the maze of pedantry. To the east, the death agony of Byzantium had begun. The old was dying. Europe trembled before the Mon-

gol horsemen and no man then living could yet foresee the
new dawn of delivery.

Perhaps the most important date in Western history is the
fall of Byzantium in 1453. For this catastrophe, due as much
to the estrangement of Latin and Greek Christianity as to the
military prowess of the Turks, turned Europe toward the
West. For Europe could only go westward. The age of the
great discoveries begins with the closing of the land routes to
the Levant, Asia, and North Africa, to European commerce,
and the appearance of Turkish naval power in the Mediterranean. The Italian and Spanish sailors, for whom the Mediterranean had become dangerously narrow waters, scanned
what must have seemed to them a second and grim alternative: to seek their cargoes in the distant East itself. Thus the
westward expansion of Europe can be seen as what it was in
fact: the seaman's flanking maneuver dictated by the victorious attack of the horseman, the Osmanli Turk. This strategic
pattern ruled the relations of the West and Asia up until our
own times. The fall of Byzantium set in motion a chain of
effects which are not exhausted yet: oceanic navigation, the
making of western colonial empires, the shift of Europe's
political and economic center of gravity from the Mediterranean to the North Sea; the eclipse of Venice and Genoa
by Amsterdam and London; and the divergence of Russian
history from the general trends of Western culture. All these
individual developments are consequences that flowed from
the same event: the Byzantine catastrophe.

It can be argued that each of these developments was inscribed in history by the logic of events remote from the
happenings at the Straits of the Dardanelles. Knowledge of
astronomy and marine techniques had advanced sufficiently
to open men's minds to the vistas of transoceanic exploration.
European peoples of the Atlantic littoral had emerged as
independent nations, who no longer acknowledged the
supremacy of the Germanic Empire, and were ready to make

their own bid for power. Mounting European population pressure upon available food resources was bound to seek an outlet in overseas adventures. The Russian people had adopted the Greek rite and succumbed to Mongol domination long before Byzantium fell, thus passing through experiences that set them sharply apart from the rest of European Christendom. Yet each of these trends might have been attended by any number of results and might have remained but vaguely defined had not the fall of Byzantium thrown them into focus. Europe had to make a choice if she was to maintain the level of her economic prosperity and the rate of her cultural development: to affront the Asiatic invader at her doorstep or to circumvent him by sea. Europe chose the latter alternative.

Within a period of eighty years after the fall of Byzantium, Europe had traced the outline maps of her overseas domination and thus of the globe. Generations of explorers, up to our own times, labored to sketch in the details but hardly changed the contours drawn by Vasco da Gama, Columbus, Magellan, Cortes, Pizarro, Verrazano, Cartier, and their contemporary cartographic interpreters. It is as if in these eighty years the horizons had widened a hundredfold. Europe burst out from her narrow promontories and embraced the earth; burst out from medieval magic and embraced life. Europe, embracing earth and life, transcended herself. Scattering the seeds of her creative powers and biological vitality to the four corners of the earth, she implanted upon distant soils a culture that was hers, yet wedded to alien environment. The age of Western culture had begun.

Europe, upon her own eastern threshold, remained on the defensive for nearly three hundred years after the fall of Byzantium. Solyman I had, by the time of his death in 1566, extended Turkish sovereignty over Hungary, Moldavia, and Wallachia. In 1681, a Turkish army besieged Vienna, and a Turkish invasion of central Europe was averted only by the alliance of Austria, Poland, Venice, the Pope, Russia, Malta, and Tuscany, the first joint European effort since the Crusades, though a defensive one, against the infidel. Again, the advance of Asia upon Europe coincided with a European spiritual and social crisis. The religious wars culminated in Europe's horrible self-mutilation, the Thirty Years' War. It was only in 1717 that Austrian forces, led by Eugene of Savoy, brilliant general, man of letters, and perhaps the greatest European in the urbane tradition of the eighteenth century, took Belgrade. It was only in 1774, two years before the Declaration of Independence, that Turkey signed the Treaty of Küchük Kainarju, imposed upon her by victorious Russia, and ceased to be a menace to Europe. Turkey now became a question, the "Eastern Question." Europe lost her fear of her old enemy and turned her diplomacy to the liquidation of the defunct Ottoman Empire. How deeply the Osmanli Turk had thrust himself into the affairs of Europe is attested by the fact that international politics still trips over the remaining loose ends of the Question.

In 1486, Russia threw off the Mongol yoke that she had borne for more than two hundred years. During that long period of servitude, Russia had not abandoned the faith which she had received from the second Rome, Constantinople. She had not become "Tatar" as some of the glib narrators of "either-or" history will have it. She did not become "Tatar," because the Mongols, clannish and noninterventionist as long as subject peoples paid their tributes punctually and in full, had no intention of operating a melting pot. But the Mongol did alter decisively the course of Russian history by diverting it from Europe. The writ of the khans of the Golden Horde isolated the Russian interior, the dukedoms of Kiev and Moscow, from the great trading towns of the Russian northwest which were closely linked to the towns of the Hanseatic League and thus to central and western Europe. While in the dukedoms a military aristocracy approximated feudalism, democracy prevailed in the northwest Russian towns. Nishnii Novgorod, chief among them, became a republic with its popularly elected assembly which, in turn, elected the chief magistrate. The influences which radiated from the northwest into the heart of Russia were cut off by Mongol conquest. The most suitable base for mounting Russia's counteroffensive against the Mongols, based upon the southern and eastern plains, was Moscow. The centralizing, autocratic tendencies of the Moscow princes were in part rooted in the central position of Moscow, placed in the midst of gentle, rolling, relatively featureless plains, in part in the nature of the struggle with Asiatic despotism. To prevail, the Moscow rulers fought fire with fire, cruelty with cruelty, guile with a cunning learned from generations of patient and supple dealings with Asiatic masters. Their centralism had its counterpart in the Mongol military organization which called for unquestioning discipline rather than individual feats of valor. These adaptations, forced upon Russia by the circumstances of conquest and liberation, did, indeed, influence the formation of the Russian character. Czarist and Soviet diplomacy with its patient groping for weaknesses in the armor of the opponent, czarist and Stalinist autocracy, czarist and Soviet administrative centralism, and the very forms of "popular democracy" imposed by the decree of the all-wise and all-powerful ruler as an instrument of autocratic manipulation, bear an oriental, Asiatic cast.*

Greek Orthodoxy was the religious pillar, supporting Muscovite autocracy. It reinforced the bars that separated Russia from the rest of Europe.

In 1439, the last of a long line of attempts to heal the

---

* "The Russian is at heart a nomad. . . . If Russia were really a proletarian society dominated by the factory and farm worker, the immense industrial progress which the regime has achieved would have been impossible." Sir David Kelly, British Ambassador to the Soviet Union, 1949–51, in the N. Y. *Times Magazine*, 23 December 1951.

breach between Western and Eastern Christendom appeared
to bear fruit. At the Florence Council, the Greek Orthodox
Church at last accepted "union" with the Catholics. By then,
it was too late.* The fall of Constantinople in 1453 was
viewed by Russian hierarchs and the Russian masses as the
punishment of God visited on the Greeks for their apostasy.
By the end of the fifteenth century, the official theory of the
Russian Church and State was formed: the succession of
the Byzantine emperors had to pass to the "third Rome,"
Moscow and its duke who remained the one and only true
Christian ruler on earth. To clinch the succession by dynastic
arrangements as well as spiritual sanction, Ivan III took to
wife Sofia, the only niece of the last Byzantine emperor,
Palaeologus. In foreign relations, Ivan signed himself "auto-
crat" and, with the arrival of the Byzantine princess at the
Moscow court, the Grand Duke openly avowed his imperial
pretensions. The Church had sanctioned the enhancement
of the throne and acknowledged the prince as its head. The
Church now claimed its rewards: the Czar's help against heresies, internal dissensions, and despoilers of its wealth. The
Czar made payment by punishing heretics and guaranteeing
the earthly possessions of the Church. The characteristics of
Russian rule emerged then and there, full blown: autocracy
and orthodoxy and their concentration in one person, the
ruler of the State and Church. The idea of the "third Rome"
runs, a red thread of continuity, through Russian thinking
up until our own times. It stirred the imagination of the
Russian pan-Slavists and intellectuals of the nineteenth century, foremost among them Dostoevski. It lives on, encased
in the bland dialectic of Stalinist Marxism, in the universal
pretensions of the homeland of socialism. It lives on in Moscow's insistence upon jurisdictional authority beyond appeal
over all Communist parties the world over; in the fulmina-

* See Edward Gibbon, *The History of the Decline and Fall of the Roman
Empire.* Vol. VI, chap. 66.

tions of the Kremlin against Marxist heretics, and lastly, in the deep-seated phobia of the Soviet autocracy toward all things Western and, above all, Western Christendom.*

With the fall of Byzantium, the link that held Russian Christianity to Western Christendom was broken beyond repair. Autocracy which owed its power to the vacancy of the Byzantine throne and the extinction of Constantinople's spiritual authority, made sure that the breach would never be healed.

The isolation of Russia from the main currents of Western cultural development up until the eighteenth century is an uncontroversial fact. Peter the Great was too much of a realist to have lavished his prodigious energies upon undoing it, had it not existed. But even after Peter the Great, who opened a carefully guarded window to the West, Russia's Western contacts remained highly selective and circumscribed by the limits of autocratic tolerance. In relation to the West, Russia's position was always and is today characterized by *ambiguity*.† To scratch a Russian is emphatically not to find the Tatar, any more than scratching the Spaniard is to find the Arab. Russia's revolt against the Mongol invader struck a blow for European freedom: Russia's unrelenting pressure against the Osmanli Turk relieved Austria and the Mediterranean peoples in the hour of supreme danger to the West. Lermontov, Tolstoy, and Turgenev are Western literary figures in the highest sense. Russian contrapuntal music and classic ballet are an integral part of Western aesthetical tradition. Yet whoever, possessed of sight, smell, and hearing, has traveled eastward across the borders of the ancient Kingdom

---

* Spengler noted the peculiar genesis of the Russian Church as a source of vast future emotional and political potentialities, ready to be channeled into a bid for world power, while Lenin and Trotsky still guided the destinies of world Communism from the cheap coffeehouses of Central Europe. Spengler's vision was in this case, as in many others, a great deal clearer than that of most of our contemporary analysts of Soviet power.

† Nikolai A. Berdiaev, *The Russian Idea*, N. Y., Macmillan, 1948.

of Poland will not have mistaken the cultural landscape gliding past the windows of his carriage for Europe. The fierce resistance of Poland to Russian encroachment and Poland's fervent self-dedication to the West are the most emphatic expression of Russia's otherness reflected in the consciousness of a Western people. One need not postulate Jung's "collective Unconscious" to uncover the source of Europe's spontaneous reaction to Russia whenever Russia moved westward. The shaggy Cossack ponies and their slant-eyed riders and the Russian infantryman with his good humor and humorless savagery stirred, in 1813, Europe's memories of a past that the tales of folklore had handed down to every man, woman, and child as vividly as if the events of which they told had happened yesterday. The memories of the warriors of Genghis Khan, Tamerlane, and Solyman the Magnificent, who raped, pillaged, and burned—in that order —were ineffaceable. To assume that Europe now has forgotten that particular, pungent meaning of Asia, is to assume that her memory has suddenly become amazingly and deplorably short. The presence now of Russia in Europe spells for the mass of Europe's peoples the return of Asia to Europe. Perhaps not the least important of differences between the American's and the European's point of view is that to the former the European's fear and aversion toward Asia or Asia in the guise of Russia appear far fetched. Hitler's rantings on "Asiatic Bolshevism" caused Americans to mistrust arguments based on Asia's alleged threats to Western culture. Yet Hitler merely exploited Europe's age-old and very real sense of insecurity.

Russia is not, and never was, wholly European. Russia is not wholly Asian and the peoples of Asia do not think she is—though the Soviets have employed propagandists recruited from Sovietized Asian tribes for publicizing Russian-Asian affinities. But an American to whom Europe's fear of Asia appears as either a dramatic pose or as a figment of neurosis should recall how close was Europe's escape from the embrace of Asia. The founding of the United States is all but contemporary with the termination of the last major Asian threat to Europe. Moreover, while Russia is ambiguous not all of her leaders are. Stalin and some of his closest collaborators *are* authentic Asians, born and bred upon Asian soil.

Never was the Western sky as blue as in the nineteenth century. The nineteenth century was the century of peace. Napoleon's fall marked the termination of an epoch of internecine wars, and the Congress of Vienna elaborated an international settlement that, but for minor changes, remained in force until 1914. The absence of general wars and the successful localization of conflicts which the Holy Alliance and the Concert of Powers could not smother into compromise, afforded the West an unprecedented opportunity. The West turned its creative powers singlemindedly to the works of peace. No other century in history contributed more to the progress of the human race.

It is easy for us to sneer at the exhibition of serene faith in progress and more progress in the future of nineteenth-century society. It is absurd to "expose" the fallacy of nineteenth-century assumptions by pointing to the failure *we* have made in applying these assumptions and in remembering what these assumptions were. The first of these assumptions was that men are sufficiently reasonable to see what their true interests are and to act accordingly. From this assumption follow all the others. Statesmen and peoples would exercise sufficient self-restraint to stop short in the pursuit of their national interests whenever that pursuit threatened to bring the roof down upon the international community as a whole and upon themselves. The abiding observance by Western statesmanship of this assumption was at the heart of the diplomacy by conference which achieved the settlement of Vienna (1814-15), of Paris (1856), and of

Berlin (1878). The same assumption underlies classical economics which supplied a conceptual systematization of what men were already doing and had been doing for some time, namely, pursuing reasonably their reasonable self-interest. The diplomatic and economic systems of the nineteenth century rested upon unwritten rules commanding the observance of, if perhaps not the great majority of men, then at least the elite controlling the levers of social action. These rules were largely those of Christian ethics. They were blended with aristocratic ideals which were suffused by religious concepts. The rising bourgeois elites of the Western nations had made this Christian-aristocratic code their own. Indeed, one of the major objectives of bourgeois political strivings was to wrest this code and the social rights and obligations which it stipulated from the exclusive possession of absolute monarchs and their courtiers. In no other country was this transfer and resultant transformation of society carried out more successfully than in Great Britain.

The history of British politics and of British thought on economics in the nineteenth century is meaningless without the ideal of the gentleman. British society expected that the public servant, trader, and professional would seek to approximate this ideal. They did—though this may surprise the twentieth-century cynic. Internationally, the British success in making the City of London the heart and center of the world market is the measure of Britain's success in making the ideal of the gentleman acceptable to others. The assumption that innumerable traders in other lands would, in their international dealings, abide by the gentlemanly code of the City, no matter how ungentlemanly they might have been at home, was justified. If it had not been, Britain would have been ruined long before the Age of Austerity.

The nineteenth century must be seen as a whole instead of an aggregate of unconnected compartments. Diplomacy by conference, Concert of Powers, code of conduct, ethical consensus, world market, free trade, and progress, each derives meaning from the other. Diplomacy by conference could have settled nothing had not the Metternichs, Talleyrands, Gladstones, Disraelis, Cavours, Bismarcks, and their confreres been agreed upon certain essentials and had they not deemed such agreement beyond the need of discussion. They could rely upon each other to do a minimum of those things each pledged himself to do and not to do a minimum of things that "were not done." These minima were immeasurably larger than the maxima of twentieth-century diplomatic conversation. Trade and enterprise were free; so were persons desirous of changing their residence. Peoples in a large number of countries enjoyed the privilege of changing their governments with the shedding of less blood than has ever flowed before or since in the pursuit of this activity.

No country reaped larger benefits from these freedoms, free trade, free migration, and democracy, than the United States. No country derived greater advantages from the then existing strategic order of things. The nineteenth century was the century of British balance-of-power policy. We discussed elsewhere the anatomy of British power. Suffice it here to note that British strategy was based upon two factors: sea power and geography. The former, because of the impressiveness of armor plate and cannon, was all too obvious. The latter was not. Britain expected that whatever threat might arise to her domination would materialize upon the European continent. It was Britain's purpose, from Cardinal Wolsey's time to the twentieth century, to prevent the junction of hostile European fleets and to interdict the high seas to that European power which, seeking to challenge British predominance, enlisted the following of other Continental naval powers. British strategic arrangements met this contingency ideally. Since any European power or combination of powers, seeking to break out from the Continent in order to strike out against the United States, would have had to run the gauntlet of British naval power and would have posed a threat to Britain, the balance-of-power policy and its instrument, the British Royal Navy, were the first defense of the United States. The arrangement did not cost the United States a penny and relieved the United States from the need of having a foreign policy and a navy of its own. As long as the United States had no need to fear Britain, there was no power on earth that she need fear.

The United States benefited beyond men's boldest dreams from the wondrous constellation of the nineteenth century. The United States remained at peace with the world, at peace to finance her growth with the monies saved on perennial military expenditures and with funds obtained from a secure and bountiful world capital market; at peace to fight small, highly advantageous local wars; and at peace to conclude without interference her own Civil War which cleared the ground for the development of American industry. However, implicit in Britain's strategic expectancy was another, a negative factor, namely, that Europe remain *the* power center whence all threats to the *status quo* would issue *and that Asia remain quiescent*. The quiescence of Asia is the reverse side of British power and of the entire fabric of nineteenth-century strategic, political, and economic arrangements. Britain had conquered her Asiatic empire by sea, and held it by seapower. But, British naval power, unsupported by land power, was incapable of meeting a major attack against the land frontiers of her Asian realm, notably Egypt and India. The penetration of Russia into central Asia and the development of a Russian railway system extending to the frontiers of Persia, Afghanistan, and the Pacific Ocean, constituted the first challenge that British sea power could *not* meet. Germany's attempt, in World War I, to invade Egypt by land, was the second; Japan's landward thrust against the frontiers of India, in World War II, was the third. The withdrawal of Britain from India was prompted by a complex of considerations that we cannot unravel here. However, the first and perhaps the most decisive consideration that shaped British policy was that India could not be held strategically except at a price of British resources that Britain was no longer willing and able to meet.

The quiescence of Asia is as much part of the constellation of the nineteenth century as are the positive factors: consensus, peace, and power. The quiescence of Asia was, as it always had been, the reciprocal of the full flowering of Western culture. Asia's dynamism had been arrested by a complex of forces. For one, the initial burst of Western inventiveness and industrial productivity had raised the technological superiority of the West, particularly in respect to weapons, to a potency which no amount of Asian skills and man power could rival. Though Russia's defeat in the Crimean War channeled Russian energies into the conquest of a vast Asiatic realm, Russia appeared, and perhaps indeed was, never less Asiatic and never more Western than in the nineteenth century. The Concert of Powers reserved for Russia a prominent and dignified place in the councils of Europe. The working European internationals of dynasts, aristocrats, and financiers had established close and fruitful connections with their Russian opposites. Most Russian intellectuals were predisposed, although for considerations diametrically opposed to those animating the ruling elites, to seek the light in the West. It was not before the nineteenth century neared its close that a few rare Westerners suspected that Russia might again incarnate the Asiatic challenge.

It is interesting to note that, the first country to Westernize having been Japan, the state of Asia appeared all the more reassuring in Western eyes. For the face of rising Japan was turned toward the Asiatic continent, toward China and the Asiatic possessions of Russia. That stance suited perfectly the diplomacy of Britain, guardian of Western universal interests. Moreover, the insular Japanese adopted, together with armor plate and rifles, the forms of constitutional government, a choice most un-Asiatic. We can see now that these signs and portents did not reveal the inwardness of Asia's situation in the nineteenth century. Asia passed through one of the cyclic periods of recuperation and rebirth that mark the rhythm of her history. The paralysis of China and the apathy of her masses made for the ease in the West's Far Eastern expansion. The resurgence of China in our times was inscribed in the rhythm of Chinese history in which expansion alternates with contraction, social integration with social disintegration. That China's resurgence should have coincided with an "Asiatic" turn of Russian history and with the most ominous schism of Western culture may be a mere accident. It is, however, the last of a series of accidents that have recurred with such frequency in the history of Western culture and of the cultures that endowed it most richly, as to suggest an astonishing regularity, if not a law of history.

The twentieth century is not the century of Asia—at least, it is not that yet. But the awakening of Asia, coincident with Western spiritual and political crisis, is neither a figure of speech nor a novelty. The phenomenon is so much a part of the Western tradition that the West would not be what it is without it. The problem it poses is the most serious one the West now meets and will have to meet for the foreseeable future. It is a strange one only to those unfamiliar with the history of Western culture.

III
Recessional

THE WEST AT BAY

HISTORY is state papers, chronicles, biographies, monuments, dungeons, palaces, hovels, ruins, battlefields, and tales. The historian, depending upon his inclination, mixes his mortar, selects his bricks, and builds his highly personal Historical Museum Without Walls. By this method it is easy to show where we were. It is not so easy to show where we are now, for the evidence is scattered all around us. There is no time to order it and one is apt to overlook the things—the "Purloined Letters"—that are under one's very nose.

We have sought to trace the origins of Western culture and its development since the point of confluence and plenitude that we call: Renaissance. What is the state of Western culture here and now? The most obvious contemporary feature is that of geographic shrinkage—not the much tauted shrinkage of the globe in terms of air travel time, but the shrinkage of the geographical domain over which Western culture indisputably holds sway. Asia has returned to Europe; Soviet Russia stands at the hub of Europe's peninsular spokes. The part of Europe that remains Western is not so much larger than that enclosed by the Roman Limes; indeed, for several hundred miles the Iron Curtain rests upon the line of Rome's farthest advance into the Germanies and the Danubian Basin. There are some differences: Scandinavia and north Germany lie to the west of Russia's dominions; however, Vienna, the Roman Vindobona, Hungary-Pannonia, and Romania-Dacia lie within the Russian orbit. Yugoslavia, the composite of lands that had at one time or another been garrisoned by

Roman legions, is a lesser ambiguity which detached itself from ambiguous Russia.

In Asia, Western culture has been in full retreat, if not to say, routed. True, before departing, Western culture had introduced the rudiments of technology. It had done so notably in India, Indonesia, and in parts of the Middle East, throughout the Chinese littoral, and, through the mediation of Japan, in Manchuria, a country that, in its present shape, is wholly the creation of Western technology. The West, by grafting its industrial techniques and administrative skills upon Asian cultures, wrought profound and irrevocable changes in the lives of the Asian peoples. The effects of Western techniques for preserving and prolonging lives are statistically measureable. But these statistical facts, as for example the doubling of India's population in the last hundred years and the raising within the same period of Indian average life expectancy from twenty to thirty years are facts suspended in a spiritual vacuum.

Though the technology of the West was thus readily available for export, the culture of which that technology formed part was not. It could not be, for it was the product of unique historical circumstances, a unique environment and a unique epoch. The West could not crate its culture with its machines, marked: Export, except for oddments (just as, in Europe, tobacconists used to place in cigar boxes reproductions of famous paintings). It could not ship its particular cultural pathology to Asian lands. If Asia thus could partake of Western culture only at random, it was at least spared its ills—or at least, some of them. And here we grasp one of the principal causes of Western crisis. It lies in the fact that the physical and psychological make-up of Western man does not correspond to his technological civilization. His spirit, his political and social institutions were formed in an epoch when he lived in close harmony with the rhythm of nature, the soil, and was attached to the land. Because Western society has tended to loose organic cohesion, it has attempted to recapture unity by organization. Lest we be understood as admitting the organic theory of culture by the back door, having cast it out by the front door, we hasten to acknowledge this analogy to be—an analogy. It is, however, one that fits the comparison of West and East tolerably well, precisely because "organic" and "organization" belong to two discrete categories of experience.

Organization is quantitative. The mass is a quantity; it is shaped by political and social organization designed to integrate, release, and curb its latent forces. It is, unlike the family or the small rural community of families that derive their form from organic functions, a thing to be formed or, rather, cast into a mold. Modern propaganda, political slogans, advertisement are, no matter how low or high their intellectual contents, primarily addressed to the anonymous, the anonymity of the urban masses. Were these appeals not keyed to the statistical notion of the average man, they would fail in their purpose. Then voters would not vote for the right program of, let us say, social welfare for the millions at so many dollars or pounds or francs per head or for the right leader who, to lead, must obtain the support of millions of citizens; customers would not purchase the product that, in order to be available at a low price, must yield profits to its maker and must be bought by millions. This, it should be clear, is not a value judgment: it says nothing about the merit of programs, leaders, and products; all may be good or bad. However, all must in their bid for public attention make themselves into the expression of the aspirations of a vast collectivity that tends increasingly to be not only the highest but the sole unit of social integration. By comparison, Asiatic society is still an organic society, despite the impact of Western technology, science, and political ideas. It is still largely a unitary society in which the preindustrial relation of man and nature has remained intact. Some acclaim the fact that

Asia has not yet cast off the binding layers of tradition as a token of continuity; others deplore it as a token of backwardness. As the case may be: it is a fact. It may be due simply to the circumstances that the machine has come to Asia only within the last generation and that Asia thus stands approximately where the West stood in, let us say, 1850. Asia, for all we know, may yet launch herself upon exactly the same course as that traced by Western industrialization. Yet that Asia has not done so may be due to fundamental differences separating the culture of the West from the cultures of Asia. It is the persistence of the organic social pattern, result perhaps of a time lag, perhaps of particular circumstances, which is at the root of the problems facing Asia in this generation. And these problems are not those of the West.

Although the introduction in Asia of Western techniques of transportation, hygiene, and agriculture and of Western administrative methods, notably public safety, resulted in preservation of life, it did not change that basic human institution, the family, and moral and religious customs built around and into it. The result was the tidal release of Asia's latent biological forces. While the increase of European population, triggered by industrialization, was accompanied by the opening up of the rich, yet sparsely settled, plains lands of America, Siberia, Africa, and Australia, increase in Asia was taking place under world conditions which precluded relief from population pressure, real or "felt," by exploitation of virgin resources.

In the countries of the West, with their reasonably efficient governments and relatively stable populations, the problem today is to expand industrial production and ensure its distribution; in brief, maintain or raise the comparatively high standards of living of the prewar era. In Asia, the problem is how the production of the commodities basic to human subsistence can be made to keep pace with a colossal increase of population. This means, of course, that the industrial production, too, must increase in order to improve agricultural technology and to provide essential services, such as irrigation, transportation, and hygiene, which will ensure the elementary safety of so large a concentration of people on so relatively small a cultivable area. But industrialization is secondary in importance to increase of agricultural production. This becomes obvious if we face up to the question: Can India and China, by emulating Japan's historical example, build up their export industries and purchase from the proceeds of exports the food stuffs they lack? The fact is that even if they could—which is doubtful—outside of Asia there is no surplus capacity for food production sufficient to meet the import demands of Asia. The problem of Asiatic human subsistence, as it is presenting itself in fairly concise dimensions, will be solved in the countries of Asia or it will not be solved at all. Again, Asia's economic problems, just as the problem of Asia's social integration, are wholly unlike those of the West. As a matter of fact, both culturally and economically the characteristics and interests of the West and the characteristics and interests of Asia are opposites. On the basis of available evidence, the forecast must read: increasing tensions and conflict. That forecast is sustained by current political developments.

The growth of nationalism in Asia has paralleled the assimilation of Western techniques. Perhaps nationalism is simply the result of Western influences, an importation; perhaps it is the spontaneous response to foreign domination; perhaps nationalism is a universal phenomenon and was latently present, although in a peculiar form, in the collective mind of Asia. No matter which of these explanations is accepted as the most plausible one, Asiatic nationalism is a rising force. The attitude of Asiatic nations toward schemes for world organization, world leagues, and world federations is notably cool. It is emphatically not the same as that of Western peoples to whom a universal sense of danger suggests the advantage of collective security in the form of a supranational organization. The new Asian nation-states are decidedly unenthusiastic about schemes for submerging the national independence, so recently won, in a world federation or the like. The exchanges between Premier Nehru of India and Premier Liaquat Khan of Pakistan over Kashmir were couched in the hackneyed language of nationalist extremism; some of the accusations and epithets employed in their controversy would have made Mussolini blush. If nationalism is something the great mass of Western intellectuals would like to get away from, their Asiatic colleagues appear to take to it with a will and an aptitude of their own. As for organizing their economic realm, the new Asiatic states have shown themselves eager pupils of the most extreme doctrines of national self-sufficiency, the very doctrines leading Western economic thought rejects. For example the Republic of Indonesia hired Dr. Hjalmar Schacht, apostle of "autarky," to advise it on how to design its international economic policies.

The leaders of Asia propose to industrialize in order to raise the living standards of the masses. Concerned as they are with the economic welfare of their peoples, they are not unaware of the fact that industrialization is the basis of modern state power. They have centered their efforts not so much on the expansion of consumer goods production as on the development of heavy industry. Thus the first fruit of Asian independence and economic planning has been guns, more guns. Though some of these guns serve to maintain the positions of these countries in the intra-Asian power game, some of them are forthrightly aimed at the West. Thus, the initial effort of Asia's new nation-states toward industrialization has been toward industrialization for political power rather than economic welfare. It is here that the attractiveness for Asians of the Soviet model of industrialization can be seen most clearly. The West's prescription for the economic development of Asia can be summed up in two words: gradual transformation. The Western method is that of the piecemeal approach. That approach seeks to preserve Asia's cultural heritage by strengthening the economic basis of human freedom. Though the self-interest of the West stands for much in this prescription, the formula imposes the least strain upon Asia's social fabric and upon the lives of the great mass of the peoples.

Adoption of the Soviet model entails for Asia the same sacrifices which the Russian people brought to its realization. The Soviet pattern was, and still is, that of economic self-sufficiency and hence of rockbound nationalism. The application to Asia requires rigid central controls and the revolutionary liquidation of the old order. In Asia this would mean a complete and momentous break with the traditional organic culture. It would mean the exploitation of hundreds of millions of peoples by forced labor in order to create the "savings," the investment capital, required by the gigantic costs of heavy industry. The kulak or the "traitor" or whatever name the victim of Soviet justice may be called is an economic necessity of the Soviet system. It is a mere matter of expediency that determines which groups of the population are singled out for bearing the burden of national self-sufficiency. If capital cannot be obtained abroad from those who can spare it for investment and if domestic savings are inadequate at home, as they are everywhere in Asia, Operation Kulak is the one and only alternative. Now, this operation would remove one difference between Western and Eastern society: it would deprive the latter of its organic nature. It would do so, however, by destroying it in one fell swoop. It would do so with a vengeance: the system that would take its place would be that of the centralized organization of the Soviet state, Asian despotism in industrial dress. It would not be that of Western industrial society.

The attractiveness of the Soviet model for Asian political and intellectual elites is not confined to its economic parts. It resides also in its built-in philosophy. When Lenin and

Plekhanov at the conference of the Russian Social Democratic party in 1903, demanded from their shocked colleagues the approval of the doctrine that basic civil liberties, "the sacrosanctity of the person," could be infringed upon or even violated if the Party leaders so decided, they not only struck at the heart of Western cultural tradition but oriented, though perhaps unconsciously, Russian Communism toward Asia. Though Plekhanov, a cultivated Western scholar, later retreated from this position of brutal denial of Western morality, Lenin did not.* Though we may charitably assume that Lenin viewed the coercion, violence, and suppression of human rights by a small, self-appointed, revolutionary elite as unavoidable evils of the temporary struggle against a ruthless enemy, the mixture of utopian faith and brutal practice became the most enduring feature of Soviet power.

Lenin's doctrine is a tempting one for Asian leaders. They are intent upon industrializing rapidly; they are faced by vast masses of peasants, illiterate and therefore incapable of reading the latest decree and instructions on how to operate a tractor or turret lathe or how to vote for the government's exclusive list of candidates; and they are insecure and inexperienced in the employment of their authority. They are tempted by the simple, though barbaric, Leninist concept of elite power. That concept is merely the "dialectic" formulation of Asia's most ancient practices of political rule. Therefore, some Asian leaders may have to do violence to the Western moral preconceptions which they absorbed, together with other matters, at Oxford, the London School of Economics, and Columbia, but not to indigenous Asian political morality.

As matters stand now in Asia, all native Asian governments are one-party governments; all have abridged, under one pretext or another, the "sacrosanctity of person"; all are violently

---

* Isaiah Berlin, "Political Ideas in the Twentieth Century," *Foreign Affairs*, April, 1950; p. 365 ff.

nationalist, and none has manifested more than purely formal interest in the blessings of Western culture—except in its technological gadgetry. These facts are so massive and so fervently avowed by Asian intellectual spokesmen, if not quite so forthrightly by some Asian leaders maneuvering for free contributions from the West's technological treasure house, that one wonders precisely where Western advocates of "meetings between East and West," draw sustenance for their rosy expectations. If Asian leaders have set out, as some of their Western admirers aver, upon the earnest quest for a meeting ground between East and West where cultures "blend," they have done so by the most circuitous road imaginable.

The "spirituality" of Asia is one of the favorite props of the Western barkers before the "world culture" shop. "Asian spirituality" is ineffable in more ways than one. The spiritual content of Western culture owes little to the cultures that held sway over the vast land masses of Asia. Its vast debt is to the Near East, impregnated by Hellenic thought and sharply demarcated by topography against the bulk of Asia. Mithraism, Hebrew religion, Christianity, and Islam, the great monotheistic religions, originated in a relatively small region that is as much a bridge to Europe as it is, geographically, a part of Asia. The great native cultures of the Asian mainland, India, Farther India, and China were and still are atheist. Neither the Hindu religion nor Buddhism, whatever their spiritual depth, can be mistaken for the severe monotheism of the great Near Eastern and Western faiths. Neither Taoism nor Confucianism are religions. The former, with its master's unique gesture of strength-in-inactivity, was never a religion. It is now, due to metaphysical modifications added in complete contradiction to Lao-tse's original teachings, no longer a coherent philosophy. Confucianism is a practical code of conduct, not a religion. Its stark pragmatism should shock a sensitive Western seeker for the good and the beautiful even more violently than the "truth as process" of Georg Wilhelm Friedrich Hegel or the naïve pragmatism of John Dewey. It is as remote from the idea of God as are the spiritual club rules of the latter. And as for the mysticism of Asia, its most active and best-heeled cults can be now found in Paris, London, New York, and Hollywood. The day is near, if it is not here, when the average Asian intellectual will have to buy the latest treatise (in English) by Ouspensky if he wishes to explore the mysticism that was Asia. Incidentally, it never was.

If Western culture is today the white man's culture, this is no longer exclusively because of the white man's racial clannishness. This is so, if for no other reason, than because the evolution of world politics has reduced the domain of Western culture to the Atlantic region. Asia has developed a racial consciousness very much her own. Perhaps hostility to the white man is the strongest common bond uniting the peoples of Asia. That this hostility is not shared, or perhaps not shared to the same degree, by the people of Japan is not a net gain to the credit of the West, for Japan, the offshore island, has drawn upon herself the antagonism of the rest of Asia. The Russians are whites. However, Russian imperialism did not encroach, at least not until recently, upon the densely settled regions of the Far East and south Asia. The anti-white sentiments of Asia are still concentrated upon the very peoples who make up the residual core of the Western world: the British, the Dutch, the French, the Americans, the Italians, and the Germans, for it was these peoples that represented Western imperialism in southeast and south Asia and in the Treaty Ports of China. Thus the antagonism of Asia is both anti-white and anti-Western. The only conception on which West and East still see eye to eye is the powerful but ambiguous one of technological progress. The West has its technology to give, the East is only too ready to take it.

Western culture, including its technology, is the product

not only of environmental factors, physical and historical, but also of a race, to wit, the white race. The question as to whether the white race is "superior" to other races is an absurd question. The white race itself is racked by doubts as to its moral or spiritual superiority over all kinds of primitive or not-so-primitive races of other colors. Shakespeare, Rousseau, and a host of Westerners deeply steeped in their own culture attributed to men of darker skin virtue greater than that possessed by their own race. Moreover, the ideology of the superiority of the *white race as a whole* was confined almost entirely to certain Anglo-Saxon population groups. It never was a popular ideology among Latins, Slavs, and the Germanic peoples of the Continent—Adolf Hitler notwithstanding. As regards matters of technologic proficiency, the white race *has* a firm claim to superiority. That superiority is formidable with respect to all other races, the yellow included. To deny this fact is either a token of ignorance or a brazen attempt to flatter the nonwhite races, though such flattery really amounts to insult. To deny this fact is to demean the authentic achievement of the white race, though technological superiority is not the full measure of the white man's worth one way or the other.

No race ever had or has now a monopoly of intelligence. Indian and Chinese physicists did work of Nobel Prize caliber: Indian and Japanese metallurgists and chemists have made the most advanced industrial techniques their own. Japanese, Chinese, and Indian textile manufacturers drove Western cotton goods from the Asiatic market. Asian mathematicians and researchers in the pure sciences have contributed important discoveries. Highest Asian intelligence is capable of mastering the same subjects which elsewhere the highest intelligence, availing itself of the requisite training facilities, can master. As for war technology, Asians have proven apt pupils and ingenious on their own account— though the efficiency of war technology is not necessarily a token of over-all technological efficiency but the result of a deliberate choice, the extent to which a nation chooses to drain its productivity into the making of weapons.

If there is any excuse for pointing out what should go without saying, it is that all kinds of unwarranted assumptions have been based upon the obvious aptitudes of Asians for learning and developing Western science and techniques. It is asserted, for example, that Asians, given time and certain historical opportunities, could have developed an industrial technology of their own or that they could expand independently the techniques they borrowed from the West, were they now cut off from the Western sources of their learning. Both assertions are, first, unprovable and secondly, from the point of view of the short-run developments with which we live or can survey retrospectively, based on highly risky assumptions. To begin with, modern industry with its power-driven tools *is* the exclusive creation of the West. Secondly, the Industrial Revolution of the eighteenth and nineteenth centuries derived its techniques from scientific methods devised by Western scientists and philosophers in the seventeenth century. Thirdly, the intellectual and moral disciplines derived from Greek thought and Christian ethics, which are the imponderable prerequisites of Western efficiency, have no counterpart in Asian thought and ethics.*

The Asiatic is "machinable"—to a degree. Western man does not only seek felicity *through* machinery, he finds felicity *in* machinery. He not only uses machinery efficiently and happily, he also efficiently and happily maintains it. It is one thing to know how to use machinery, it is another thing to repair it, improve it, renew it, and conceive it anew in response to new requirements and inventions. That the West still leads in this respect by a wide margin is borne out by statistical data such as that for inventiveness (patents) and

---

* André Siegfried, *L'Âme des Peuples,* Paris, Hachette, 1950, pp. 212-17. (Published in the U. S. as *Nations Have Souls,* G. P. Putnam's Sons, 1952.)

real income per head of population and of gainfully employed industrial labor. The facts are so plain that they seem
hardly worth stating. But the Asian menace to the Western
way of life—in the form of war or competition—and the Asian
promise—in the form of marketing opportunities and economic co-operation—have been so inflated that the bubbles
require pricking.

The only major menace here and now to the Western "way
of life" is contained in that way of life itself. If Asia is a
menace, it is a latent one. To release that Asian menace, the
West itself has to breach the protective dikes.

The West invented the machine driven by steam, combustion, and electricity. From this invention issued a new
technique of production: mechanization. Mechanization has
made the West what it is today. Mechanization is the instrument of Western power. It is the fruit of science. However, technology and science are not the same thing. The
Greeks, for example, possessed deep insights into nature; they
did not employ their understanding of the laws of nature in
the quest of material progress. It was, in all likelihood, the
northward shift of Europe's political and economic center of
gravity that provided the incentive for the technical exploitation of scientific theories. A harsher climate called for more
solid man-made comforts than did the milder skies of the
Mediterranean. Science thus stepped from the study into the
workshop, and the problems of the workshop began to nag
imperiously at science. The philosophers still sought to explore nature for exploration's sake, but science could no
longer remain indifferent to the application of its findings,
for new challenges to pure research issued from application.

The technology of the West is inconceivable without
scientific methods of thought, so alien to the Asian mind.
However, the mechanization in which Western technology
achieved its highest expression to date is not identical with
science; it is a technique. By virtue of this technique man

made the forces of nature his servants and extended immensely the leverage of muscular energy. This is the precise meaning of mechanization. Mechanization gave rise to a new, unprecedented form of society. Science, put at the service of industry, transformed itself into a discipline for making the facts of nature conform to the needs of man. Science, put at the service of industry, became the servant of the will to power. For man possessed of such powerful tools sought to subject the resources of the entire earth to his bidding.

The age of mechanization opened with a raid on the natural riches of the planet. As the plunder reached fantastic proportions and began to discommode the very peoples who had engaged in it, science was at last called upon to devise remedial measures, "conservation." Experts disagree on the extent of the damage, but not on the plain fact that huge damage *was* done. The impatient exploitation of natural resources at an immensely accelerated rate wrought the marvels of mass production. The West reveled in its plenitude of things. It became only belatedly aware of the fact that it was drawing heavily on its capital.

For nearly two hundred years the West enjoyed serenely the monopoly of science and mechanization. The balance of power between the West and East, so precarious until Prince Eugene stormed Belgrade, was suddenly upset in favor of the West. Asia, awakening to the fact that the West's irresistible sweep across the globe had been triggered by its techniques, sought to assimilate the latter, not so much because of admiration but because of will to self-preservation. The machine is now the common property of all non-Western peoples, except those marooned on the remotest ledges of Toynbee's cliff. To handle an instrument is not so difficult; to make it and to replace it, to renew incessantly the bold onslaught upon the obsolescent—Schumpeter's "creative destruction" as the motive force of industrial development—that requires disciplines by which the West still abides with incomparable devotion.* It is in the steadfastness of this devotion that the secret of Western power is found. Outwardly, the power of the West is protected by the armor of its technology. But that armor is but the child of the flesh and bones of Western prowess. The gravest danger to the West is not the chinks in its armor; these Western ingenuity is sublimely capable of closing. The living culture of the West is nourished by sources that are as varied as its distant origins. The real danger is the drying up of these vital sources. Western technology is a product of Western culture. The West, by letting that culture go to rot and by putting its faith in the thing that culture made, technology, may bury under its own scrap and rubble the springs of its life. The danger to the West arises from its very domination of nature. Man may master ever vaster natural forces; he may no longer master himself.

* See Joseph A. Schumpeter, *Capitalism, Socialism, and Democracy*, 2nd ed., New York, Harper, 1947; pp. 81 *passim*.

MACHINE AND MASS

MECHANIZATION brought to a head, though it did not cause, the crisis of Western culture: alienation of man from vital beliefs, alienation of social groups from society, alienation of whole peoples from the Western community. Mechanization, by creating new forms of social life, challenged society to assimilate these new forces to its traditions. The challenge was not met, it is not met yet.

Society is by definition organized society, the integration of individual wills into a social order. Organized society is, at any given moment, a compromise between traditional habits and new methods which are in the course of making their influences felt. Western society is no exception to this generalization. However, there is a difference between Western society and preindustrial societies. All human societies, in order to remain vital, must operate the compromise between tradition and innovation. Now, the making of this compromise has turned into a desperate race. Never before was the development of an organizing principle less a matter of free choice. The structure of Western society is undergoing not slow cumulative changes, but a sudden drastic morphological change, at once all inclusive and irreversible. For the machine, itself, is a rigorous organization. The wide diffusion of machine technology, the great increase of population, and the increased proximity of cities to cities and peoples to peoples gave rise to an ever more inclusive trend toward social readjustment in terms of organized patterns. Traditional, organic society—the family and the community that the human eye could survey as Pericles could

still survey the assembly of his 5,400 free-born fellow citizens
—was swamped by quantitative problems far beyond its spatial range and moral-political authority. These quantitative
problems called insistently for the creation of ever larger
administrative units. The growth of administrative organization entailed a cumulative process of depersonalization.
Human society tended to approximate the machine, that
"most exact and dynamic organization perfected by man." *

The likening of social and political organization to "machine" and "machinery," though a habit of speech more current in America than in Europe, acknowledges forthrightly
the power over men's lives of mechanization: it is from the
machine that society takes its cue. The perfect machine is
perfect collectivization, for each part can be replaced by a
part rigidly conforming to its standard of identity, and the
operation of each part is a function of the operation of all
other parts. Thus the organization of society in response to
the machine and, unconsciously or consciously, on the pattern
of the machine is tantamount to collectivization, no matter
what the political ideology by which a society professes to live.
Indeed, the trend of Western society has been toward organization, depersonalization, and collectivism.

If there is one development within the last one hundred
years, common to all Western peoples, it is the rapid diminishment of autonomy, the autonomy of the family, the local
authority, the market, the Church—and the person. If the paid
hands of volunteers of "human progress" propaganda should
care to dispute the phenomenon by spurious references to
diverse freedoms with which man in the most advanced Western societies is allegedly blessed, they should be required to
state how the following questions were answered a hundred
years ago and how they will be answered today. Within any

* Roderick Seidenberg, *Post-historic Man*, Chapel Hill, Univ. of N. Carolina
Press, 1950, pp. 27-30.

Western nation, what is the percentage of families that have resided for more than, let us say, twenty years, in their present place of residence? What is the percentage of those who have abandoned their place of residence in that period? What is the longevity of families, how many families remained, within the life span of one generation, a unit? How many broke up? Does the head of the family decide such questions as the schooling and professional training of the family's minor members (the question whether parents decide if their off-spring should enter the military being charitably omitted)? What argument other than that of the potential owner (and if necessary, the builder's) is required to build a house, a factory, a hermit's shelter? What agreement other than one's own is required to engage upon foreign travel? How large a part of the population is engaged in administrative activities, notably the "public services"? How large a part in manufacturing, agriculture, and handicraft, notably the "private sector"? These questions can be multiplied at will, one for each social activity, without affecting in the least the end result of this comparative inquiry. Organization has grown, so has the size and power of the administrative and managerial apparatus. The stature of man, of family, of organic—or if one prefers the term, "informally organized"—social units has diminished. It is bumptious nonsense—or worse—to assert that within the last hundred years Western society has come closer to the ideals of institutional patterns "cut to the stature of man."

The dangers of "gigantism," the trends toward, and relish of, bigness in government, industry, skyscrapers and bombs have not escaped the notice of thoughtful observers. A growing international literature attests to the preoccupation with the problem: how to restore organic society, man's dignity, and his harmony with nature? Various remedies have been proposed such as increase of local autonomies by constitutional provisions,* decentralization of cities by the creation of "community centers" and "garden belts," † the creation of "plant communities" by transferring a share of "plant government" to the workers.‡ Various hopeful signs have been noted by the "communalists" and "decentralists" such as the tendency of certain industries, especially new industries, to eschew the construction of giant plants and to select rural areas rather than urban agglomerations as most suitable plant sites; the growing independence of commercial traffic from those old transportation bottlenecks, the railway junctions around which large cities have been built; and, on the political plane, a better informed public that participates—or at least "has been given the facts" necessary for participating—in national politics. The philosophies of these schools of thought are based mainly on fortuitous "self-curing" developments which they purport to discern, on the technical manipulations of technology for the purpose of "humanizing" technology, and on the organizational manipulation of organization for the purpose of "loosening" it and returning its control—or, at least, part of it—to smaller bodies.

Communalist and decentralist ideas are being vigorously propounded in the United States, Britain, France, and the smaller highly industrialized countries of Europe, by a small devoted band of thinkers, managers, and engineers. They provoke healthy debate. They are being tested in interesting practical experiments in city halls and factories. However, this fight against "gigantism" has not won a significant victory anywhere. The big cities are still getting bigger, their rural margins are being swallowed by slick building projects that are no more "personal" than were the old blocks of

---

* See especially Adriano Olivetti, L'*Ordine politico delle Communità*, Rome, 1948.

† See Lewis Mumford, *The Culture of Cities*, N. Y. Harcourt Brace, 1938, and *The Condition of Man*, N. Y. Harcourt, Brace, 1944.

‡ Peter Drucker, *The New Society*, N. Y., Harper, 1950.

tenements, though they shrewdly exploit the cliff dweller's longing for green pastures. Vast bureaucracies are still growing vaster. They breed a new kind of efficiency, namely, the effortless efficiency of developing new controls, intervening intimately in the remaining "private" sectors of social life, and creating those permanent emergencies which are the routine posture of modern society and call for compliance with virtually any abridgment of personal freedom as a civic duty.

The unassuaged appetite for material satisfaction is growing while consuming. It is impossible to open, anywhere in Western lands, a popular magazine or a daily paper or turn the plastic key to the ether without arriving at the conclusion that ultimate felicity *can* be had through machinery. Professions of self-denying ordinances and of devotion to things of the spirit are contradicted, more often than not on the same page, by unblushing promises of the grossest pleasures of the flesh and of satisfaction of group and individual selfishness. Evidently, the true nature of this propaganda is not revealed by the overt professions of the "mass media" but by their role in the general scheme of things. If privately owned, it is their mission to sell things; were they to fail in that mission, they would be forced out economically. If publicly owned, it is their mission to "sell" political dogmas and administrative policies; were they to fail in that mission their management would soon be dismissed by the ruling group or party.

The age of mechanization, administration, and "gigantism" is the age of the masses. The very word "masses" is charged with ideological dynamite. There are the "'masses" in the flesh. They crowd the ball games, and jam Forty-second Street and Fifth Avenue at five o'clock. There are the masses as a tendency. This tendency has suggested the term "massification," a word as unlovely as the tendency to which it is applied. The term arouses instantly the intense responses of

various schools of thought, ranging all the way from traditional liberalism to traditional conservatism. To the former
the "masses" is a pathological development of modern society. To the latter, the "masses" is the shapelessness that has
invaded the realm of "form," manners, and tradition, if it is
not that dangerous beast, the mob. To the collectivist, "progressive" or whatever we may call a foe of traditional social
stratification, this explanation is, at least so he avows, rank
heresy. For the "masses" are simply you and I; the term is
meaningless, for the "masses" simply do not exist, for you
and I are not the mass, we are the Public. Or, the "masses"
are simply those who are not allowed to share in government
and the good things of life; they are "mass" because society
does not admit them to forms of social integration. Or, the
"masses" are the good people, their brow sweatstained, the
"working masses" or "masses of toilers" as opposed to sloth-
ful spongers and lustful exploiters of the great majority of the
people. The "masses" are the innocent, the industrious, and
the brave. The concept of the "common man" adds a slightly
different tilt to the meaning of "masses." To belong to the
"mass of common men" is to be deserving, a badge of honor,
not of opprobrium. Even these few examples should illumin-
ate the shades of meaning that attach to "masses" and the
ideological freight the term is made to carry. Tell me what
you mean by "masses" and I will tell you what your politics
are, whether you know what they are, or whether you claim
to have no politics whatsoever. One's position in the universe
of political ideologies can be determined with considerable
precision by one's attitude to the "masses."

We have touched upon the problem of collective—group or
national—psychology in one of the preceding chapters. We
noted that the treatment of "misunderstandings" and tensions between peoples, alienation and hostility, in terms of
the psychology of individuals in a society, affords no insights,
except wrong ones, into the problem of Western culture, or,

for that matter, any culture or relationships of cultures. The transposition of the concepts of individual psychology to the field of international society, as, for example, that of the frustration-aggression sequence, "easily leads to the ridiculously untenable proposition that individual mental health is a panacea for the whole problem of intergroup and international conflict." * It follows that the attitudes of a group are not equivalent to the attitudes of the majority of individuals in that group, with culture operating as the catalyst of individual attitudes. Were this not so, then the tendencies of a group, society, or nation at any given moment would be the mere aggregates of the tendencies of the individuals, or at least of the great majority of individuals, within it. The latter hypothesis is, of course, untenable. It might have been a valid one in the feudal age when political tendencies were entirely confined to a small segment of the population and when the bulk of the population, the peasantry, had no defined political tendencies. Then the individual tendencies of knights could indeed be equated with the tendencies of knightly society, and that was all anyone from king to page needed to know. Evidently, modern society's tendencies are not so simple. Were they so simple, then no modern nation would go to war, since the great majority of individuals opposes war.

This conclusion then suggests to us the importance of "media" of all sorts for transforming individual tendencies into something quite different from "individual." Indeed, this conclusion directed contemporary research in social psychology (or psychological sociology) toward the formulation of such concepts as "elites," "attentive public," "leadership," and "power structures." These formulations say less than they imply. What else do they assume but the existence of a something that is not "elite," not "attentive," that is lead and

* David B. Truman, "Political Behavior and International Tensions," *World Politics,* Vol. III, No. 4, July 1951, pp. 548-49.

that obeys "power"? That something is the "masses," not the
mass of medieval peasants who as a dynamic social factor did
not exist, but the mass of people within the modern state who
can read, to whom political arguments are addressed, and
who are presumed to weigh these arguments, to arbitrate their
merits, and to give their decision as expressed by the ballot.
Thus the millions are on the one hand presumed to possess
the same discrimination as the "elites," the "attentive public," the "leader," and the group in "power"; yet the fact that
the latter minorities, some infinitesimal, are singled out and
are presumed to function separately or even independently
betrays the existence of a gap. What is this gap if it is not the
void that separates the few from the many, the articulate
from the inarticulate, form from mass?

In a sense the "elite" few and the "attentive" many, the
"public" (informed or not so informed) and the "leader" are
married to each other. One has no existence without the
other. Each contemplates the other with an odd mixture of
emotions. All attempts to bury this strange relationship of
modern mass society beneath savant formulations and glib
hypocrisies will not exorcise its ghost. That ghost has haunted
democracy for a long time, certainly before Aristotle exposed
it as an earthly accomplice of popular rule.

The "mass" does exist. It is not a chimera. Leaving aside
for the moment the etiology of "mass," let us examine its
behavior. Evidently, the line separating "elites" from the
"mass" is not fixed. If certain conditions are given an individual loses his "elite" status and is swallowed by the "mass,"
and the "attentive public" loses its discriminating adjective
and turns into a simple "public"; that is, a mere mass of educated men and women obeying the same stimuli the less
erudite "mass man" obeys. Not even the most contemptuous
critics of the masses, as for example, Ortega y Gasset and
Gustave Le Bon, assert that formal social status as, for example, membership in a ruling group, aristocracy or "good so-

ciety," guards the individual against absorption by the mass. The "mass" is not a static thing but a dynamic relationship, to wit, an everchanging relation of the shapeless anonymous to integrated society; there is not only a circulation of "elites" but a circulation between "elites" and mass. In a certain mass situation, as, for example, panic, a meritorious member of the political or spiritual elite may behave like a stampeding "mass man"; an insensate, illiterate half-wit, by his example of calm and indifference to danger, may behave like a leader and savior. However, one must guard against analogies between the mass that can be spatially defined, the mass at the game or at the political meeting or at the scene of a disaster, and the mass we speak of when we refer to the pressure of "mass opinion," the aspirations of the "mass of common men," and other kindred manifestations of the anonymous which we can apprehend only by inferences—if we can apprehend them at all.

We infer from certain changes in policies, standards, and slogans that these changes are the effects of a blindly working will, not of rational deliberations. We acclaim these changes as desirable or undesirable depending on our ideals or prejudices. (It goes without saying that no one who has given the phenomenon, mass, a thought deems himself part of the "masses": this goes for mass psychologists, admirers and defenders of the "toiling masses," or any one who writes about masses or deals with them, and, especially, for those whom the masses have chosen to lead them.) But we note that the changes do not correspond to individual tendencies and we cannot help noting that not infrequently the mass wills crucial changes that are the exact opposite of what nearly all individuals in society profess to want and in all likelihood do want. It is precisely through the gap of this contradiction that the irrational enters. Without the concept of "mass," the "irrational" has no meaning in politics. Indeed, for a society that was so distinctly not a mass society as that of the eighteenth century, the "irrational" had no political meaning at all. Mass and leader are reciprocals; the society of the eighteenth century knew no "masses," no Führer.

In the modern sense "mass" is latent energy; it is action. Even at rest, the "masses" exercise pressure. Psychologists ascribe to the individual a certain emotional and intellectual formation, the normal one distinguished especially by the pre-eminence of consciousness. In mass situations, however, a release of emotional forces weakens and, in extreme cases, submerges the powers of the intellect and moral will. The individual then loses his identity and disappears in the mass. This is the mass situation in the historical sense: the storming of the Bastille; the collective rapture evoked by Hitler-in-the-brewery. This process, however, is independent of a specific place or occasion. It is at work wherever man loses his identity or so alters his conduct that he blends with the other members of the mass into a new entity. This entity is the mass in the psychological sense, that is, the psychological mass. It is this psychological mass that alters the physiognomy and the spirit of Western culture. Its giant specter hovers over all public affairs, the deliberations of the politicians, the industrialists, the merchants, the diplomats. In politics, it is no longer the political issue itself that dictates strategy, as, for example, deflation versus inflation, but the anticipated reaction of the masses and the likelihood that this or that alternative can be imposed, with the right kind of propaganda, upon them. Politics thus becomes a gamble in mass psychology. In diplomacy, the task is no longer to anticipate a move by the opponent, but to anticipate its effect upon the psychology of the masses, one's own and the opponent's. This is the meaning of "direct" and "open" diplomacy, a contest for mass opinion in which the techniques of propaganda, commercial advertising, and allied arts are more important than the techniques of diplomacy proper and the concrete diplomatic issue.

Thus twentieth-century politics, business, diplomacy, entertainment, art are so many games played with and against the masses. The stakes are vast, for the mass is the source of vast power. The game is played under the eyes of the millions, the watchful mass. The perfection of the player's performance is attended by a decrease in spontaneity; the game is "staged." The "spontaneous demonstration" at the Nuremberg Party Rally or on the Red Square are the most brazen exhibits of rehearsed mass effects. However, they are not so remote in principle from the techniques of contemporary Western politics. The carefully rehearsed informality of "fireside chats," the taking the masses into the political leader's confidence about highly complex national or international issues, the leader's off-the-record remark dropped casually after months of systematic sampling and polling of public opinion, the publicity attending public hearings before congressional or parliamentary committees, are part and parcel of mass techniques. So is the journal of the reminiscing statesman scanned before publication by battalions of staff members and public relation experts and then candidly offered (in one million copies, first printing) as intimate revelations. So is public diplomacy, a drama staged for the benefit of the mass audience.

And yet here again yawns the gap. Never before were the intricacies of public administration so inaccessible to the great mass of citizens as they are today. Never before were so many administrative decisions, which are in fact legislative and judicial decisions, made in the inner sanctums of bureaucracy and not in the public forums of legislatures and courts. Never before was the routine conduct of international affairs shrouded in denser clouds of secrecy and the tiniest breach of "security" punished more rigorously. The gap has opened beneath the feet of the Muses. The novelist pours his soul into that rare work of excellence, destined for the discriminating few, and by a stroke of magic, the resultant book, with some skillful prompting by hordes of expert publicists, advertisers, jacket designers, and salesmen, achieves overnight the rank of a best seller. Miraculously, too, the moving picture rights are bought, for a large sum of money, by a leading producer with assured outlets before the first copy of the book is sold. One need not risk exposure to the caustic remarks dropped, off the record naturally, by commuters on the New York-Hollywood shuttle, to fall prey to gnawing doubts.

Never before have the masses been invested by constitutional provisions and the eulogies of politicians, academics, and sales executives so categorically with omniscience. Their judgment, they are assured, is the ultimate arbiter of the nation's foreign policy, the statesman's moral fiber, the automobile's quality, and the artist's creation. Yet never before were there as many experts and never has the expert received greater acclaim and emolument precisely because of his possession of expert knowledge, knowledge possessed by him and him alone. In view of the high differentiation of skills in modern society this cannot be otherwise; but this is precisely what the fiction of the man in the street as the incarnation of good judgment and as the repository of information—of *all* the facts—cheerfully denies.

The presence of the masses as *the* decisive factor upon the public scene, noted more than a century ago by numerous observers belonging to virtually every political and philosophical camp, has suggested the conclusion that Western culture entered into the "mass age." Whatever validity adheres to this conclusion is degraded by its summariness. For just as medieval folkways lived on beneath the individualism of the Renaissance and still linger on today, so the organic society continues to function beneath and by the side of organized society, mass society. Moreover, the Age of the Masses is a misnomer for it implies that the masses rule. This they do nowhere, nor have they ever done so in history. Rule in a mass society is exercised by the leader or leading elite that at once is subject to mass pressure and channels it and renders it dynamic. Mass and leader are the aspects of the same phenomenon: disintegration of organic society. If this epoch is the Age of the Masses, then it is also the Age of the Leader, and it is the concrete historical occasion that suggests the placing of the emphasis on either mass or leader. If Age of the Masses is a meaningful designation it is so as an evocative formula in cults. The Cult of the Elite calls upon the chosen few to defend the temple of culture against the barbarian-from-within. Aside from the fact that the cult of elitism is the refuge of the snob and misfit, it seeks to prove the impossible, namely how to step across one's own shadow: how did the barbarian-from-within manage to outwit the elite and how does the elite propose to expel from the city the masses which it itself let in? Decrying elitism as plain fascism, the Cult of the Masses proclaims that all is well, that individuality is not lost in the mass but that, to the contrary, man gains true liberty by losing himself in the mass, for he thus escapes the irksome social pressures that curb his individual urges and inhibit his expression of self. The mass man is thus more truly man than the individual warped by social pressures. He is endowed with an innate wisdom not unlike Rousseau's noble savage. The masses are thus apt to be right, for they are guided by a higher wisdom, namely, "collective" wisdom. Those who in their pride refuse to submerge themselves in that deep and broad common pool are left high and dry, alone with their sterile intelligence.

The Cult of the Masses (which should not be mistaken for the Marxian cult of Mass Action) builds its mansion upon foundations that history has proved to be shaky. The myth of the collective wisdom of the masses is itself an abject concession to irrationality. To begin with, there is no means of proving that anything resembling collective wisdom exists. Though it is true that leaders would frequently have chosen the wiser path had they listened more attentively to what the masses wanted, it is also true that they frequently would have managed better had they not listened at all. If the masses are all-wise, why then is the age in which we live and in which the masses *are* the decisive factor, the age of the greatest catastrophes and most fantastic brutalities, the age of wars to extinction, and the age of victories without peace? It seems the devotees of both cults claim too much.

The mass is ethically as well as intellectually neutral. It is neither "good" nor "bad," like the machines and the gadgets which delight and enthrall it. The masses are one aspect of the great Western crisis. The mass and mass civilization are most certainly not the cause of that crisis but one of its consequences, though perhaps the most important one. One may decry or acclaim the masses for being what they are. However, they are what they are, not because of choice or intrinsic development; they are what they are because the development of Western culture has made them thus. They are the creatures spewed forth by the alienation of the Social Mind.

THE GREAT SCHISM

THE RISE OF Western culture from the Renaissance to the threshold of the nineteenth century can be seen as the ascendancy of an affirmative idea that gained dominance over the minds of men: dualism. Dualism, implied by Greek philosophy and Roman practice, becomes the explicit characteristic of Western thought and action. From the Renaissance onward, Western theologies as well as lay philosophies affirmed the duality of the temporal and the divine. By the nineteenth century the logical last step, implicit in philosophical dualism, had been taken. The separation of Church and State, the domain of God and the domain of Caesar, had been written into the constitutions of most Western nations or had been informally accepted as a principle of practical government.

The great secular philosophies of the nineteenth century proclaimed this separation as man's ultimate step upon the path to freedom and as the very charter of Western culture. For this emancipation from the super- and preternatural removed at last the awkward wrappings of medieval tradition which still overlay that superlatively efficient instrument: the Western mind. The ultimate and sole arbiter of its employment in any and all tasks was secular morality. Peguy's remark on Descartes' method, namely that "it is a morality, the morality of thought and a morality for thinking—because his conduct is his thought—and that Descartes embodied morality because . . . he developed his thoughts deliberately as actions . . ." proudly affirms the claim of Western secular thought to be a law unto itself. Western man is "the man who directs his thought as action and whose action is guided by the rules of conscious thought, capable of controlling itself." A Greek thinker of philosophy's Golden Age, returning from the Elysian Fields to this earth, would instantly recognize in this statement the ultimate consequence of the train of thought he set in motion; however, he would also discern the vengeance of hubris stalking his proud heirs.

The development of modern technology, we have noted, was "given" in the *idées forces* of Western culture. Industrialization and increase of population were corollaries. The tendencies unleashed by the impetus which the Renaissance imparted to Western society, reinforced each other. All this seems clear to us and would seem to, let us say, Leonardo da Vinci or Bacon, perfectly logical. As a matter of fact, the most prescient minds of the late seventeenth and of the eighteenth century envisioned a future world in which the forces of nature would be made to do man's work and men's lives would be less at the mercy of disease and the elements. What they did not foresee and what only at the beginning of the nineteenth century the wisest men saw was that the traditional structure of Western society would prove incapable of accommodating the changes, each in itself beneficial, which its genius had wrought. Within the context of the ideals of Western culture, industrialization is beneficial, for it not only increases the power of man but, by making his life more secure and comfortable, allows him leisure to develop his mind and contemplate the good and the beautiful things of this earth. Since longevity and health induce a zest both for work and for enjoyment, these gains redound absolutely to the benefit of mankind. What development, unforeseen by all but a handful of Western minds, poisoned the brimming cup?

Up until the beginning of the nineteenth century, all political and social ideas were backed by the binding sanction of a transcendental order. No matter how revolutionary a political or social idea may have been then, its advocates and its followers sought to obtain for it religious sanction. Society accepted and rejected it by invoking the arbitrament of Christian ethics. We need not split hairs over the unanswerable question whether all men did so in fact; they most certainly acted as if they did. Religious sanction was a conservative agent: it maintained the existing order of things. It did not necessarily conserve this or that regime or form of government; it did, however, supply a firm frame within which change occurred and which barred the political and social system to the invasion of extremist forces. Moreover, it supplied a compendium of expectancies that appeared plausible to the great majority of men and thus made their lives secure, secure not against suffering and death, but secure against the fear of suffering and death.

All this was changed when the nineteenth century began. It was changed with climactic suddenness as though the combustible materials that had accumulated in the hidden recesses of Western culture had suddenly burst in flame. The tremendous power of resistance that Western culture had built up over the centuries, still contained throughout the nineteenth century the conflagration. It attests to the bold optimism of that century, the last that built its faith upon all the great ideals that gave birth to Western culture, that many of its wisest men believed that the fires could be quenched. Western man in this century has lost his optimism together with the ideals that nourished it, for searing catastrophes blanket the horizons of his vision.

The social structure of Western culture failed to meet the crucial test of industrialization, of the development its own brilliant vision had called forth. It had come close to attaining perfection: the blueprint had called for two compartments to accommodate the spiritual and the temporal. That division had been the very feature that accounted for the strength of the structure: in one compartment man was to have been free to render unto God what was God's; in the other he was to have been free to determine his own destiny by shaping his social and material environment according to the dictates of his reason. In sum: to act as if God did not exist. This arrangement or, if one prefers, accommodation, had yielded brilliant results so long as each compartment remained intact and carried its full share of the burden imposed upon the structure as a whole by the nature of man. The arrangement was a delicate one at best. It is no exaggeration to say that since the beginning of Western culture, the most searching thought of Western philosophy was addressed to precisely the balance implicit in that arrangement. Its precariousness haunted all great thinkers of the Western Age. The tragedy of Western culture is that the balance should have broken down at the very moment when industrialization and its social consequences subjected the entire structure to a new and most critical test.

Industrialization and capitalism unleashed the flood of material productivity. They also unleashed the flood of human procreation. Western society managed brilliantly the integration of machine with machine and of all the machines into a system for creating vast economic wealth and, internationally, political and military power. It failed conspicuously to channel the human flood into the green fields of its spiritual tradition. It succeeded in integrating the masses of people, that owed their very existence to the advance of science and technology, with the machines devised by science and technology—as if they themselves were machines. It did not succeed in integrating them as men into society. And like machines, that have but functional coexistence, they were cast upon what Alfred Weber called the proletarian dump heap. Hitherto stable groups were broken down into social classes and the human fragments of this process, deprived of status and rights, were swallowed by that negation of integration: the masses. The process of fragmentation thus culminated in the separation of Western society into two spiritual camps, Disraeli's "two nations."

The disruptive forces did not assail all of Western society with the same thoroughness. Here and there the structure held. Ingenuity and sheer luck succeeded in containing the schismatic forces. But at certain focal centers the schism was final. In Europe, the alienation of the industrial proletariat was abetted by the indifference of the new masters, namely, the industrial and financial bourgeoisie, who had joined the older ruling elites or had subverted them. The new masters were only too eager to derive their warrant from secular morality: if man was the master of destiny, shaping his social and material environment according to his reason and if reason was a law unto itself, then problems of social adjustment could be left to the workings of reason. And what was more reasonable than the workings of the market in which that most reasonable economic law, to wit, the law of supply and demand, adjusted all relationships, including that of employer and wage earner? As for spiritual authority, its social domain was rigidly fixed. Though the domain of reason within which man acted as if God did not exist, had immensely grown, the new bourgeoisie who had won its place only by dire struggles against the old order leagued with spiritual authority was determined to bar the latter from interfering with rationality, especially the rationality of the market. If the bourgeoisie accepted the schism of society either as a "natural" result of the workings of economic laws or, at best, as a temporary condition that the working out of these laws would ultimately remedy, the revolt of the Western intellectual made certain that the schism was complete. The very purpose of Marxian doctrine was to complete it. The idea that the proletarian had been cast out from traditional society and could never return to it, is the cardinal assumption of Marx and Engels, and, though perhaps less clearly stated, of all contemporary collectivist doctrines. It was no accident that bourgeois intellectuals—and virtually all revolutionary intellectuals of the nineteenth and twentieth century were members of the bourgeoisie—should have compounded the finality of the schism. For they, too, knew how to claim the support of secular morality: if man is the master of his destiny and if thought is action and action thought, then by what sanction was man to be prevented from pursuing thought to its logical conclusion and to drive action to the ultimate goal fixed by thought? No one can read *Das Kapital* without being struck by what it presumes as a matter of course and does not even care to submit to the test of proof, namely the complete rationality of all social processes including the formation of moral authority and the perfect correspondence of cause and effect in all human action.

Marxism enlisted at once in its cause the scientific method of social analysis and the techniques for political mass action. It thus appealed most powerfully to bourgeois intellectualism and to the masses who wanted to be given what they could not bring forth from their chaotic depth: leadership and action. The propagandist effect of its doctrine on the displaced masses was to imbue them with the conviction of no return, of everlasting isolation from the rest of society. It was thus Marx who "made" the proletariat, perhaps more so than all the economic forces he pretended to describe. If the proletariat is a "class" it is because a hundred years ago Marx made it conscious of being one. It is this consciousness, so deeply felt ever since by the European working masses, that completed the separation of the "two nations." The proletariat deemed the spiritual values of traditional society mere screens for the interests of the ruling classes, whereas it regarded itself as the bearer of the universal truth that would set mankind free from want and class hypocrisy. By contrast, traditional society became the more conscious of itself and its broken unity the more the other camp persisted in isolating itself in dour hostility. This deadly juxtaposition sharpened the conflicts over political and economic power, and the ambiguity of class morality opened the way to moral relativism. The void created by the erosion of spiritual values was filled by "ideologies," systems of thought designed to cloak political and economic interests. "Ideologies" are mass products in the true sense: they are designed to fit mass situations and to engender mass action. They represent the highest perfection in subverting ideas, the chaste concepts of reason, to action; they represent the final, deepest degradation of reason.*

Ideologies are relative because they are determined by particular interests and not by concepts of reason and ethics held to be universally binding for all men. The fighting ideologies of our age accuse each other of lacking absolute validity. They do so quite rightly, for none pays more than lip service to the universal ideas and universal spiritual truths that are the lodestars of Western culture. The ideas assembled in these ideologies are only valid relative to a particular assumption as, for example, the class character of capitalist society. The truths these ideologies claim are only true relative to an exclusive and arbitrary set of values, as, for example, the superiority of one race over the other. The resultant confusion and the negation of all "self-evident truths" are so many blows struck at the structure of Western culture which rests upon the arc of verifiable concepts of reason and binding "self-evident" truths. The blows could not have told against the structure of transcendental concepts that had been reared by three centuries, had the roots of these transcendental concepts not become dessicated abstractions. These roots had drawn their nourishment from immanent and transcendental powers, "known instinctively" as conferring meaning upon

* See Alfred Weber's searching and moving meditation on the destruction of the European intellectual and spiritual heritage which he served so long and so wisely. *Farewell to European History*, New Haven, Yale University Press, 1948; pp. 68-71, *passim*.

the fabric of human society and nature. The meaninglessness of life and nature is the common starting point of the disintegrationist philosophies that sprang up in the second half of the nineteenth century and attained their greatest popularity after World War II. Man is a thing, life is an absurdity, nature is an aggregate of facts, society is a shell within which each man faces alone a crowd of strangers met by chance or statistical accident. The bleakness of this vision is surpassed only by the countenance of a big industrial city on a rainy Sunday afternoon.

The disintegrationist philosophies of our times originated in the Hegelian system, or rather in its breakdown. They owe their principal debts to Hegelian historicism and to Marx's historical materialism that turned Hegel on his head. That debt was grimly acknowledged by Positivism, the philosophy of social mathematics and hence of perfectly organized boredom. Auguste Comte, anticipating the "neurosis of our times," spent a year in an insane asylum shortly before the publication of his definitive work, *Course in Positive Philosophy*. The debt to Hegel was acknowledged, though more obliquely, by Wilhelm Dilthey and Martin Heidegger, the midwives of contemporary existentialism. According to Dilthey man does not have a nature but only a history. Taking up this proposition, Heidegger directed his attention to human existence: man not only has no definable nature, but his "essence" is in his existence; he is what he is because he exists. Human existence creates and transforms the social and material structures surrounding it. Human existence is not the "I" isolated by Descartes and Kant as the subject of experience, but the One, that is the anonymous Everybody and Nobody to whom are addressed such normative banalities as: "One does not sit down in the presence of ladies standing on their feet; one does not eat peas with one's knife." Heidegger's clue to human existence is anxiety: man is anxious about being in the world; and through anxiety, anxi-

ety without any discoverable object ("free-floating anxiety"),
he discovers the world.

We need not enter upon the ontological and epistemological ramifications of existentialist thought to catch its meaning for, let us say, the French and German generation exposed
to the "anxieties" of the last twenty years, which have
mounted from economic insecurity in the thirties on to the
climactic denouement in World War II and then to the
permanent precariousness of the post-Potsdam era. Its meaning for the educated men and women of that generation, who
were not professional philosophers, was in the meaninglessness of all and everything except "one's" own existence.
From this renunciation of society—and there is a great deal
about renunciation in Heidegger's work and that of his
French and German disciples—there is only one easy step to
submerging "oneself" in powerful collectives. Since man's
essence is in his existence and not in transcendental ideas, and
since society is a mere distraction from oneself and one's own
existence, it does not matter greatly what collective ideology
one chooses so long as it screens one against one's anxieties,
at least one's social and economic ones. This interpretation
is certainly far from fair to Heidegger and Sartre's philosophical insights, of which not a few are deep and, in the latter's
case, set forth with the literary verve of the great Humanist
tradition. However, what matters here and what justifies the
inclusion of this system among the disintegrationist philosophies is how they are understood, not what they purport
to say.* Since they do say what they say in a language that
strongly appeals to a sense of isolation, a sense of not belonging to society, that has so skillfully been nurtured by earlier
disintegrationist philosophies, they cater wittingly or unwittingly to the disruptive forces loose in our society. Their
affirmative ethical statements—and they do purport to pro-

---

* See for a concise statement William Barrett, "What Is Existentialism?"
PR Series, No. 2, New York, *Partisan Review,* 1947.

vide man with ethical maxims for meeting his desperate plight—are swamped by the more fashionable statements of negation.

Another example of disintegrationist philosophy is Karl Mannheim's "sociology of knowledge" that owes its heaviest debts to Hegel, Marx, and Dilthey. According to Mannheim, all human thought is "existentially determined." This means that, as Marx put it, "thought" is dependent on "reality" and hence on the "class" structure of one's mind, and that, as Mannheim puts it more succinctly, there are no valid concepts of reality and truth except those relative to whatever place a social group occupies in the stream of the historical process. Mannheim's sociological relativity affects not only value judgments and political aspirations but all theoretical thinking itself. Science thus is no longer immune to the "class" characteristics of the scientist. It should be noted that Mannheim did not despair of the possibility of gaining genuine knowledge. He viewed our times as times of crisis, in which different types of knowledge coexist. However, the existence of groups with antagonistic interests and experiences precludes the validity of any theory of "one truth." Mannheim himself hoped for a "dynamic" type of thinking as opposed to "static" bourgeois thinking. Thus, by his own choice, he re-enforced the distinction between antagonistic sciences, which correspond roughly to antagonistic social interests. Though the absurdity of this theory is instantly revealed as soon as it is applied to the natural sciences, it is less obvious when applied to the cultural sciences.*

A physicist may have strong views on the political purpose for which atomic energy should be used. But no one who has ever watched a physicist at work will care to assert that, while at work, he gives thought to its political implications. That cultural scientists, even while they labor at their discipline,

* See Paul Kecskemeti, "Technology and Class Consciousness," *Modern Review,* Vol. 3, No. 2, Jan. 1950; pp. 138-47.

are apt to note their work's political implications and be swayed by them is plausible. It is not plausible that all cultural scientists, at each step of their investigations, consult their political or "class" conscience—except where they have to, as, for example, in Russia. While the theory of "sociology of knowledge" thus claims far more than can be proven by scientific observation and experiment and is, moreover, subject to its own strictures—who takes care of the caretaker's daughter?—it has met with enthusiastic reception in "dynamic non-bourgeois" quarters. Like Marxian propaganda, this philosophy creates, by its appeal to those who are ready to be appealed to, the situation it professes to analyze. Its devotee can talk without qualms about "class conscious" geneticists and "proletarian art." As for the latter, it does not exist—except made to order by highly sophisticated practitioners of bourgeois antecedents with an eye on public subsidies or promotion in the Party.

The disintegrationist philosophies swept the intellectual scene of Europe. They supplied the intellectual ballast not only of the Marxian mass movements but also of their rival authoritarian ideologies. Upon the ground of relativism, Communism, Fascism, and National Socialism meet in intimate communion, and it is their mutual efforts toward the devaluation of all values that has made their frequent collaboration with each other so easy. In the United States, the disintegrationist philosophers were accorded the cordial reception extended to all novelties; they did not gain a large following; and their effect upon the thinking of the great majority of educated men and women has been nil. This circumstance alone, were it not for other and more massive evidence, suggests that in the United States the schismatic tendencies that have ravaged Western culture beat against a structure far less fragile than is that of European society. The United States is still one nation, not "two nations" as was

Disraeli's England and as is every major European country today.

The United States perfected the very methods of mass production which, because it stresses the production of things that will satisfy the taste of the many and not of the few, stands in a close relationship to the formation of human "masses" in the meaning of the term stressed in these pages. Though this relationship does exist, it is not a cause-effect relationship. As we have pointed out, it was changes in the spiritual climate that, in the nineteenth century, favored the jungle growth of the "masses." Mass production did make the process cumulative. The bleak factory and its shoddy products did create the impersonal, anonymous ambience of the mass man's existence. But the mass man was not created by them; he was created by the traditional society that could, but would not, gather unto itself the members of the diaspora. In brief, it was not machine mass production that created the mass man but society that dealt with men as if they were machines. This simple fact would be hardly worth noting except that it has escaped not a few observers of the American and the European scene. The oversight is at the root of some of the most irksome misconceptions about the United States and its influence abroad which have gained acceptance in Europe. These misconceptions have one point in common: American mass production methods are blamed for the increasing "massification" of Europe and the materealism of popular attitudes toward life, letters, art, and public affairs. Indeed, the brunt of European criticism of American cultural influences bears upon this point. Now, as any schoolboy knows, the Industrial Revolution began in Europe, not in America, and Europe had developed, by the end of the nineteenth century, mass-manufacturing techniques that were no whit less effective than those employed in the United States. The United States imported about as many of these techniques from Europe as Europe imported from the United States. The symptoms of industrial malaise appeared in Europe long before they occurred in the United States. When these symptoms did become noticeable in the United States, they were far from trivial. They did not, however, portend a revolutionary, irreparable break with traditional society. For the separation of society into two spiritual camps without inner contact did not take place in the United States. It is this circumstance that more than any other sets the United States apart from Europe and Europe apart from the United States.

That the United States became the greatest industrial nation on earth without alienating its industrial population from the rest of society and that it maintained its spiritual unity intact—at least, compared with Europe—is due to the concurrence of diverse developments, some engendered by deliberate action, some by incredible good fortune. Among the latter and perhaps the most fortunate is the historic setting. The United States was founded before the outbreak of the French Revolution and before the full impact of the Industrial Revolution was felt in Europe's settlements overseas. While the Founding Fathers perceived clearly, perhaps more clearly than their European contemporaries, the new forces impinging upon the political and economic structure of the West, they were able to trim their sails in relative calm before the onset of the storm. The Constitution is distinguished by a calm deliberateness and ripe assurance. The constitutions of Europe, which were wrested from traditional authority either by violence or the threat of violence during the turbulent decades following the French Revolution, were marred by haste and contradictions. The rights which the American Constitution granted the people appeared to have been given—and indeed on the whole *were* given—with full awareness of their implications and in a spirit of generous trust in the people's wisdom. The rights granted by European constitutions appear, by comparison, to have been granted either without awareness of what they meant or grudgingly under duress. Thus the American Constitution was not only a law of the land in the legal sense but the expression of a free consensus that preceded the making of the Constitution and was henceforth to underlie it.

The United States incorporated happily in its Constitution the very features of representative government which the revolutions that were soon to sweep Europe, sought to impose upon reluctant rulers. The American achievement was the work of men who, as a group, were the very embodiment of the spirit of the eighteenth century. That century at its high noon marked the fulfillment of the promise held out by the Renaissance. The foundation of the United States virtually coincided with the last years of that magnificent epoch in which the labors of a hundred years suddenly bore such abundant fruit. It was the end of an epoch in which one man's mind could still bracket humanist learning, natural philosophy, and the art of government. From the heights of this epoch, the enlightened mind could survey all that had been and relate his own position in time to the long course of western history. The men who made the Constitution, to the country's miraculous good fortune, stood at the summit of their times. Being Englishmen, to boot, they escaped the one encumbrance that weighed upon the generation of Enlightenment: its infatuation with its own brilliant abstractions. Being Englishmen, they retained in the brightest era of intellectual skepticism, a healthy skepticism toward the intellect.

The foundations of American unitary society were laid. Subsequent developments but strengthened its unitary characteristics. The "melting pot" became the very school of adaptation. The classlessness of American society from the 1830's on was not only a matter of institutionalized equality but also the one and only working concept under which men of all lands and all social strata could be assimilated rapidly into American society, rapidly enough to join in the pressing tasks of economic development. Since spiritual authority had never been wedded to the state and each creed enjoyed the toleration of the other, the division of the temporal and spiritual realms never became a serious political issue. Because religion did not, could not, claim temporal authority, it retained all the more effectively its hold upon what it had to claim: the allegiance of the faithful.

IV
The Happy Configuration

THE WESTERN DIALOGUE

THE SINGLE most important fact about Western culture here and now is its survival by the grace of American power. The Western community survived because the United States assumed the guardianship which had slipped from the hands of Europe. The West accepted together with American guardianship the hegemony of the United States. So unsubtle and so massive is the reality of the United States' hegemony that its impact is felt as a traumatic shock no less by the people of the United States than by those of Europe. It is as if the Western peoples recoil before what they themselves have wrought. For what they wrought does violence to their most cherished preconceptions. Was not the struggle of the Western peoples against the hegemony of one power in their midst the true meaning of Western history? Were not the wars against Germany, just as those against Napoleonic France, fought to this end? Was not the liberation of the many from the subservience to the one the noble cause that raised these wars above the ignominy of senseless carnage? And what is the meaning of national independence if it is not cultural freedom? Only to ask these questions is sufficient to conjure up a host of ambiguities. Is the subservience of Europe to the United States less real because the United States has not sought it? Is the impact of American ideas and things upon European cultures less profound because the United States did not impose them wittingly or gave no more than Europe eagerly took? Is the Americanization of Europe a mere figment of Europe's conservative imagination or is it not the logical consequence of Europe's decline and dependence upon the United States?

The identification of cultural autonomy with political independence, which fixed the ethical position of American foreign policy in two world wars, may derive from a grave error as to the nature of both culture and politics. Indeed, the history of our times suggests not only that the identification of culture with nation *was* in error, but also that the attempt to order international society according to the principle of national *and* cultural independence was the cause of universal abridgment of all liberties, the national and cultural ones included. However, whether in error or not, the idea that cultural freedom and political sovereignty are inseparable dominated, and still dominates, Western thought on culture and politics.

Western culture, viewed through the lens of common preconceptions, is a unity composed of national subcultures, each nourished from common sources and enriched by ceaseless cross-fertilization, yet each possessed of a distinct national physiognomy. Like most generalizations on human society, this hypothesis is plausible up to a point and not susceptible to exact verification. It happens to be the hypothesis that underlies the stated purpose of American initiative in world affairs. If it were not so then the Wilsonian concept of national self-determination and the Rooseveltian formula for international order would be devoid of sense: congeries of groups and individuals are recognized as sovereign nations by the hallmarks of their common culture. If they do not hold in common a distinguishable culture, by what moral authority can they be subjected to one and the same political authority? It is not the least paradox of our times that no other nation is more forthrightly committed to the concept of the identity of national independence with cultural independence and to everlasting vigilance against the encroachments of political hegemony the world over than is the

United States, and that the United States now exercises a political hegemony that far surpasses in plenitude of power the boldest attempts at Western domination. This paradox is not paradox at all *if* the concept of national culture as warrant of political independence can be shown to be a fallacy, a tragic one at that. Be that as it may, the paradox, seeming or real, is at the core of American-European problematics. For the contradiction of American avowed intent and political reality masks the one massive, unsubtle fact about Western culture, here and now: if it were not for the power of the United States, Western culture would be no more. American hegemony is the condition of its survival.

The rise of American power above the power of any and all members of the Western community is the one truly revolutionary event in the history of the twentieth century to date. For it is the one event which the much abused term, revolution, fits both in the dictionary meaning of the term— a total and radical change—and in the meaning of Marxian semantics applied to international politics—the culmination of the process of capitalist imperialism.

Internationally, the Russian Revolution has turned out to be no revolution at all: Stalinist expansionism followed the tracks of the armies of Alexander I. Its strategic gambits are substantially the same as those which led Alexander I via central Europe to the checkmate of the Congress of Vienna. (A diplomat present at Vienna in 1814 or at the Berlin settlement of 1878 could, upon his release from purgatory, be briefed in a few minutes on the Russian Question which his latter-day colleagues now face.) The current eruption of Asia is, as we have noted, not a radically new phenomenon of Western history, but a return to the routine of two millennia. Russian expansion across Inner Asian and Far Eastern frontiers stolidly pursues objectives that were staked out and sometimes attained by such staid servants of the czars as Muraviëv and Kuropatkin. The revolutionary slogans under which Stalinist Russia proceeded to its tryst with czarist expansionism were the small coin of Marxian exegesis minted in the second half of the nineteenth century. Though Marxian ideas bore the venerable patina of age and were the common property of every literate European, there occurred no Marxian revolution in Europe. The very fact that there has been none, although theoretically there should have been a long time ago, has forced even the most intransigent Marxist into the position of gradualism. Nothing has contributed more to this unrevolutionary quiescence than the participation of socialist and Communist parties in bourgeois governments. The problem posed today by Stalinist Communism in Western Europe is not a revolutionary problem. It is surely not one in terms of *social* revolution. It preoccupies the European counterintelligence services rather than the European intellectuals: the Communist parties and Stalinist agents in Europe are adjuncts of Soviet military power, not the bearers of a breathlessly expected social message.

There was a time when Europe questioned Russia, asking her the vital question about the classless and stateless society that was to have emerged from the spring tide of the Bolshevik Revolution. It asked Russia the question all the more ardently because the idea was its own idea, sprung from the depth of European thought. It was precisely the strength of the Bolshevik appeal that Europe's question was not addressed to a particular Russian "experiment" but to the manifestation of a universal idea that happened to have alighted upon the soil of Russia. Europe asked Russia about itself rather than about Russia. When the Bolshevik Revolution turned out to have been no revolution at all but a changing of the guards in an oriental palace, the questioners fell mute. The political formations of Communism in Europe today are formations of organized fear: the ideological residue of Communism is the residue of nostalgia. Europe's intellectual Communists are romantics. Neither Communism's storm troopers and secret agents nor Communism's residual brotherhood in the faith care to ask Russia anything worth knowing concerning the state of utopia. The Russian Question is a question of hard and fast military-political strategy: the intellectual phase of Europe's relation to Russia is finished.

The question Europe now asks is addressed to the United States. That question, too, Europe asks about itself. For every vital question that one asks of one or of many men one asks about oneself. Not that Europeans are incapable of asking "objective" questions about America and of coming up with "objective" answers. The long line of European explorers of the American scene furnishes impressive evidence of Europe's ability to engage in analysis no less rigorous than that practiced elsewhere in the fields of the social sciences. Despite a raft of critical, sometimes very critical, reviews, evaluations and re-evaluations of the findings of Alexis de Tocqueville, Lord Bryce, Hermann Keyserling, Bertrand Russell, André Siegfried, and Geoffrey Gover, their findings on the American scene command an impressive and impressed American public. This is so perhaps precisely because the ultimate question they asked America is not about America but about themselves and thus about Europe and about the fate of Western culture. This is so perhaps because American explorations carried out by Americans, often applying methodological devices far more refined than those employed by European observers and possessed of knowledge far more complete as to the intricate patterns of American culture and subcultures, halt at the limits of the American scene and suggest questions that, however clever, do not call for a universal answer. For the same reason, the American explorer of the European scene, searching for America's own image in the last mirror of the gallery of European facts and fancies, elicits a response that Europe denies her own self-analysts. It is as if America and Europe, searching each other, ask the same question, the question of their common fate. This dialogue is the dialogue of Western culture. Once that dialogue ceases and Europe and America know about each other all that is worth knowing, Western culture will dissolve in the void of its own indifference. Then American guardianship will guard nothing but a museum, a shrine of nostalgia. Then the rest, just as in the case of the ended dialogue between Europe and Russia, the Russia of the alleged revolution, is silence.

The question which Europe now puts to the United States is the question of man's relation to society. It is the same question which Europe put to Russia. Indeed, Europe had asked this question of the United States long before it searched and rejected the answer given by Soviet Russia. Ever since the foundation of the United States, Europeans pondered intently American political and social developments and deemed them revolutionary and surpassing, in their startling innovations, the most profound changes that had occurred in Europe, the French Revolution included. De Tocqueville wrote:

> The American legislators have succeeded to a certain extent in opposing the notions of rights to the feeling of envy; the permanence of the religious world to the continual shifting of politics; the experience of the people to its theoretical ignorance; and its practical knowledge of business to the impatience of its desires. The Americans, then, have not relied upon the nature of their country, to counterpoise those dangers which originate in their constitution and in their political laws. To evils which are common to all democratic peoples, they have applied remedies *which none but themselves had ever thought of before; and although they were the first to make the experiment, they have succeeded in it.* The manners and laws of the Americans are not the only ones that may suit a democratic people; but the Americans have shown that it would be wrong to despair of *regu-*

lating democracy by the aid of manners and laws. If other nations should borrow *this general and pregnant idea* from the Americans, without however intending to initiate them in the peculiar application they have made of it; if they should attempt to fit themselves for that social condition which seems to be the will of Providence to impose upon the generations of this age, and so to escape from the despotism of the anarchy which threatens them; what reason is there to suppose that their efforts would not be crowned with success? *

De Tocqueville's question, put to America, is clearly about Europe; for he continues:

It may readily be discovered with what intention I undertook the foregoing inquiries. The question here discussed is interesting not only to the United States, but to the whole world; *it concerns not a nation, but all mankind....* When I consider the present condition of several European nations—a condition to which all others tend—I am led to believe that they will soon be left with no other alternative than democratic liberty, or the tyranny of the Caesars.

My aim has been to show, by the example of America, that laws and especially manners, may exist which will allow a democratic people to remain free.

Tocqueville's "inquiries," from which these passages are random selections, are permeated with the thrill of the new. The new American society had, within the forty years of its political independence, laid its hands firmly on the problems which tradition-bound European society still sought to smother by the repetition of empty formulas. These problems had crystallized under the pressure of boundless energies

* Alexis de Tocqueville, *Democracy in America,* Chapter XVII. Italics are mine.

called forth by the sheer bigness of the physical tasks facing the new state bracketed by vast seas and an immense hinterland. America had spontaneously devised solutions for which Europe had groped so painfully and so unsuccessfully. Goethe's famous stanza to America, the happy country that need not forget a past and mourn ruined castles, expressed Europe's wonderment at America's good fortune. To America is revealed, in a flash of inventive genius as it were, what Europe had been searching for, what Europe knew to exist, but what Europe, caught in the stultifying labyrinth of its lush theorizings and its intractable historic realities, could not reach.

It would be a gross oversimplification to conclude that Europe then sought in the emergent realities of American society an answer to "problems" of the Industrial Revolution, though a solitary thinker like Tocqueville may have suspected the connection. The great mass of Europeans, the educated ones included, did not know that these problems existed. Unawareness of the precise nature of these problems, particularly of that of the machine as an agent of population dynamics and hence of social dynamics, is perhaps the most striking characteristic of nineteenth-century thinking on political economy, the speculation of Karl Marx included. It is most striking for us who have read to the end of the chapter and now know the plot of the story. Though intelligent European observers of nineteenth-century America may seem obtuse in the light of our hindsight, they did grasp one fact that derived from the Industrial Revolution. That fact could be observed most advantageously in America, is still perhaps the most important fact about America, and now challenges European society on its own ground. That fact is: social mobility.

It is now fashionable to "qualify" the testimonies of such inquisitive strangers as Tocqueville, Dickens, and Lord Bryce by references to their "class-status" and the social position of those Americans whose company these travelers kept or are assumed to have kept. Despite this gratuitous assistance on the part of the "sociology of knowledge," the findings of these Europeans, even suitably "qualified," are the most valuable record we possess on one aspect of America's particular culture and Western culture, social mobility.

Not a few European liberals sought social equality in America. They deemed equality a civic good; they were, from what they had heard and read before they came, predisposed to find what they sought. Not a few European conservatives sought in America facts which would refute the Rousseauesque idealizations of American society; they found not equality but a parvenu society and bad manners. It is not surprising that liberals and conservatives did not agree as to whether American society was egalitarian; it is striking that they unanimously testified to its being mobile. Unlike their opposites in Europe, poor men became rich virtually overnight; rich men lost their money and took to manual labor; men changed their professions as they changed their shirts which, by European standards, they did fairly often; farmers left their farms and hired themselves for wages to urban entrepreneurs or turned themselves into businessmen; a considerable part of the population was ceaselessly changing its geographical habitat and no one appeared to think all this unusual. If there was equality of a kind upon which the European observers could agree, it was the equality each American had which allowed him to share in the dynamism of a society which refused to set in the mold of conventions and traditions. The United States had broken with static traditions of organic society, yet it had found a new principle that insured the unity of its new society in the making: mobility or, for the device is fraught with a dynamic meaning, unity in diversity. To this day, the United States remains "mobile." It is the least definite country within the writ of Western culture. The best book about France written, let us say thirty years ago, stands today, but for mere chronology, in no need of revision. The only kind of meaningful book on America would be one written in not less than ten-year installments.

From the vantage point of the mid-twentieth century we now see clearly that the question Europe asked of America in the nineteenth century was how to solve the problem of social alienation posed by the Industrial Revolution. America was, and still is, a classless society. America's constitutional arrangements did confer equality of a kind, though at the start not nearly as absolute as the guarantees of equality conferred by the French Revolution upon every citizen. In this respect, the United States could teach Europe little. Its true message was that of equal opportunity in a race that started anew every day and of a broad popular consensus as to the basic rules under which everybody could enter and run the race. As for the prizes to be won, the sky was indeed the limit.

If Europe did not fully understand the answer America had given, this was because Europe, fascinated by the race and the prizes, did not grasp the nature of the rules. That America was, in the age of monarchies, a republic helped rather than hindered Europeans attempting to gauge the nature of democracy, as the nineteenth century understood the term. True, the American Constitution marked the zenith of eighteenth-century creative political thought. But democracy enshrined in the wisest constitution did not explain social mobility. As a matter of fact, the Constitution and democratic usage alone could have brought forth all kinds of society, the most hardened class society and despotism included. What made America the unique mobile society of Western culture was not formal arrangements, though these were indeed propitious, but moral and psychological forces playing upon a unique environment. What *made* America was the character of its people pitted against the challenge of a vast continent.

The United States attained statehood in the eighteenth

century and before the outbreak of the French Revolution. The leadership of the new state embodied the spirit of the age perhaps more characteristically than the elite of any other Western country. The eighteenth century was at once fiercely rationalist and tolerantly urbane, boldly adventurous in science, politics, and love, and rigidly bound by conventions of social deportment, warfare, and religious devotion. Its great men—the intellectuals of the rising bourgeoisie, free-thinkers, revolutionary philosophers, and flamboyant free-booters in literature, trade and sex—adhered with virtual unanimity to the forms of aristocratic conduct.

The eighteenth century, deceptively simple because of the refined harmony of its decorum, marked a culmination of the tendencies which had been loosed by the Renaissance: the transcendence of organic society by individual freedom. The Age of Enlightenment enjoyed an unobstructed view all the way from the summits of antiquity to the emergent shores of man's new dominion in which free reason would unlock all riddles and subject all passions to its noble discipline. It is this poised assurance, sustained by intimate familiarity with the history and philosophy of the ancients, punctilious observance of an aristocratic code of manners and firm reliance on the power of man's mind to cut across prejudice and passion to right solutions, that permeates the achievements of the Founding Fathers and appears to render them impervious to time. So powerful is their stamp, the stamp of a profound sense of measure and judicious balance, that a French observer of our times can assert emphatically that "the United States is the last Western country in which the great ideas of the eighteenth century have retained their luster." * So indeed they have, untarnished by the blood that the French Revolution spilled in their name and still luminous amidst the immense accretion of political philosophies

* Bertrand de Jouvenel in a lecture to the members of the Cercle Allais, Paris, April 8, 1951.

and ideological moods cast forth by the nineteenth and twentieth centuries. The longevity of the Founding Fathers' creation owes much to the sublime moment of the eighteenth century; it owes no less to the fact that the Founding Fathers, rationalists though they were, were men of action. They were men of action because they were Englishmen and consequently they knew how to put thought to the service of action. The center of gravity of the English national character rests upon action. By contrast, that of the French rests upon thought. The Frenchman, in action, takes his cue from thought and makes action serve thought.

The Englishman cultivates the will rather than reason and emotion. This scale of preferences is clearly manifest in English education, English manners, and in the very speech of the English people. Englishmen, bending their will to action and acting for action's sake, are materialists in the literal sense: action needs tangible and material objects on which to exert itself. This "materialism" does not exclude disinterestedness and the most sublime self-sacrifice. On the contrary, "materialism" of this sort is self-denial: "To thought [the Englishman] opposes the barrier of empiricism; to passion the iron gates of self-control." * It is, however, this subordination of all other vital forces to the will, that explains the Englishman's material success. His practical sense, his sense of action, and his feeling for the use of material objects as means of actions, are at the root of a philosophy of life that has been attributed traditionally and specifically to him, namely the philosophy of utilitarianism. Utilitarianism is tolerance of thought, although that toleration oscillates between the limits of indifference and cynicism. Will to action and utilitarianism are "English" character traits that have attained an even greater dominance in the American character than the English. For the challenge of the American

* Salvador de Madariaga, *Englishmen: Frenchmen: Spaniards,* London, Oxford, 1928, p. 17.

environment elicited the exercise of these traits on a grand scale.*

Since collective life manifests itself mainly in action, it is the domain of action. Within this domain, the value of co-operation—the multiplication of individual efforts—can be detected at once. As men of action, the English had a genius for co-operation and spontaneous organization. This genius, put to the task of organizing a new state, a new economic organization, and countless new communities, surpassed itself. American organization and efficiency—the sublimation of action for action's sake—and that instinctive group self-control, one of the most striking features of the contemporary American scene, owe their most important debt to their English heritage. The English genius for co-operation is also the ancestor of an American character trait noted by contemporary observers, the sensitivity of the American middle classes to group signals and to the "veto" of the peer group, a phenomenon summed up in David Riesman's term: "other-directed man." †

England's, too, is the Protestant ethos that assigned so powerful a guiding role to individual conscience yet managed to reconcile that doctrine with predestination. Since man's punishments and rewards were inscribed in the book of Providence, it was sinful to cavil at one's estate upon earth, including the estate blessed with ample earthly possessions. The severe Protestant ethics brought about ascetic training for the postponement of enjoyment, enjoyment of heavenly rewards for just labors on earth. Yet that training bore earthly fruits—despite the other-worldliness of its objec-

---

* "The American is imaginative; for where life is intense, imagination is intense also. But his imagination is practical and the future it forecasts is immediate. . . . He is an idealist working in matter." George Santayana, *Character and Opinion in the United States,* New York, Scribner, 1920, p. 175.

† David Riesman in collaboration with R. Denney & N. Glazer, *The Lonely Crowd,* New Haven, Yale University Press, 1950; pp. 19-26.

160   *The Happy Configuration*

tives—and self-denial abetted capital accumulation. Moreover, the guidance of conscience freed the individual from reliance upon priestly mediation and, in the last resort, traditional authority. Thus Protestant conscience replaced the direction from without of ecclesiastical and social hierarchies by the inner direction of man alone with his God. In post-Renaissance Europe, the growing complexity of life was engendered by differentiation of skills and the impact of industry and trade upon agricultural and guild society. The Protestant conscience provided the directional guidance for coping with these new and ever-changing situations and for steering the vessel of progress in accord with the winds ordained by Providence. The older faith was reluctant to place so much discretion in the layman's hands. England's break with Catholic tradition and the subsequent proliferation of nonconformist sects released in the English character psychological drives toward individual exploration of nature, individual investigation of mind and society, and individual pursuit of enterprise. Though these drives stirred powerfully other peoples of northern and western Europe into activities that broke "the cake of custom," England, partially by design and partially by accident, fell heir to much of their intellectual and material achievements. England's mediation thus endowed America with ideas, techniques, and customs that French Calvinism and the Protestantism of the Germanies, Scandinavia, and the Lowlands had wrought and which England herself had assimilated to her own tradition.

At the beginning of the nineteenth century, the three principal elements that had gone into the making of the American character were these: the genius of the eighteenth century, the genius of the Anglo-Saxon race, and the genius of Protestant Christendom. Obviously, so summary a judgment must be understood as a shorthand notation; obviously, the compound was not unalloyed. From the very start of North American settlement, the most heterogeneous cultural influences vied with each other. At the time of the American Revolution a score of highly developed subcultures, owing little or nothing to Enlightenment or Anglo-Saxon Protestantism, had taken root in American soil. From the very start, the cultural influences of Europe underwent varying changes—in some instances changes beyond recognition—in the process of assimilation to social and geographical conditions that in many respects differed profoundly from Europe. These qualifications, necessary as they are, do not detract from the validity of our thesis: the dominant character traits of the new nation derived from the unique consolidation of political thought at the zenith of Western culture: the Englishman's will to action at the high tide of its vigor, and the liberation of religious conscience from all authority but its own. These coincident factors beckoned the first wave of immigration that started after the Napoleonic Wars and came to an end about 1880, which consisted chiefly of Englishmen and Scots, Germans and Swedes, Jews and Irishmen. At first glance, the Irishman's presence in this company appears to involve a contradiction. Upon closer examination, that contradiction is revealed as a paradox, no more and no less of a paradox than is the Irish character itself: the Irishman, whatever may have been the economic motivations of departure from his isle, was as well prepared as his fellow-Celt, the Scot, to receive the "signals" of a society that was Anglo-Saxon in character yet had cut its ties to Established Church and transferred moral authority to individual conscience. Far from an obstacle, this proved the Irishman's golden bridge to the American community. A good case can be made for the contention that, had England herself built that golden bridge, the "Irish Question" would have been settled long ago— just as its attenuated duplicate has been settled in this country. Be that as it may, the Irishman just as his fellow-immigrants from western and northern Europe came to seek a new life endowed with freedom of faith, freedom of action, and freedom of political convictions. And this was precisely what the Happy Configuration promised. That promise was kept, at least for the great majority of immigrants. It was kept so convincingly and so spectacularly in terms of social and economic progress that Europe increasingly took this promise to be the promise of the future, its own as well as that of America.

These last pages are meant as but an impressionistic paraphrase on the American character, an unashamedly impressionistic one at that. Far more learned investigations on the American character, equipped with psychological and anthropological terminology, have not turned up any important insights overlooked by so "impressionistic" a writer as, let us say, De Tocqueville. The topic that concerns us here is not so much the complex skein of American culture, but those of its features that insured social mobility. Among these, the threefold ones of the Happy Configuration were of capital importance. The history of Latin America appears to supply corroborative evidence, though of a negative kind. Physical opportunities similar to those offered by North America, beckoned the European immigrant. There appears to have been no cogent reason why Latin America should not have rivaled the United States—except that its culture barred, and in most Latin countries still bars today, free social circulation.

The conjunction of the three basic traits of the American character accommodated a broad range of newcomers and profound political, social, and ethnic changes, allowing immense enlargement of the physical realm, geographic and economic, of the United States. In the process of accommodation, and precisely because that process succeeded in accommodating so vast a variety of new developments, new basic traits were added. The nature of this accommodating process, its swiftness and pragmatic shifts and turns, makes it well nigh impossible to answer with any degree of accuracy such questions as: Is the United States still a Protestant country?

is it still Anglo-Saxon? and, most difficult of all, is it still the Republic established by the Founding Fathers? However these questions are answered, the answers will elicit many objections and not a few very angry ones at that. Scientific criteria are not available, for the questions concern matters that statistical treatment—as, for example, church attendance, breakdown of population according to "national origin," and frequency charts of Supreme Court decisions—reduces to pedantic absurdities. What is important here is the extent to which the ideas that presided over the birth and growth of the United States and impressed upon it features so distinct from Europe, still dominate the United States today. For, let us repeat, in the eyes of Europe—and perhaps in the eyes of mankind—the American experience is pregnant with answers to a universal question: what is man's place in industrial society? To this question, the United States supplied the one positive answer given in the nineteenth century: the creation of an industrial society that was free and classless. The United States, unlike the European industrial countries, passed through the Industrial Revolution and remained *one* nation.

True enough, historic and natural setting favored the American experiment. The history of the United States opened with the liquidation of a large segment of the ruling class. The initial instability of social status set in motion a chain of social changes. Up until the last third of the nineteenth century, the expanding frontier not only provided opportunities for escape from the pressures of industrial society into adventure but also a splendid training in social organization. Frontier society challenged at once the initiative of the individual and his capacity for co-operation. Frontier society did not ask the newcomer where he came from and what he had been, but what he could do—and practically everything remained to be done. The frontier thus became the school not only of the pioneer, self-reliant and boldly enterprising—the rugged individual of the great American saga as well as the cliché—but also of the group. Communal improvisation and informal team play raised a thousand towns from the wilderness, nurtured intense civic pride, and infused the life of American communities with a "civic-mindedness" and autonomous flavor which has evoked the wonderment of a long line of European observers. Not only the geographical dimensions of the frontier but its innumerable tasks, especially those of building new communities out of a wilderness, gave free scope to social mobility. Had farmers not managed to turn themselves into townsmen, soldiers of fortune into pillars of the law, lawyers into tradesmen and tradesmen into judges, gamblers into investors, and laborers into entrepreneurs, these tasks could not have been done. If the overflow of energies generated within the older settled centers nourished the expansion of the frontier, the frontier spirit radiated back into the communities from which the pioneers had departed. Its venturesome restlessness, prowess of improvisation, directness of speech, and equalitarian manners kept American society as a whole from settling into a rigid mold.

The relentless spread of industrialization helped to integrate a great American internal market. It displaced the handicraft artisans. In their place arose a proletariat, new in American life. However, that proletariat itself was fluid and refused to conform to the Marxian pattern. The proletarian lifted himself—by sheer industry or bold imagination, by comparatively easy access to expanding educational facilities or simply by a knack that satisfied a special demand of the market's unlimited appetites—into the ranks of the capitalist and managerial classes. Neither political nor social barriers blocked the path to this upward circulation. Though contemporary folklore and propaganda may have overglamorized the from-rags-to-riches procession, the average man had abundant concrete evidence that men no more privileged than he had managed to join that procession. In brief, the American proletarian, like most everybody else, was an optimist. The European proletarian was a pessimist. In Europe, the proletariat became a tradition and through that tradition aware of itself. In America, the proletariat was a state of transition. It was not "class conscious" because it did not view itself as a class apart from American middle-class society but rather as the aspirant in the anteroom of manual labor which opens into the parlor of business. Similarly, the ethnic minorities waited in the anteroom of assimilation for admittance to the fold of American society. To a considerable extent, proletariat and ethnic minority overlapped: in industry, the less desirable, the "dirtier" jobs requiring brawn rather than skill, were filled by immigrants who had not yet mastered the ways of American society, notably its language.

Successive waves of immigration and the workings of the system of education kept the "class lines" fluid. In each generation certain ethnic groups were kept from full social participation in dominant groups. They were, however, never the same—witness the Irishman, German, Jew, and Scandinavian. Though the not so subtle barriers confronting the raw immigrant were only too frequently replaced by subtler ones confronting his native-born sons and grandsons, these did not stand in the way of the attainment of riches and political power. More important still, despite the resistance of ruling groups—who themselves were the product of constant transformation—the upward penetration of ethnic or religious minorities was irreversible. In Europe, this had never been so. Toleration of ethnic and religious minorities had always been subject to revocation. Minorities who had gained equal status with majority groups found themselves, again and again, fettered by new shackles of discrimination. American proletariat and ethnic and religious minorities knew themselves as participating in a forward movement that despite temporary lags, obstacles, and inequities, led toward a goal others had manifestly attained and that they themselves could attain. The process of expansion, geographically, economically, and socially, was neither neat nor orderly. But disorder and instability, often the very ferocity of the struggle and the hot passions that it fanned, were themselves aspects of the vitality of social growth. It has of late become the fashion, especially among the followers of stagnationist economic doctrines, to ascribe that growth and the dynamism of American society up to the Great Depression, to the workings of the frontier and to the economics of geographical expansion and population increase. In the light of these theories, American capitalist society was simply rescued from economic stagnation and a hardening of the class structure by the safety valve of expansion and the opportunities of a growing market. This theory, which, incidentally, is first cousin to Lenin's theory of imperialism, does not explain why the frontier in, let us say, Latin American countries and in Russia did not exercise the same benign function. It attributes to the invisible hand of geography and population dynamics regulatory powers which older economists ascribed to the market. To deny the importance of the frontier in American history is to deny the most massive fact in the history of the nineteenth century. But the potentialities of the American frontier, in order to become "fact," required a social and moral setting without which they would have been as socially inconsequential as they remain to this day in Latin America and Russia. That setting was given in the United States by the accommodating heritage of the Founding Fathers, the English character, and the Protestant conscience. National morality and faith were vague in idea, but inexorable in spirit. They were the gospel of work and the belief in progress. By them every man could live. All men were free, but not free to alter or challenge that gospel and that belief.

THE REVOLUTION OF RANK

"En obéissant à tous, chacun a le sentiment de
n'obéir qu'à lui-même."

—J.-J. Rousseau

TOWARD the close of the nineteenth century forces impinged upon the development of the United States which
blurred its message to Europe and cloaked it in disquieting
ambiguities. More than two thirds of the wave of immigration
that descended upon the United States between 1880 and
1914 originated in the Latin south and Slavic east of Europe.
Unlike the preceding wave, its driving force was not so much
the search for political liberties and pioneer adventures as
escape from the pressure of the extreme poverty that ground
down the masses of Europe's most backward regions. Large
numbers of immigrants were recruited by organizations such
as steamship companies, industrial concerns, and immigration
societies. Personal initiative was replaced by directed mass
migration. The newcomers from the feudal lands of Europe
tended to remain more passive in their responses to American
political and social institutions than had been their predecessors from western and northern Europe where the ideas of
democracy and individualism had taken root. For Slavs and
Latins the language difficulties were greater; so was the educational distance separating them from the older settlers. The
large majority of the immigrants professed the Roman Catholic faith or one or the other of eastern Europe's orthodox
religions. It was the impact of this "alien" mass that confronted the United States with a problem of assimilation on

a truly gigantic scale. Even if the ethnic and cultural origin of the new immigration had been less remote from that of the receiving society, its sheer mass—twenty-two million between 1880 and 1914—would have taxed the country's capacity of absorption. Heretofore, the solution of that problem had been left chiefly to the immigrant himself, haphazardly assisted by his neighbor, employer, fellow immigrant, and, perhaps, the local community. Now the problem concerned the nation. It imposed upon its social structure strains different from those it had to cope with during the preceding hundred years. The social structure had to accommodate itself to the influx of new human and cultural elements—different in kind and, most certainly, in magnitude. The United States *did* cope with the problem. The seemingly impossible task *was* accomplished—and accomplished in a far briefer period of time than most American and European observers of the times thought possible. It was accomplished under pressure.

The process of assimilation that had been continuously going on since the foundation of the country and even in colonial times now lost some of its spontaneity. Assimilation became a national policy complete with its administrative and educational systems. The melting pot became a mill in which citizens were ground out to uniform specifications. The immigrant himself soon took these specifications to be standard marks of quality not unlike those he learned to look for in the universe of economic satisfaction. Precisely because of that drive toward assimilation to which he was subjected and his genuine desire to comply with it, genuine albeit powerfully solicited, the immigrant tended to be keenly aware of his "otherness" long after he had attained formal status. Unlike his predecessors—the innumerable ethnic and religious minorities who, in the preceding two centuries, had sought and found in the United States a haven for their "otherness" and had bethought themselves little of their formal status—the new immigrant inclined to chafe uneasily under the residual burden of his "foreign" culture and to seek anxiously to slough it off. This sentiment which we may call anxiety to conform was abetted by education, the group—especially the immigrant's own—and the market, the labor market as well as the market of mass-produced goods. In European middle-class society the genuine reason which had prompted the son to identify himself with the father as responsible head of the family was put in doubt by modern industrial and urban conditions of living. In America its validity appeared doubly dubious in the light of the immigrant's experience with the struggle of assimilation. In America, the attitude of the son toward the father was more complex than in Europe since children of immigrants adjusted more quickly and easily to the new environment. The surface of traditional respect for parental authority wore thin. The son tended to identify himself with the group, especially that of his "peers" in age and education. The immigrant father, uncertain of his moral veto power and more often than not deprived of his economic veto power as well, was thus not only incapable of restoring his moral authority but was himself only too anxious to conform with the mores of ruling groups.

The collapse of parental authority in immigrant society and the identification of the immigrant's children with "peer groups," especially with groups of great numerical strength, affected American society as a whole. The public school acted as an effective transmission belt for the assimilation of older American society to the attitudes of the immigrant. Traditional American aversion to authoritarian forms of *personal* relationships was now re-enforced by the readiness of large masses of immigrant youths to trade parental authority for *group* authority as the price of admission to full membership in society. But this development added a new twist. Heretofore, aversion to authority had been the reciprocal of the will to self-assertion and hence to freedom from one man's authority. Democratic manners had been a concession to one's fellow man and group for one's autonomy in relation to both. Now, however, good style of social intercourse frowned upon differentiation. All had not only to pretend to be alike, but try to be alike. The "peer group" now assumed far greater authority over the individual than an older America had cared to concede it, but had conceded to family and church, and, though more reluctantly, to the community. For the "peer group" demanded and obtained a transfer of individual conscience to itself that the older social institutions had not exacted.

Obviously, we are not confronted here with a trend unique to the United States. In Europe as well as in the United States, the most important change that took place toward the end of the nineteenth century was the shrinkage of self-direction in the productive process. The trend was to increase production in enterprises of increasing size and to develop and to tighten the discipline of the work process within each such enterprise. The technical character of manufacture demanded discipline. The movement of the workman had to be timed exactly to the motion of the machine. Millions of once independent farmers and craftsmen became disciplined machine tenders. Standardized machines operated by standardized manipulations allowed for little or no variations in the worker's skill. The growing number of standardized products, pressed upon the consumer by increasingly refined methods of commercial propaganda, called for a standardization of consumer tastes. In all industrial countries, material power and material satisfaction increased with the unfolding of these new techniques of production and distribution. In all industrial countries these new techniques fostered the development of mass characteristics that, though most clearly discernible in the economic realm where production catered to the tastes of the many rather than the few, gradually extended their sway into politics, journalism, and, finally, the arts. Although the attribution by Europe of these characteristics to American society, and to American society alone, was based on a misapprehension—the moat in Europe's eye—American society did reveal the features of the international trend most rapidly and most impressively. For, in America, a conspiracy of circumstances imparted to that trend cumulative force.

An immense, rich territory, a large internal market, the conditions under which the Civil War was fought and the victory of the industrializing North, the heavy capital investment and technological contributions by Europe's most advanced countries, all these factors favored the growth of large-scale enterprise and mass production. However, the assimilation of large numbers of immigrants—many of whom brought only their hands to the American market and who were incapable of absorbing any but the most rudimentary instructions and yet were docilely prepared to engage in monotonous, hard work—called for the development of machines and working methods—a technical discipline—that could put unskilled man power to work. On the other hand, immigrant wages swelled the national demand for consumers' goods. The immigrant received, by way of advertisement and more subtle pressures, rudimentary instruction in how to spend his money and join the ranks of the consumer. Here, too, his presence in the American economy suggested simplification of methods and of slogans as well as products, for the expensive goods were beyond his financial reach and his tastes were as malleable as they were uncertain.

It would be grossly misleading to picture the immigrant as the principal agent of the mass production developments that reached so high a perfection in the United States. He was in the main a passive agent. Moreover, the new techniques integrated native farmer, craftsman, and backwoodsman with equal ease in the processes of production and consumption. All that can be claimed for the last mass immigrations is that they powerfully re-enforced prevailing trends. These trends were, economically, toward mass production and standardization of product and, socially, toward an identification with the "peer group," the group of one's peers in age, education, and on the income and consumer level. Obviously, the increasingly large number of people who worked in large enterprises and had been taught to derive satisfaction, and indeed did derive satisfaction, from mass-produced goods, slogans, and amusements were no longer the independent, self-directing Americans of the old philosophy, the Threefold Configuration.

In the first decades of the twentieth century the American national character underwent profound changes. In America, these changes gave rise to gnawing doubts which were to find first and perhaps most poignant expression in a rich body of creative writing. To European eyes, the American "personality" appeared far less sharply drawn than it had been toward the end of the nineteenth century. In one respect, it was now, by virtue of the completion of the European ethnic spectrum, more European than it had ever been. But precisely because of its ethnic comprehensiveness, the American "personality" now seemed more alien to, let us say, the individual Frenchman, German, Englishman, Italian, or Pole. In the nineteenth century, it was still possible for the European to visualize the American personality in the image of, let us say, a nonconformist Englishman whose eccentricities were tempered by a solid German education. Inadequate as such a stereotype may have been, it contained a hard kernel of truth. Uncle Sam's features are idealized, albeit not unusual, physical distinctions among the men of northwestern Europe. They are a relative rarity among the men of southern and eastern Europe. They are, incidentally, a rarity among the passers-by in the streets of today's American city. More important than Uncle Sam's idealized physical appearance was his moral stance and his universal message which reverberated in Lincoln's homely rhetoric. To Europe, that message was as simple as it was authentic: it promised liberty and unity.

Europe had won the former in the great struggles for political and national liberation in the first part of the nineteenth century—only to lose its essence to the divisive canker, class conflict, that had corrupted its social organism. Americans were free and in their freedom reconciled to one another. Somehow, in the first decades of the twentieth century, that message had become garbled. The greatest danger now facing America and Europe is that the message will no longer be understood, that the clanking of the apparatus, the blare of the "mass media," and the martial trumpets will drown it out altogether. It is idle boastfulness to speak of a "new message." People do not improvise historic "messages." They cannot change at will their character to meet the specifications of an international popularity contest. If they are gifted, they invent new words and songs to honor the theme of their youth. America can renew its message and can expand it to encompass the realities of modern Western society, realities that America has done so much to forge in the crucible of its own inventive energies. To do so, America must answer its own pressing question, the question that Europe, too, asks itself yet wants America to answer.

Perhaps the most significant intellectual development in the United States here and now springs from the realization of a growing number of social scientists that new categories of thought must be brought to bear upon the universe of their discourse. One may rightly ask: what is remarkable about applying new ideas to a field in which the most obvious characteristic is change? However, the most striking impression which the Western discourse on social questions throughout the last hundred years conveys is the persistence of the stereotypes of Marxist affirmation and anti-Marxist rebuttal. Not only the Marxian but his intellectual opponent spoke of the "proletariat" and "social classes," "wage workers" and "entrepreneurs," "socialism" and "capitalism" as if these concepts actually corresponded to and exhausted concrete social alternatives. Though not everyone was a socialist or a Marxian, everybody accepted, wittingly or unwittingly, the categories of Marxian dialectic. It is this circumstance rather than their contributions to science which raised Hegelian philosophy and Marxianism to the potency of destiny. In Europe, the dominance of Marxian thought and of thought that negates Marxian thought, yet is its dialectic slave, is still unbroken. Capitalism *is* capitalism and socialism *is* socialism and both are what they are now and forever everywhere. In Europe, the controversy was so intense that the disputants were too harassed by the pressure of arguments to keep an eye on what they were arguing about. Yet all the time the subject matter was changing. Now the realities no longer fit the arguments of either side. This intellectual estrangement from reality—from life—is but one symptom of the disease we called social alienation. The spokesmen of the "two nations" cannot understand each other's speech, for that speech is as empty of living content as were the theological disputes of the late Middle Ages, stultified as much by "dialectical" argument as by estrangement from the common faith.

In America, the outlines of the new society (and possible future society) were more sharply sketched than in Europe. Its features were: technological progress and shift of emphasis from production and "work" to consumption and "play"; the numerical increase of the middle class swelled by the expansion of the professions, bureaucracies, and service industries; the self-identification of large numbers of factory workers with the middle class and the extension of the middle-class way of life beyond the bounds of middle-class occupational status; the great increase of middle incomes and of the middle incomes' share in the national income; the instancy and greater accessibility of communication and the pervasiveness of its media. These developments had solved a good many of the social problems most European theoreticians and politicians were still talking about. They created new problems which most European and not a few American theoreticians and politicians failed to note. The new alternatives presented themselves no longer in the stark forms of the Marxian juxtaposition. Property had lost some of its former psychological and even some of its physical advantages. There had been a regression of the acquisitive urge. There had been ascendancy of security as a life goal, garlanded by the gay festoons of leisure and play. It was no longer easy to draw the neat Marxian line between "exploiters" and "exploited." The scale of possibilities within which the individual could make his social choice was no longer a vertical one of Upper, Middle or Lower Class. He was now mostly constrained to make his choice between one and the other life styles of the New Middle Class—the New Middle Class that numerically exceeded any and all other strata of population. He could no longer rise to the Upper Class which had become an anachronism. He sought security rather than risk and relied on group solidarity as protection against loss of status. The social choice was thus to *be* of the New Middle Class or not to be of any class. The choice was not that of joining sides in the social struggle, to stand for or against private property, to be a "capitalist" or a "toiler." The choice was not one between dialectic opposites, but between marginal alternatives.

The features of the new society are still vague and by no means as firmly etched as were those of its predecessor. In a sense, this discussion takes certain trends for granted and places in the past what the reader may view as the likely or unlikely development of the future. However, the evolution of the last twenty years, roughly since the beginning of the New Deal era, has tended unmistakably in the direction of our "society of marginal differences" and away from the horns of the Marxian dilemma. More important still, this interpretation corresponds to the society in which the majority of Americans believe they live in or *could* live in but for certain modifications. Whatever these certain modifications may be, they are not conceived of as revolutionary alterations. What has masked the American trend from European observation is the persistence in Europe of the old vocabulary that owes so much of its crudity to Marxian slang and its counterpart, the anti-Marxian vocabulary lifted from the Marxians by their embattled foes. That vocabulary is still popular on both sides of the Atlantic. No wonder that Europeans still view the complex American scene as the square arena in which "capitalists" battle "socialists," "free enterprise" stands at bay before the "planners," "entrepreneurs" exploit "wage laborers," and "depression" stalks "prosperity"! Perhaps no Soviet propaganda trick has succeeded more brilliantly in Europe than the identification of the American economic system with European capitalism of the Karl Marx vintage.

If the Marxian counterfeit has, in European eyes, distorted the outlines of American society, non-Marxian platitudes on "standardization" have not helped in correcting the European vision. The myth of American uniformity is, in Europe, about as popular as is the Marxian cliché of American capitalism.

The standard aperçus of visiting Europeans, offered after a two weeks' dash through plants, night clubs and lecture halls, on American "standardization" reveal a stunning imperviousness to facts.* The American consumer has a far greater choice of goods, quantitatively *and* qualitatively, than has the European. American industry "standardized" an incredible variety of products. Most European "standardized" products are drably uniform; European mass-made goods are, as a rule, shoddy. American industry, bidding for the custom of a large, alert and restless public, succeeded in squaring the

* See Peter Drucker's witty essay "The Myth of American Uniformity," *Harper's*, May 1952.

circle: it devised "standardized" methods for satisfying a great variety of tastes and wants.

In America, the trends toward a new society—trends that antecede the New Deal and were implicit in the character of American society—did not escape thoughtful observers who, however varied their philosophical premises and interpretations, shared one distinction: they were refreshingly undogmatic. If Veblen gave the impetus to American social analysis, his successors paid their debts to him by breaking new ground. Upon its soil Veblen's seed blossoms, free of Veblen's idiosyncratic weeds. So odd a company as Peter Drucker, James Burnham, Elton Mayo, Harold Lasswell, and David Riesman, divided by profound differences of method, intellectual posture, and didactic purpose, appear teamed in kindred undertakings: to get "behind" the economic process. Their social analysis concentrates upon differences of personality and status more subtle than those engendered by bare economic necessity as Marx understood it.* These differences, although they originate in the workings of the economic system, curve back upon the economic process and subvert economic laws by noneconomic aspirations. How far this approach has been pushed is shown by comparing Veblen's notions with those of, let us say, Riesman. Where the former is still preoccupied with production and seeks for a solution that will maximize it as well as its social usefulness—by transferring control of the economic apparatus from "conspicuously" spending financiers to functionally minded engineers—the latter takes for granted technology's capacity for dealing with the problems of production and views the problem of what to do about its bottomless cornucopia as the one that most baffles American society now. Where the one still worries about how to make the cake bigger and how to cut the underprivileged majority

* See David Riesman, *op. cit.,* p. 294.

in on the "leisure" of the upper classes, the other is concerned with what the *privileged majority*—the New American Middle Class—will do with its privileges, to wit, its mechanical possessions, its leisure, and its play. Between these terminal points of view, puritanism and hedonism, production ethics and consumption ethics, sociology of scarcity and sociology of abundance, there has burgeoned a variety of schools of thought. The talk of their exponents is of distribution rather than production, the worker's status rather than his wages, business as a system of power rather than a system of profit, personality rather than class. It is not proposed here to determine how closely these notions correspond to observable facts. Technological progress may run, despite the assistance of atomic energy, into unexpected obstacles, especially those posed by exhaustion of raw materials. A steady rate of technological advance, if not the maintenance of present production levels, is the cardinal assumption of all "abundance" philosophies. Future population growth, which must remain stable or decline if technological progress is to insure a higher standard of living, may play all kinds of Malthusian tricks. Businessmen, even those who were exposed to the subtleties of cultural and social analysis, may still seek profit rather than power. Workmen may still prefer a fat pay envelope to a meaningful relationship with their job and fellow operators. There is ample evidence that these atavistic trends still persist. To American Marxists, not a few of whom have been long exposed to the arguments of noneconomic sophistication and have learned to package the old Marxian stand-bys in a smoother vocabulary, the class struggle is still the thing and the worker's alleged affinity for middle-class culture is so much hooey, a clever smoke screen designed to mask the pitiless exploitation of the many by the few. Moreover, were Marx alive today, he would be quick to assert that not only religion but also leisure is the opiate of the masses. All these objections notwithstanding, these new doctrines, attempting to turn the flank of both traditional liberalism and Marxism, are highly relevant to the image the New Middle Class has of itself and its future. Moreover, from the sum total of these arguments emerges a fairly convincing statement of American hopes and fears.

The hopes, if not the expectations, are grounded on fair statistical evidence: * Measured in dollars, the New Middle Class constitutes a formidable part of the total population. The changing distribution of income is most clearly revealed by the increase in the proportion of the population in the income group, that is, from $2,000 to $5,000. In 1929, about ten million families—28 per cent of the total—had incomes in this range while by 1946 this group included twenty-three million families, or about 50 per cent of the total. The rise is also strongly manifest in the increasing number of families with incomes from $5,000 to $7,500. Looking at the situation in the reverse way, the percentage of families with incomes of less than $2,000 shows a sharp decline from 65 per cent in 1929 to 40 per cent in 1946. In aggregate dollar terms the families in the $2,000–$7,500 in 1946 received one hundred and eleven billion as compared with thirty-eight billion in 1929. Nowhere else in the world are average incomes so high and is national income so evenly distributed.

Appearances do not belie the statistics. Peaks and valleys of living standards are increasingly flattened out into an undulating plain of marginal differentiations. The rich, entangled in taxation and status obligations, either cannot spend conspicuously or have grown too alert to the censure of the public and their own group to throw their funds about—except for the benefit of publicly approved causes. "Conspicuous" spending is now a fashionable practice chiefly among

* See Harold G. Moulton, *Controlling Factors in Economic Development*, Washington, D. C., The Brookings Institution, 1949; pp. 285-290. See also Selma F. Goldsmith, "Appraisal of Basic Data," *Studies in Income and Wealth*, New York, National Bureau of Econ. Research, 1951; Vol. 13.

the hierarchs of Hollywood, who feel they owe it to their public and their sponsors, and among the gangster bosses who thereby assuage their frustrations. As for the plenitude of gadgets, their possession is no longer an indication of either wealth or status. Not a few rich drive Fords; not a few working men drive Buicks. There is approximately one automobile on the road for every four persons of all ages. Significantly, among the purchases of high-priced cars, there are not a few members of ethnic and social groups that suffer from "denials of sociability" and must seek consolation in "conspicuous" possessions. An expensive television set graces the average humble home, at least in areas accessible to television broadcasts. The millionaire vacates the big house in the suburbs made untenable by high taxes and dearth of domestics, and seeks shelter in a city apartment; the salaried employee and worker moves into snug air-conditioned "units" of suburban developments. Not a few of the poor rich, traditionally inhibited about buying on long-term credit, feel that they cannot afford, and often in fact cannot afford, to acquire household labor-saving devices that the well-to-do poor will add to his trove of gadgets as a matter of course. The metropolitan cinema palace and increasingly, concert halls and "democratized" opera houses with equanimity admit, for a standard fee, millionaire and proletarian.

As for the street scene, it has been impossible for a good many years to distinguish readily by differences in dress and ornament between members of classes. Again, conspicuousness in dress seems to go with membership in groups of frustration, ethnic or otherwise. Or it goes with professional status, as for example the movie star, or with local holdouts as, for example, Texas oil and cattle barons. Obviously, differences in goods offered for consumption exist, are explicitly stated on the price lists, and confer some kind of distinction on the purchaser. These differences, however, are mainly marginal—so marginal indeed that it takes all the arts of sales promotion to put them across to the customer: the differences between Fords and Mercuries, Chevrolets and Dodges, streamliner coaches and Pullmans, the Paris model of Fifth Avenue *couture* and its simultaneous reproduction by the low-priced department store, Georgian brick dwelling and ranch-type house, would have baffled the rich or poor customer only thirty years ago.

Differentiation is nowadays achieved in part by choice of materials and ornaments rather than basic features of the product, and in part by a coy and covert snob appeal directed at the connoisseur whom the advertisement respectfully pats on the back for his powers of fine discrimination. In brief, the distinction of the product is precisely that its distinction from a like product is small and that awareness of this distinction confers distinction upon its possessor. It is an open question which we will leave to the expert to answer, as to whether advertisement still "pays" or has become an outlet for the narcissistic impulses of the managers and their public relations counselors. No one can prove convincingly that the buying public responds to some of the subtleties that emboss the patient product or chooses haphazardly from a supply of goods that, as far as basic features are concerned, has become fairly inelastic. The trend in consumers' tastes is toward refinement. That refinement is found in wrinkles. These need not be trivial, especially as regards the aesthetical satisfaction they furnish. Much of high culture is "wrinkles." The days of sumptiousness and ostentation are gone, except in public spectacles available to most everybody at moderate prices or free of charge. The days of the fun-of-interior-decoration and the joys-of-cooking, expertly rationed to modest budgets, are upon us. The vogue of unostentatious refinement has swept the nation to a high plateau of genuine good taste and sense of quality without which there is no joy of living. Millions of Americans mix their soup with sherry and bless their steak with claret. Millions of Americans buy decent reproductions of masterpieces, ancient and modern—some indeed daringly modern and controversial—and reproductions of the splendid pieces in wood and metal created by American craftsmanship in the eighteenth century. A surprisingly large number of workers, it is reliably reported, have emancipated themselves from Grand Rapids and taken to functional furnishings. The ubiquitous presence of and preoccupation with "wrinkles" has sent many a housewife of modest circumstances to museums, the sophisticated magazines, and even to books, if only to the splendid cookbooks that are such helpful and moving reading.

The trend toward refinement and sophistication which is attested by the care bestowed upon it by the mass media, sales promotion, and by the concrete evidence of better cooking, more discreetly cheerful chintzes and a notable upgrading of public entertainment, especially of good music, has led to a profound change in popular attitudes toward gadgets. Most Americans take their gadgets for granted and the prestige value of gadgets is declining. If there is prestige attached to gadgets it is especially to those that help their possessor to do without gadgets and restore some operations to nature, as, for example, the prestige of the barbecue pit and of the leg-powered bicycle. In this respect Americans, somewhat of blasé *beati possedentes,* are the least gadget-minded people in the world. The ludicrous veneration bestowed upon mechanical contrivances as marks of individual distinction by, let us say, the French and Latin American press, is unthinkable in America. In Europe, the introduction of familiar American gadgets is frequently met either with naïve wonderment or a crude appetite for possession that leaves visiting Americans with a mixed sense of superiority, compassion, and disgust. In Asia, possession of American hardware such as cars and radios, not infrequently elicits a ferocious sense of power, highly deleterious to public safety and native culture. And as for Russia, present-day Soviet pride in gadgetry, somewhat clumsy gadgetry at that, would have embarrassed an American vacuum-cleaner salesman of thirty years ago.

The preoccupation with differentiation and more subtle differentiation in what is called the "American-way-of-life"—which comes to resemble increasingly the New Middle Class's way of life with its comfortable width not too narrow, not too wide, and its easy gradients—is clearly enough inscribed in the things Americans seem to want and in their routine value judgments which assume the dignity of an ideal. American society not only *is* middle-class society, it is becoming more so. American youth is moving in the direction of the society-of-marginal-differences. The campus of any American college, the corridors of any American high school, can serve as laboratory experiment. If youth dreams of the high adventures of amassing possessions, life in mansions, and shuffling corporate equities, then its dreams are sealed in its subconscious. Its habits of dress are those of unostentatiousness in deviation from the mean, not unlike those of their elders, only more so. They do not rule out color and fetching wrinkles nor a studied negligence, if not to say slovenliness. But they do not err on the side of eccentric elegance or obtrusive self-assertion. As a matter of fact, the genuine interest in "wrinkles" has brought the generations nearer to each other than they ever were: the same kind of slacks, the same lipstick, and the same hair-do grace without a ripple of self-consciousness both mother and daughter. And as for youths' dreams and practices of sex they are, however biologically conservative, remarkably free of financial and social considerations compared with the caveats about the wrong side of the tracks, maintaining the upkeep of family mansions, and similar warnings that squelched Victorian love and still interfere with the eugenics of the European bourgeoisie.

In sum, the New Middle Class disposes of a store of things and values that far surpass in excellence that possessed by any other proportionate population segment in history. The

American way of life may not be the facsimile of the suburban bliss that smiles upon the convertible coupé in the *Saturday Evening Post* advertisement, but it is the nearest imitation of it in the world of animate things. It is moderately priced and accurately calculated to fit a moderate budget, so accurately indeed that there is no margin, financially. The material fit is tight, and the psychological fit is even tighter. The emphasis on marginal, small differentiations requires a fairly strict observance of extreme limits which bound one's choice. To stay within these limits requires a keen sense of balance. The shifts from one status to the other, one permissible social attitude to the next are delicate. Primitive impulses, the winds of passion, are dangerous intruders in this social world which depends for its equilibrium on complex psychological team play and which has ceded so much of its terrain of maneuver to the bastions of security. Hence its fears. And since its fears are those of losing status—depending not so much on individual initiative, as does wealth, but on the toleration and approval of others and of "groups"—these fears are fears of the anonymous. The threats of anonymous dangers from the realm of international politics re-enforce the sense of insecurity of a society that has given precious hostages to security. Hence its anxieties.

America is uneasy; America is tense. The United States, for the first time in its history, faces the threat of war to her continental possessions. The United States fought many foreign wars during the 175 years of its existence, more wars than any power except Britain, within the same space of time. These wars were mostly fought abroad; none of these wars caused severe losses in American lives and property. Now the American people expect that their homes will be the principal target of the enemy. They surmise that the attack will be pressed home with weapons, known and unknown, endowed with apocalyptic powers of destruction. They believe that the decision of war and peace does not lie with them but with the inscrutable rulers of a people about whom no one but a handful of men possesses first-hand knowledge. Since these assumptions and forebodings of the general public correspond, at least in their essentials, with the estimates of political leaders and their experts, the threat of war alone supplies ample ground for worries that, far from abnormal, reflect a healthy concern with self-preservation. However, anxieties bred by the fear of war agitate the unquiet spirit of a society which is unsure about itself. American society was undergoing profound changes when World War II blanketed the unsolved problems of transformation by easy unanimity in response to the peril of the nation. The resurgence of foreign peril in the late forties again suspended the meeting of American society with itself. It is as if its innermost anxieties had been transferred to a series of international emergencies. These emergencies, dire as they were, offered opportunities for escape from intimate and grave dilemmas, of which government, groups, and an increasing number of individuals eagerly availed themselves. Thus, for example, no one can argue convincingly now as to whether the problem of full employment has been "solved" by the introduction of a variety of fiscal techniques and legislative devices or whether it was "solved" by the man-power requirements of war economy or whether it is even a meaningful "problem" at all. No one can say now how many members of the New Middle Class would have found their "status" had it not been for the expansion of the military establishment and a host of agencies that owe their existence to foreign necessities, felt or real.

Featherbedding is a general phenomenon. Featherbedding is a practice in which the intelligentsia now engages as skillfully as organized labor. The proliferation of "made" jobs has never been confined to the more obvious pasture of sinecures, the bureaus of government. The twilight zone of specialization in industry, commerce, academic institutions, philanthropic undertakings, and recognized professions expanded rapidly long before the advent of "emergency" agencies of government and a large standing military establishment. The twilight zone of specialization is now the habitat of a vast population armed with a vast variety of degrees and certificates. In industry, the once fairly determinate zone of production engineer, plant manager, and personnel director now shades almost imperceptibly into the vague domain where industrial psychologists, morale builders, public-relations men, investment councilors, legal aides, stylists, and kindergarten supervisors support management in its efforts to grapple with a host of problems of which not a few arise from the congestion in the domain of expertness or the fertile imagination of the experts themselves.

In academic institutions, minute differentiations within fields of specialization not only deepened scientific and scholarly insights but also the entrenchment of the specialist in his job, the usefulness of which can be ascertained by only one expert opinion: the incumbent's own. Academic institutions have pioneered in the production of all kinds of standardized marks of competence and derive a large part of their income from the universal demand for degrees. In all societies of status from Byzantium to Germany, distinction derived from the recognition of the collectivity and not from birth, wealth, and individual deed, a certificate of competence—a degree —is the claim check to a job. To obtain this claim check the candidate must pass an examination. The United States has passed from the era of "learn while you work" and "you are the man for the job if you can do it" into the era of examinations. This alone marks the extent of the great transformation that separates contemporary American society from that of the 1920's. A whole generation of the New Middle Class has gone through the mill of examinations and is going through it now. In part, this grinding process was triggered by the introduction of the merit system into the civil service of federal government and many state and local governments

as well; in part it has been set in motion by the crying need
for bringing order into the expanding fields of specialization;
in part it has been brought about by the guild-conscious
professional organizations of specialists who *have* passed the
prescribed examination. From the twin drives for uniform
professional standards and the professional's security against
"unfair" competition flowed many consequences, some highly
beneficial to the community, some merely curious, and some
pernicious to the public weal. Undoubtedly, public health
has on the whole gained by rigid standards of medical education. It is doubtful that the professionalization of many chari-
table, public assistance, and neighborhood activities has
greatly improved the ministrations of the agencies concerned.
It is certain that these agencies are now burdened with larger
payrolls, and that many able volunteers, especially women
seeking worthwhile work without remuneration, are now deprived of fulfilling occupations. The volunteer in the service
of the community, lacking the fig leaf of certificate or degree,
is now relegated—whether in hospital ward, home service,
or poor relief—to the least desirable jobs. Among these, money
raising is the one job professionals are most willing to yield
to the volunteer without examination.

Professionalization and specialization, marginal differentiation of status and security of status, all these related horizontal aspects of a highly developed and rigorously organized
society are projected vertically into the structure of that society, its hierarchy. Big Business anticipated Big Government.
The bureaucracies of the great corporations developed fairly
complex distinctions of rank that were to their holders often
as important, if not more important, than the financial remuneration attached to them. But the expansion of government and especially of the military establishment has
immensely increased the popular prestige value of rank.
Differences in official rank correspond in one respect closely
to the situational differences in the New Middle Class which,

we noted, are less obvious though not less meaningful than social classifications based on income. The hierarchy of rank is a hierarchy of marginal differences within a rigidly circumscribed range, outside of which roam people without rank and hence of indeterminate personality. The difference between a first and a second lieutenant is about as marginal to the civilian bystander as is that between a Chevrolet and a Dodge to the pedestrian; both are deeply meaningful to the connoisseur and to those within the inner circle where these differences confer distinction. Undoubtedly, the personal acquaintance of millions of Americans with military organization and the growth of a large standing military peacetime force have made the American public more rank conscious than it would have been had the universe of rank been confined to the civilian bureaucracy. The military, however, provided a truly popular training in the operation and appreciation of a value system that had been developed, though less methodically and less forthrightly, in the shelter of the large corporations, federal government and trade, labor and cultural associations. The military establishment for many Americans, especially for members of the New Middle Class, supplied the kind of graded satisfactions—in lieu of the dazzling rewards of the successful captain of industry or finance—which American society of the thirties had learned to seek. It supplied security; it also supplied a social status that required no other justification than itself: one *is* a colonel, one does not work at being one.

The bureaus of Washington afford ideal conditions for observing the system of rank at work and its capacity for infinite refinement. Unlike the clerks of some of the older highly bureaucratic states, American civil servants are not distinguishable by portable badges of rank. However, their respective positions in the hierarchy are invested with minutely graded insignia of office. The most obvious one is spatial: shared occupancy of office space or sole possession or tenure of a suite including secretarial and waiting rooms. The furnishings range, by staggered gradations, from functional office furniture to Georgian reproductions or replicas of Duncan Phyfe and all kinds of furnishings having no functional or utilitarian significance. Ornaments, such as wall maps, photographs, and portraits of high incumbent or recently departed officials, especially those bearing dedications, are as expressive of the tenant's rank as would be braid on his sleeve or brass on his hat. Protocol prescribes the means of displacement, from group conveyances such as bus to the largest and latest model Cadillac limousine and private plane, with or without sleeping quarters and lounge, again according to the passenger's rank. The summary treatment accorded here to the painstaking labors that competent officials have lavished on arranging and rearranging these minutiae of protocol barely grazes the surface of an exciting phenomenon, relatively unknown to the man in the street remote from the seats of government. To the many hundred thousands of public servants occupying these seats, from fireproof swivel chair to period *fauteuil,* the system supplies satisfactions as well as stimuli as vivid as those another generation derived from the pursuit of wealth or social position in the now obsolescent context of memberships in expensive clubs and "best society." Not a few members of that fading "best society" and its associated economic organizations such as corporate directorates and the great law firms have transferred to the official hierarchy. Not a few of the great and many lesser managers of industry have adjusted themselves to the pace of the various government organizations, in which they now hold office, and the prerequisites attached thereto.

There is ample evidence, to which Washington contributes an important, though not the only exhibit, pointing to a development more significant than that which James Burnham discerned and labeled the Managerial Revolution. America's new status society, though it is the successor of the society dominated by holders and manipulators of titles to wealth, such as bankers, brokers, or plain coupon cutters, does not tend toward the domination of managers, that is, persons who do not "own" but "manage," be they managers of big corporations, big labor unions, or big government. The New Society bears the unmistakable features of Rank Society. Its social differentiations are those of rank rather than function. If the passage from Babbitt's America to the America of the Civil Servant, 11th class, can be dignified with the term revolution, then that "revolution" was the Revolution of Rank.

The rise of American rank society has not escaped the notice of Europeans. Its representatives are in full view everywhere in Europe: the officials of American occupation governments in Germany and Austria, the staffs of a host of agencies ministering to the economic and military needs of Western Europe, and an endless stream of miscellaneous emissaries of the American government. American voices speaking to Europe are the bland voices of officials. European travelers, returning to the United States after an absence of several years, profess themselves impressed by the growing bulk of officialdom. Europe finds in the likeness of the United States familiar features. America is becoming more "European" yet at once more enigmatic. For the orderly ascent up the ladder of rank is not that free and lusty movement that, Europeans once thought, would keep American society loose in the joints. American society is still a classless society, but it is no longer mobile. The spidery web of rank blurs the image of "equality" once so clear to the envious gaze of Europe. In the eyes of Europe, America's New Society is not so new.

And is it so new? Perhaps no other writer has recorded more sensitively the stirrings of that new society than David Riesman has in his *The Lonely Crowd*. Riesman distinguishes between three "ideal types" of social character: the tradition-directed, the inner-directed, and the other-directed person. The tradition-directed type corresponds roughly to what we have called organic society. The behavior of the individual is controlled by traditions that are handed down piously through the generations. Religion and ritual supply orientation for everyone within the rigid limits of clans, castes, and professions. Tradition insures conformity. Chronologically, tradition direction, the mode of control of feudal and agrarian societies with their stable populations, is succeeded by inner direction, the mode of an expanding society in which social barriers become fluid, technological shifts upset the economic and population balance of agricultural society, production of goods increases, and colonialism and imperialism release restless energies into geographical space. The greater range of choices and of initiative demanded for coping with new problems cannot be encompassed by the inflexible code of tradition and calls for a more elastic and "self-steering" character type. The source of direction of the individual is "inner"; it is the body of precepts implanted in the child and youth by its elders that guides the man toward predestined goals yet leaves the choice of the road to his judgment, his conscience. This mode of social behavior Riesman designates: inner direction. It corresponds roughly to the life style of Western culture which we saw emerging from the Renaissance and crystallizing in the Threefold Configuration of eighteenth-century Rationalism, Individual Will, and Protestant Conscience. As Riesman sees it, "inner direction" is now giving way to "other direction."

Other direction is the mode of social behavior prevalent in societies faced by slowing population growth and, in the fullness of time, population decline. The peaks of technological creativeness have been reached. The maintenance, expansion, and refinement of productivity has become a routine and no longer demand the bold initiative and painful self-denial that went into scientific and industrial pioneering. There is plenty of capital and, since the machine is doing man's work more and more efficiently, plenty of manpower. Inventiveness is systematized by collective research. Capital formation is nurtured by the large corporations' cautious write-offs, dividend policies, and "fair trade" policies, and by government fiscal policies. These supply the balanced diet of even industrial progress. "Scarcity psychology" gives way to "abundance psychology." The society of producers gives way to the society of consumers. Training in social behavior includes increasing doses of training in consumption, leisure, and play.

In the smaller families of highly urbanized and industrialized communities, there is a relaxation of older patterns of discipline: one or both parents are absent for the better part of the day, be it at work or working at consuming. The children, whose birth and number are largely a matter of parental discretion, are tended by institutions, from kindergarten to grade and high school. The child is taught to conform to the standards of the "peer group," the age, and the class-graded collectivity of school and neighborhood. The parents, themselves concerned with their popularity in the circle of their peers at work and at play and leisure, "make [the child] feel guilty not so much about *violation of inner standards,* as about failure to be popular or otherwise to manage his relations with . . . other children." *

The pressure of conformity in adolescence is in maturity re-enforced by the mass media: movies, radio, newspapers, and other vehicles of popular culture. Thus the source of guidance is one's contemporaries, known in the flesh or known through vacuum tube, screen, or print. The guide is the current in which one is borne away. These standards of conformity are implanted early in life; they, too, are "inner." But they are continuously modified from "without." It is only the process of "paying close attention" to others, their con-

* Riesman, *op. cit.,* p. 22. Italics are mine.

duct and their "signals," that guides the "other directed" along the path of life from the first tender group experience to consumption of the group-approved cemetery lot.

Riesman's thesis, a masterpiece of Alexandrine sophistication, is carefully hedged by qualifications: his types are "ideal" types. In all ages, all three sources of direction shaped social conduct simultaneously. In the tradition-directed Middle Ages inner-directed monks and other-directed courtiers were deviations from the norm. In this, the other-directed society, tradition direction and inner direction retain their guiding power over large segments of the population as, for example, farmers and scientists, slum dwellers, and the residual Victorian middle and upper classes respectively. Moreover, one and the same individual may, and nearly always does, shape his behavior by mixing the sources of direction. In all ages, "inner directeds" were other directed in certain kinds of social behavior and so forth and so on *ad infinitum*. Riesman's value judgments are restrained. If his distaste for "other directedness" occasionally appears to get the upper hand, he views the other directed person as peculiarly fitted for coping with the pressures of modern society and as capable of becoming a full man as were his characterological predecessors. Riesman views the dominance of other directedness in modern culture as flowing rather from international trends, capitalism, industrialism, and urbanization and not so much from the character-forming experiences of a particular people. These qualifications notwithstanding, he addresses forthrightly his critique of other directedness to American society. The other directed, he suggests, finds himself particularly at home in America due to "certain constant elements in American society, such as the recruitment from Europe and its lack of a serious feudal past."

Riesman's "other directed" type is the stereotype of what we called the New Middle Class, predominantly urban, "white collar," and salaried. It perhaps does not master, for mastery connotes passions that it spurns, but certainly operates the vast and intricate mechanism of modern industrial and bureaucratic America. Since history repeats itself but never quite repetitiously, some of its features are new, some are old, very old indeed. New is the sheer size of the New Middle Class. Unprecedented is the technological power the levers of which lie in the hands of the New Middle Class. At no time in history have so many commanded the services of so large an amount of power and had so broad a latitude for leisure. Never were so many capable of receiving as many "signals" and accessible to as many "signals" emitted by so many senders. The New Middle Class, collectively, has more, does more, and can do it faster than any society before it. But does that not exhaust its features that are genuinely "new"? The social characteristics of metropolitan living are not new. The heightened awareness of others and the sensitive alertness to the ubiquitous pressures; the withering away of the family and the increasing authority of seen and unseen crowds; fashions, fads, and conformity—these and related features of mass society recurred in every one of the great cultures of history such as the Roman, the Byzantine, and the Chinese. There are indeed nuances such as, for example, the peculiar attributes of rank, that should be recognized as true innovations contributed by the New Middle Class to the lore of metropolitan and bureaucratic diversity in conformity. But even these nuances perfectly match the general characteristics of mass society drawn to life so vigorously by, let us say, Oswald Spengler and Ortega y Gasset who, incidentally, were agreed—however far apart they were on other matters— that mass society need not be (and, in fact, never was) "proletarian" and may contain (and, in fact, usually did contain) *all* classes. There is little in the make-up of American bureaucracy, except perhaps its inordinate propensity for organizational charts and reorganizations, that cannot be found in the characterizations of older bureaucracies by Mosca, Pareto, and Michels. The short supply of jobs palpably related to the *production* of goods and the long supply of seekers for jobs related to distributing, appraising, and taxing goods or merely writing or talking about them are not new phenomena. The oldest chronicles report exactions by the drones and scribes levied upon the national product.

The face of the New Middle Class, so alert to subtle differentiations and so imaginative in the creation of marginal differences, so uniformly good looking with its accent on youth and so tastefully attired, is strangely inexpressive. Its gestures, tolerant, sophisticated, and controlled, are as pleasing as the motions of a superb chorus and as impersonal. The team is perfect and all members watch one another much too carefully to step out of line. The goal is no longer the elusive one of "keeping up with the Joneses" in an everlasting race for riches, but in "keeping up with them in the quality of their inner experience." One does not emulate one's fellow citizen, one *is* he and everybody *is* everybody else. Anonymity is civic virtue.

The "ideal type" of the New Middle Class is most certainly not the epitome of *the* American character. David Riesman, for one, does not suggest anything of the kind. However, there are abundant signs and portents that point to the unfolding of a trend: Big Business, Big Pressure Groups, and Big Government and their bureaucracies; professionalization and its professional guilds; security of tenure and hierarchy of rank—these are not random notions about contemporary American society. The design of the pattern, fuzzy as it may be at the edges, is perfectly clear: authoritarian society. An authoritarian society is one in which authority rests with powerful collectives. Whether these collectives obey the command of a single individual or of a group of individuals is not a question that affects the nature of authoritarianism one way or the other. The emergence of flamboyant personal dictatorships in this century rather obscured than clarified the conditions that are sufficient and necessary for the imposition of authoritarian rule. The *Führer* and the Big Brother are not necessary; they are mere names given to anonymity; they are not persons. Authoritarian society can do perfectly well without them, as late Roman, Chinese, and Byzantine history shows. The emperors hardly ever contested the power of the bureaucracy. Most of them were either masters of ceremony or top bureaucrats themselves, and despite innumerable re-organizations, the bureaucracies survived virtually intact and unaltered by the wear and tear of the centuries, including occasional attempts at fundamental reforms and even "demo-cratization." Anthropomorphic authoritarianism is a conces-sion to the monarchic past and to organic society with its clear-cut father-son relationship. It is not necessary under ad-vanced conditions. The apparatus is self-operating. And if personalization of authoritarian power were to suggest itself for the sake of educating marginal groups (among whom the father image retains its authority, together with a consistent ego and superego derived from father-son relationship), then a disc or sound track can supply the personal touch. Big Brother canned is as appropriate for the occasion as he is "fresh" off the hustings.

It is argued that the multiplicity of pressure and veto groups and government agencies and, lastly, the struggle for power within these collectives check and balance authori-tarian tendencies and that a kind of invisible hand thus regu-lates the political market and keeps it "free." To begin with, this argument admits implicitly that *representative* govern-ment no longer does the job and that the functioning of the democratic process must now depend on chance collisions of the "interests"—a kind of Heisenberg law of politics. But more important still, the protagonists *are* admittedly collectives and immensely powerful ones at that. They are rivals for authori-tarian control. Far from being opposed to the nature of the thing, they all want it, though each wants it for *itself.*

And if in national and international politics conflict is *the* thing, so are alliances and combinations. There is a tragicomic touch to the theory of "pluralism" according to which the private citizen remains the arbiter in the battle of the behemoths. And so he may—until the behemoths stop battling or one has finished off the other.

Creative art does not always tell us what a society is but it tells us where a society is going. In the United States, the Victorian novel told us relatively little about contemporary manners. The purlieus of gentility were not so extensive as the reader unacquainted with the American scene was asked to assume, and the manners were mostly bad or clumsy. However, the Victorian novel expressed what many Americans wanted: the refinements of an older culture, "graciousness." A generation later, much of what the Victorian novel assumed as given because it reflected the reader's aspirations, had come true: preoccupation with good manners and form had become a national characteristic. The protest novels and "social message" plays of the early thirties such as *Tobacco Road* and *Grapes of Wrath*, did not protest conditions that could be generalized into the then prevailing American "way of life." The realism of these literary insights into slums, flophouses, and dust bowls was all the more convincing since hardly any reader or theatergoer had ever been to these places. Europe took avidly to American social-protest literature. It is not surprising that most European readers visualized America as an endless procession of Oakies, Jeeter Lesters, Negro convicts, and sweat-stained drunks stumbling across the ruins of a ruthlessly materialistic society. Obviously, protest-literature stood in the same relationship to contemporary realities as did the Victorian novel. Both "assumed" more than the facts warranted. Both projected social trends, the one toward more "gracious living," the other toward more "social justice."

During the war, formal and informal censorship and the mobilization of artistic media and the artists themselves, deflected creative trends toward the "war effort." It is doubtful that even today creative literature has freed itself from the peculiar inhibitions of wartime experiences. Its tendency is to protest against a pall of conformity that it associates with war and militarization and their peculiar emphasis on unblinking authority. It protests against violence, particularly that meted out by military weapons. Or, if it does not protest, it frankly seeks and offers escape, escape from war as well as from the tolerant, sophisticated, and subtle nullity of middleclass civilization, its purring gadgets, and its mass media. The contemporary novel has no illusions and no heroes. The battle against exploitation, intolerance, and all kinds of social injustice has been won; the victory is all too complete. Silence has fallen on the battlefield whence tycoons and fascists have been driven and the lonely victor is haunted now by his own unidentifiable anxieties. Whereas the moral tenor of the literature of the thirties was keyed to guilt, social guilt, that of the postwar writers is keyed to anxiety about the myriad crude or subtle pressures of a closed society, about the shape of things to come, and about the very purpose of living. Contemporary literature is ambivalent. It is, in this respect, unlike that of the thirties which knew what it wanted and proclaimed it with missionary zeal. Contemporary protest literature protests authority yet seeks its secure shelter; it repeats the social message yet shrinks from the image of Utopia.

The contemporary novel, spun around psychopathological personalities or from the web of academic psychology and psychiatry attests the prestige of the clinical approach to the mind.* It is the literary expression of the ambiguities that have crept into the value system of American society. Though the psychological novel begins with Stendhal, it is, in its present state, a new literary form. Not only is it equipped

* See Merle Curti, *The Growth of American Thought*, New York, Harper, 1951; p. 779.

with the tools of psychology and psychiatry which its author may handle more or less artfully, but the hero of the novel is the "neurotic personality of our times." The individual character, normal or abnormal clinically or morally, is caught up in irreducible contradictions of society. There are no norms. Words lose their meaning. Thus the creative effort is not so much directed at the composite effect of words, the story, but at the meaning of words. The story is not in what the characters say or do but in the meaning that they give to or withhold from their words and deeds. This preoccupation with the meaning, the literary stance of philosophical and ethical relativism, is, also, not an unprecedented development. Late Roman, Byzantine, and Chinese literature and philosophy were concerned rather with the intricacies of meaning than with the things that words meant. It is not surprising that between the meaning and the meant an ever-widening gap opened, and that these ancient cultures lost, in the literal sense, their meaning for all but the experts on meaning, the Mandarins. That this tendency now troubles American literature—and not only the "little magazines"—can easily be ascertained by a random choice of current novels and short stories. On the didactic level, American literature, popular novels, and short stories are weighted heavily toward problems of "adjustment," adjustment to the group and its fashion and manners or adjustment simply to the situation one is in. What is important here is not how plots are solved or the didactic purpose conceived of, but that the problems seem to matter more urgently than adjusting or failing to adjust one's conduct to inner standards, or, for that matter, fixed standards of any kind. Moral standards are situational, not personal.

The moral standards of traditional society are still impervious to frontal attack. The devotional words of American speech are still those of traditional society. They are "freedom," "liberty," "self-reliance," and "individualism," and not yet "security," "group," "rank," or "state." "Democracy" is still "good government" and "good government" is "democracy." * The ideals of the eighteenth century, enshrined in the Constitution, still command the homage of the citizenry; action is still America's manly ideal; and the Protestant conscience still furnishes the words of judgment applied to social conduct. But the ambiguities of meaning have filtered into the devotional words themselves. "Freedom" is "Freedom from Want" and hence "Freedom" is "Security." This proposition is perfectly logical. However, the devotional words of the American tradition were not words of logic but words of belief. The question is not whether this or that meaning can be associated logically with them but whether their emotional content survives the dialectic operation. Admittedly, semantic exercises are of no great importance; they do not change the nature of things. They are, however, symptomatic of gnawing uncertainties. A raft of learned studies on public opinion, on politics, and private opinion on sex have furnished impressive evidence of the cleavage between standards codified in law and avowed by public authority and common standards of behavior and beliefs. It can be argued that such a gap existed in all societies past and present and that in contemporary American society new methods of research merely illuminated its depth and width. In nineteenth-century America, graft in politics, unscrupulousness in business, and all kinds of hypocritic shenanigans were as flagrantly at odds with publicly avowed standards as, let us say, the doings of certain pressure groups, criminal rings, arbitrary bureaucrats, and innumerable average men and women in the privacy of their homes or in the dark of night are today. In many respects, the contemporary scene compares favorably with that of the older America: public graft is, nowadays, mostly petty; corporation presidents are pillars of public trust

---

* "Conscience is still at work here; a deep sense of values is involved—a sense of what it takes to make the full man." G. T. Robinson, "The Ideological Combat," *Foreign Affairs,* Vol. 27, No. 4, p. 529.

and spend millions on publicizing it; public manners are the best in the world; even gangsters and racketeers aspire to the better things in life including originals of the postimpressionists; and the mass media deleted the last vestiges of forthright ribaldry from their contributions to popular culture.

The regression is manifest in the subsidence of passion. The watchword of the New Middle Class is tolerance, not passion: if it disdains the acquisitive rage of the tycoon, it also spurns the passionate zeal of the reformer. For its emotional budget does not provide for the luxury of passion. The New Middle Class finds, perforce must find, its emotional outlet in tolerance, not passion. For to be popular is to tolerate and to be tolerated, and popularity is the indispensable lubricant of a society of rank. Obviously, the limits of that society are the limits of its tolerance. Hence its "intolerance of intolerance." A hierarchical society allows no room to passions except one: collective resistance to the eccentric, especially the passionate reformer.

The Revolution of Rank has been all the more profound for having been accomplished without those jarring incidents that attended most events to which historians accord the ambiguous designation: revolution. It was by definition a disciplined revolution by a social stratum to which disciplined behavior was all the more natural because it required no particular conscious effort of self-denial and was, so to speak, built into the character by education. Further, the emergent social system corresponds to the existing economic system with its highly differentiated production and products, hierarchy of plant and hierarchy of goods, and thus merely "socializes" the standards of industrial efficiency. Efficiency is its compelling slogan. Thirdly, like every great revolution, the Revolution of Rank was carried out with the consent of the public. The American public, despite the apparent disorder of the democratic give-and-take, is the best disciplined in the world, precisely because its discipline is learned in the school of production and consumption, and not in the barracks. Its drillmaster is the expert, not the sergeant; the voice of command is that of impersonal efficiency and practical education, not that of leader and doctrine. The discipline of the American people, a generation ago the least docile of the West and certainly the most fantastic and erratic, is all the more effective because it is effortless. The performance of the American people at war was, both to its enemies and its allies, a wholly unexpected revelation. The ease with which production geared to peacetime demands swung into the making of history's greatest store of weapons baffled friends and foes alike. American discipline, so matter of course and so perfectly attuned to the pace of modern technology, created in a matter of months what the cruder and more primitive discipline of the Germans and Japanese, despite much fanfare and grinding of wheels, had not wrought in years: a colossal, smoothly operating war machine. The American military performance attained its most impressive heights in the massing of matériel and complex organizations rather than in solitary flights into epos although these, too, were not lacking and revealed unrivaled capacity for heroism. Britain's proudest hour was indeed the Battle of Britain, Russia's the Battle of Stalingrad. The great moments of the United States were the clocklike timing of the landing in Normandy, the Task Force in the Pacific joining the horizons, and any moment any day in thousands of American plants. Unlike the great military nations of Europe, the American people did not learn discipline in the school of war but in the school of modern technology and urban living, on the assembly line, and in the rush-hour traffic. It is this schooling that has made them the greatest military power and the most patient nation of the twentieth century.

Discipline was not one of nineteenth-century America's conspicuous virtues. It was surely not one of which Americans cared to boast or which the *émigrés* from Europe's ancient military states esteemed as the noblest of civic virtues. To the older inhabitant and to the immigrant alike the American way of life meant individualism and decentralization. These two words sum up the meaning of nineteenth-century democracy in America. In the twentieth century, by contrast, technology and city assemble large numbers of peoples in tasks requiring disciplined co-ordination and the subservience of the individual to the collective. Discipline and centralization sum up the meaning of the realities of American democracy in the twentieth century. Discipline and centralization have given the American people their high standard of living in peace and victory in war, wealth, and world power. Yet the price of wealth and power is the disquiet of the American spirit. The facts are what they are. Yet the beliefs are those of the past. America stands at the fork in the road: the technical and organizational armature of American power is that of 1952; the ideals Americans profess are those of 150 years ago. André Siegfried, pondering the America of today and recalling the America he knew as a youth, concludes his comparative essay with De La Rochefoucauld's maxim: "Man often thinks that it is he who chooses his way while that way is chosen for him; and while his spirit draws him in one direction, his heart leads him imperceptibly in another one." *

The American people seek their guidance in the ideals of Western culture at the high noon of the spirit; their very power pulls them toward goals that, however lofty, were not inscribed in the message that set them upon their course. Here lies their dilemma, and Europe's dilemma, too. For America is the guardian of Europe's future, and America is uncertain of her own.

* André Siegfried, *L'Âme des Peuples,* (Paris: Hachette, 1950) p. 186.

V
Europe, The Troubled Mind

THE BURDEN OF THE PAST

T HE MOST important single fact about Europe is this: Europe, only a generation ago the center of world power, is now debated ground. De Tocqueville's prophecy has come true: the nations of Europe are "stopped, or continue to advance with extreme difficulty," whereas America and Russia "have suddenly assumed the most prominent place among nations" and "sway the destinies of the globe." * In World War II Europe, and not any single European nation or group of nations, was defeated. England and France, nominal victors, retained but the shadow of their former might; Germany was struck from the list of Great Powers with a finality that, obscured though it was by the confusion of the victors, was clearly inscribed in world trends of population and economic growth.

Europe is debated ground. Upon it is renewed the struggle that Europe waged unceasingly from antiquity to the threshold of her greatest age: the struggle against Asia. As in the past, the menace of Asia presses now upon a Europe that is plunged into a general malaise compounded of lassitude of power and the alienation of society. Strategically, the clock is turned back to the epoch of Tatar and Turkish invasion, and spiritually, to the age of the great schisms that divided Western Christendom from the closing of the Middle Ages to the seventeenth century. History artfully designed the proper geographical analogy: the West at Bay now stands where it always stood, facing the resurgent East. Elbe, Neisse, Danube, Leitha

* De Tocqueville, *op. cit.*, Chapter 18.

are the rivers of extreme peril. At their banks, Rome sought to stem Barbarian invasion, European chivalry went down to defeat before the Mongols, and the combined forces of the Empire stood off the Turk. That Europeans, steeped in the history of their small continent, should draw these historical analogies and deem them fitting, may seem to Americans another symptom of Europe's sickly, engrossing concern with her past. Has there not been a change in the scale of things? Is not the base of Western culture extended across the Atlantic and is the conflict between East and West not as wide as the world? And does not the global range of intercontinental power deprive the narrow rivers of Middle Europe of their historic strategic significance? That Americans consider the answer to these questions as self-evident and that Europeans accept these answers as valid *from the American point of view, yet not from their own,* strikingly illuminates the "lag" that separates European from American thinking. America's world political perspectives have immensely widened, for America now "sees" Europe and Asia from the angle of her continent. Europe's eastern angle of vision remains unchanged, the nearness of the object of perception blocks the distant views.

It is now easy to see what only a few men saw before the last returns of history were in, namely how long ago the decline of European power began. It is now easy to see that war was merely pushing that which had been falling. To begin with, the Europeanization of the globe—by conquest and the diffusion of European culture and technology—had never been a one-way process. The impact of European power upon older cultures, though subjecting them to political domination, evoked their long-dormant vital forces and implanted not only the notions of European law and technical civilization, but also the idea of European nationalism in the subject peoples. Only upon territories settled by peoples of European stock did "Westernization" mean the spatial extension of

Western culture's writ. In the East, including Russia, "Westernization" meant the adaptation of Western ideas and techniques by another culture, but not the replacement of that culture by that of Europe. In this sense, Americans were not "Westernized"; they were Western from the beginning; Russia was "Westernized," yet did not become Western.* Europe thus called forth the forces of resistance to European domination and endowed them, perhaps more prodigiously and carelessly than any other conqueror, with the skills, institutions, and, especially, the weapons that could be turned most effectively against herself.

The European Age never signified a domination as absolute as the reader of, let us say, Marxist writings on imperialism might be led to assume. European domination, compared with that of older empires, was always uncertain and methodically sowed the seeds of its own disintegration. The Sepoy Mutiny and the Taiping and Boxer rebellions were handwriting on the wall; the rise of modern Japan was at once the triumph of "Westernization" and the most signal failure of Europe to retain control of the process it had set in motion. In this sense, it can be said that the world's European Age began under the auspices of artillery and closed when artillery met artillery. Europe wrought a change in the scale of things and in the end that change reduced the scale of Europe. European technology provided the means of transportation and communication necessary for the organization of effective government over vast continental areas: the optimum unit of national government today is about five to ten million square miles and a population of one hundred and fifty to two hundred millions. If European technology supplied the tools for erecting large and powerful non-European states, it reduced the nation-states of Europe to midget size that precluded efficient economic organization as well as mili-

* See Hajo Holborn, *The Political Collapse of Europe* (New York: Alfred A. Knopf, 1951) p. 8.

tary defense. Because of their small size and relatively small populations European nation-states did not reap the full benefits from the techniques of mass manufacture which they themselves had done so much to devise, a condition that is now painfully apparent but could have been easily discerned, a generation ago, by any alert student of economics. Indeed, the new methods of mass manufacturing redounded most unambiguously to the benefit of Europe's non-European apprentices, the United States and Japan, whereas in Europe their introduction exacerbated international and social tensions. These tensions were long contained by the diplomacy of Britain and the doctrine of free trade, re-enforced by Britain's naval power sheathed in the velvet glove of financial controls and the prestige of British manners. However, Britain's predominance was never absolute.

The myth of the British Empire was, and still is, at the root of the confusion about much of European history up until 1939 and the seemingly precipitate decline of Britain from a position of world power. The British Empire was never an empire in the proper sense, as was the Roman or as is the Russian today. The narrowness of its domestic base, the heterogeneity and dispersal of its possessions, and the very nature of its economic policies and professed political ideas, set severe bounds to British imperialism. Britain thrived on competition, so did her competitors, and so did, by the grace of this circumstance, the non-Western peoples, even some "subject peoples" who were on the road to Westernization. As the travelers on that road increased, the terms of trade as well as the balance of trade turned against Great Britain. In 1912, a Royal Commission assigned to the investigation of Britain's declining share in world trade, proffered findings and conclusions that hardly differ from those which, thirty-five years later, formed the basis of Britain's request for American economic aid. The pattern was then clear; the only difference after World War II was that it had become more so. Britain was always more sensitive to, and perceived more keenly, shifts in international trade than her Continental rivals. The latter, whose gains in trade were made at Britain's expense, for a long time did not note or care to note that Europe as a whole was slipping. However, this, too, was in keeping with the total lack of solidarity that strikes us now as the most conspicuous feature of what is called the European Age. Europe lavished upon the weak the very tools that had made her strong, and the competitive ardor of her peoples insured that this operation was transacted upon a strictly competitive basis. Prodigality and lack of solidarity—these were the causes that hurried the European Age to its close.

The great problems of history are simple—so simple indeed that every schoolboy knows how to solve them. Obviously, any reasonable Greek knew how absurd was the Peloponnesian War which delivered victors and vanquished alike into the hands of foreign foes. The problem was how to reconcile the major powers of Greece, Athens and Sparta; unite the city states; and confront the foreign foes with a powerful alliance. Surely, no one could fail to see that fratricidal struggle could ultimately benefit no one but the lurking Persians and Macedonians. Yet the Greeks, the most reasonable of reasonable peoples, perversely insisted upon quarreling with each other. It is as though their gods had blinded them to the most obvious dictate of reason, self-preservation, and as though they had become estranged from the common devotion to the guiding ideal of Greek culture, sense of measure in all things. The Greeks did not solve their simple problem, and Greece was ground to dust between the millstones of Macedonian and Roman power.

Obviously, Europe at the beginning of this century had but one reasonable alternative: unification. The other, the perverse alternative, was: self-mutilation and perdition. In the nineteenth century, it could still be reasonably argued that a war between European powers was a contest over the international balance of power with the rest of the world standing respectfully on the sidelines. The Napoleonic Wars were the last reasonable bid for world power. Had Napoleon won, the European Age might have issued into several centuries of Europe's uncontested domination over the entire globe. Henceforth wars between European powers could change the balance *within* Europe; they could no longer reverse the trends that diminished the power of Europe in relation to non-Europe. To the contrary, wars *within* Europe could only accelerate these trends. By the beginning of the twentieth century it had become clear to all men not bereft of sense that a general European war could only redound to the detriment of all of Europe, victor and defeated alike. Cecil Rhodes, Lord Haldane, and like-minded men in Germany and the United States, laboring for the creation of an Anglo-Saxon-German block, lacked neither wisdom nor sophistication. Had they succeeded, the European Age would have been extended indefinitely although—or perhaps, because—its principal trustees would have admitted the United States to partnership. The problem and its solution, both were simple.

The conditions under which World War I was brought to an end did much to conceal the true dilemma of Europe. The full weight of American power had not as yet been cast into the scales when Germany collapsed; Europe was thus deprived of the last act that would have spelled out the plot of the drama: if America did not actually "win" the war, it could have done so most convincingly given a few more months. Britain and France thus nurtured the illusion—which their statesmen (who knew better) did nothing to disturb—that *they* had "won" the war. The Bolshevik Revolution cast a lurid veil over the realities of Russian power and its unfolding demographic and economic potentials which had been rapidly building up since the end of the nineteenth century.

The consolidation of the Soviet regime; American industrial and financial might so massively manifest in its contribution to European economic reconstruction; and, last but
not least, the willful doings of Japan while the West had
been looking elsewhere, supplied crushing evidence of how
decisively the center of gravity of world power had been displaced. Yet so heavy was the burden of the past upon the
mind of Europe that no one, except for a handful of men,
seemed to grasp the blinding fact. Europe was confronted
with the choice of reconciling her nations to each other or
of reaping the harvest of anarchy and thus following the
Greek example, familiarity with which formed part of European education. A handful of men labored in vain: Briand's
United Europe scheme faded into the shady shuffles of
Geneva; Coudenhove-Kalergi's books were widely read and
favorably received—except by the statesmen who mattered.
There is not a shadow of doubt that, in the light of reason,
France and Great Britain should have tried to forge the
unity of Europe; there are solid grounds for assuming that
they would have succeeded had they agreed to try. For, from
1919 to the beginning of the thirties they alone were *the*
Great Powers of Europe. There were then innumerable arguments, some highly plausible, showing why the solution was
impracticable or should not be tried. Plausible or not, none
of these reasons were relevant in the face of the *other* alternative: European disunity and mutuality in disaster. So signal
a failure to solve such a simple problem posed so starkly
cannot be ascribed to a lapse in logic. Logic was Europe's
forte from which flowed her unique achievements in science
and technology; Europeans knew more about history and had
written more about it than any race before them. Europeans
were shrewd enough businessmen and statisticians to read
the trends of world trade; and, as for diplomacy, the heirs
of Talleyrand and Castlereagh possessed a treasury of precepts that spelled out clearly the general interest of Europe.

The cause of Europe's failure cannot be found in lack of knowledge or even prescience. Europe "knew" yet acted as if she did not. Her failure was moral not intellectual. That moral failure spawned the one attempt at European unity that mocked the idea of unity and compounded all the forces that hurried the European Age to its close: the Hitlerian bid for European domination. Hitlerian Europe was a travesty of Europe. A travesty of logic is not illogical: it is antilogic. Hitler was possessed of logic of a kind, the deadly logic of the demented whose thoughts unfold rigorously from a fantastic premise. That premise was that European unification could be consummated in an act of orgiastic nationalism. However, to burden Germany—or even Hitler—with the guilt for Europe's failure is to degrade history to a child's tale told by an idiot. Europe's moral crisis begot a grotesque monster: German racist ideology. But that ideology, however hideous, was the uncontestable offspring of European society: the Europe of Disraeli's Two Nations. It was the genuine product of Europe's Industrial Revolution.

THE HORRIBLE SIMPLIFIERS

THE ASSOCIATION of Liberalism and Nationalism throughout the first half of the nineteenth century was not, as it now may seem when the former has lost its ardor and the latter its reason, a chance meeting of opposites. It was the last attempt to join the Two Nations that faced each other in bitter hostility within each European nation-state. In that attempt, Liberalism and Nationalism stood indivisible. The Rights of Man wedded to the Romantic, the political ideas of the eighteenth century joined to the ideal of nationhood: the community of traditions, folkways, and speech—this was the spring that was to have restored the verdure of Europe's earth, blighted by the Industrial Revolution and eroded by skepticism. Mazzini's nationalism affirmed national individuality within, not against, common Western culture. His nation was the intermediary between man and universal society. To be an Italian was to be a fuller man and thus to enrich the common treasure of mankind.* To be sure, this was not the Olympic cosmopolitanism of Goethe, representative of the eighteenth century, with its emphasis on "the common sense of civilization." Nor was it that strutting prejudice, the idolatrous nationalism of the twentieth century.

In the peoples' risings of the 1830's and 1840's, Liberalism and Nationalism fought on the same side of the barricades. After the Revolution of 1848, perhaps the most crucial in the line of Europe's revolutions which failed, Liberalism and Nationalism parted company. It is no mere whim of history

* See Hans Kohn, *Prophets and Peoples*, N. Y., Macmillan: p. 76, *passim*.

that the publication date of the *Communist Manifesto* is 1848, for in that year Europe's last hope of closing the breach of alienation was crushed. Henceforth, the traditional society and the dispossessed of the Industrial Revolution were at war and both surrendered free will to the inevitability of class struggle. Marxian fatalism fed upon the bitter disappointments that the defeat of the Liberal-National alliance had left in its wake. If that defeat sealed the solidarity of the dispossessed, it drove traditional society behind the ramparts of the State. Traditional society held the instruments of rule, the levers of production and the passkeys to education and thus to its own citadel of power. Traditional society was the master of all it surveyed. The price of its power was fear: incapable of healing the wound of alienation and of embracing the millions whom the Industrial Revolution had uprooted, traditional society faced the stony hostility of the masses. Traditional society incanted the canons of the vital beliefs that hallowed its traditions, and denied their substance, the brotherhood of man. Marx's materialism turned the degraded values of traditional society against itself. The anguished voice of the faith that spoke through the encyclical, *De Rerum Novarum,* fell upon deaf ears; had Europe but known it, that unheeded voice was the voice of judgment. The void left by the erosion of vital beliefs was filled by secular mass ideologies which corresponded to the broken halves of what had been one European society: Nationalism and Communism. If Marx and Engels and Lenin were true heirs of the revolutions that failed from 1789 to 1848, so were Count Gobineau, Edouard Drumont, the anti-Dreyfusards, Houston Chamberlain, Dostoevski, Mussolini, Rosenberg, and Hitler. The coming of the mass ideologies rings in the Age of Travesty: if the *Communist Manifesto* was a travesty on the Rights of Man, so Mussolini was the caricature of the Mazzini who wrote: "The Europe of the peoples will be one avoiding alike the anarchy of absolute independence and the centralization of conquest."

Nationalism was the refuge of traditional society that refused to face up to the task of reconciling the nation with itself. The power politics of late nineteenth-century and twentieth-century Europe, unlike those of the eighteenth century, were not only, and perhaps not mainly, concerned with enlarging the nation's power in the society of nations but also with "exporting" the social crisis into world politics. In that sense, the First World War was a monstrous maneuver of diversion. The desperate attempt to patch up the rotting structure of national society with patriotism was probably the principal cause of war, and not the clash of rival imperialisms as the Marxian theory of Imperialistic Wars proposes. The streamlined mechanics of the operation were revealed by Mussolini and Hitler, but the basic tools had been perfected long before World War I. If any fuller proof were needed for the reality of what we called social alienation, it can be found in the pathology of stricken European society. The one and only organizing principle which the ideology of nationalism brought forth was militarism. That Communism withered to that same concept of social organization is characteristic of its common roots in social alienation. Both nationalism and Communism, derived from social alienation, found their characteristic form logically in barrack society. Nationalist militarism must not be confused with the military organization of the eighteenth century. The latter was based on an aristocracy for which war was an avocation, and not on the nation as a whole. The peoples did not participate in war and war was "limited." The militarism of nationalism is all inclusive; its base is the entire nation, it is compulsory and its hierarchy is not one of caste, as was that of eighteenth-century military organization, but one of rank.

The attitude of the ruling classes of traditional society toward the state was ambivalent. The state was their refuge from the wrath of the dispossessed. However, the entrepreneurial and professional middle classes as well as the older estates, aristocracy and church, looked askance upon the growing power of the military and administrative bureaucracy of the state, i.e., rank society. True, no fine line of demarcation could be drawn between traditional society and the new rank society. A rank society, composed of professional officers and clerks, had existed long before the Industrial Revolution, but it had been the servant of traditional society and largely staffed by the ruling classes, especially the lower orders of the aristocracy. The rise of modern nationalism and militarism, vast standing armies and vast military administrative apparatus ramified with ever larger sectors of the national economy, engendered the growth of a huge bureaucracy. The more unwieldy and the more entrenched that bureaucracy became, the greater waxed its power. Because of its very size, bureaucracy recruited its members from all strata of the population, and admission to its hierarchy was gained by the route of examination rather than by titles of birth or wealth.

The social *immobility* of traditional society in the age of nationalism and militarism heightened the attraction of bureaucratic careers, especially for the white-collar middle classes. In Germany and France, for example, bureaucracy supplied its members not only with a safe, though moderate, livelihood, gained at a modest effort, but also with a society of its own. That society was ruled by its own etiquette and conventions, its own rewards and punishments. Rank society was exclusive, more exclusive than the "best society" of birth, wealth, and the ostensible rulers of the state. "Best society" entrusted the bureaucracy with the routine tasks of administering the state, the army, ever larger sectors of the national economy that supplied the army, the public finances that supplied the huge funds for paying for the army and its supplies, the educational system—and the "social problem." If nationalism and militarism were the instruments which traditional society had forged for curbing the masses, bureaucracy systematized and administered their application. In this process traditional society, its attention diffused over the world of business, politics, and the art of living, was forced to delegate ever larger powers to its servants, military and civilian bureaucrats. Once started, the process was cumulative: the bureaucracy *became* the state. It is not easy to assign exact dates to the chronology of this process. More likely than not, the European nation-states that went to war in 1914 were then already ruled effectively by their respective bureaucracies and not by their ostensible rulers, monarchs, parliaments, and financiers. The alleged responsibility of the latter for the outbreak of the war is another myth of heated Marxian and post-Marxian fancy. Traditional society did not "want" war. If a responsibility for war attaches to Europe's traditional society it is that traditional society mounted a machine which it could not stop and which could not stop itself because of its own momentum. In World War I, bureaucracy came truly into its own for its reach extended to every phase of national life. World War I is said to have been a total war. It is more accurate to say that it was the first war between total bureaucracies. Walter Rathenau's planned economy of wartime Germany was the precursor of the Administrative Age in which we now live.

Though after World War I the state in Europe ostensibly relinquished some of the most stringent controls imposed during the duration of hostilities, it did not jettison the administrative apparatus built up as a wartime measure. To the contrary, nowhere was the bureaucratic personnel substantially reduced, and in certain countries, especially the new nation-states of Eastern Europe, the number of government servants increased considerably. This tendency reflected a universal trend, namely the relative slowing up of the increase in industrial workers—the proletariat—and a relative increase in the so-called white-collar groups and persons engaged in "service industries," especially the biggest of all "service industries": government. Thus the structure of European society was composed of three parts: traditional society (businessmen, politicians, bankers, clergymen, academics, physicians, artists and writers, aristocrats, statesmen, farmers, and monied contemporaries); the working population or "proletariat"; and the bureaucracy. The latter increasingly assumed the role of arbiter between the two former; it represented the state; it operated the nation.

More important still, military-civilian state bureaucracy was the principal agent of socialization of the means of production, whether by outright alienation of property or by confiscatory taxation. Socialization was carried out with the warrant of emergency legislation enacted for the purpose of winning wars and paying for defeats. It mattered little whether Marxian parties were able or not to form governments: when they attained the heights of command they found them occupied by the bureaucracy that, administratively, had performed the socializing operations effectively though with little or no awareness of the "dialectic" process. The non-Marxian parties, too, could do no better than accept the accomplished fact, despite programmatic protests. The surprising unanimity, for example, of Europe's major Socialist parties after World War II on one point, namely nationalism, is not surprising at all. British and German Socialists are—shades of Marx!—virulently nationalist not so much because of a sudden dialectic shift to the doctrines of Mussolini and Hitler but because of the simple fact that their own programs were executed by the servants of bourgeois bureaucracy and that European political-parliamentary socialism lost its *raison d'être* except as a means of controlling the laboring masses, a mission that bureaucracy was only too willing to entrust to socialists. On the other hand, nowhere did progressive regimes, socialist or crypto-socialist, find the established bureaucracy troublesome. In Germany, the bureaucracy served with impartial loyalty Emperor, Weimar Republic, and Adolf Hitler; in France, functionaries imperturbably stayed at their desks under Tardieu, Léon Blum, Daladier, and Pétain. Even in Russia from whence capitalists, landowners, and priests had been driven, a surprisingly large number of czarist officers and officials ministered to the administrative needs of the toiling masses. The peculiar and permanent position of the bureaucracy in the life of Europe's nation-states throughout the last hundred years has escaped not a few American historians and political scientists. In Europe, the phenomenon compelled attention. It necessitated a considerable revision of the Marxian interpretation of the struggle for power in capitalist society: evidently, a third party had joined the class struggle—only too ready to relieve both capitalists and proletariat of the irksome burden of power.

The one major European country that stood aside from the general trend toward the ascendancy of the militarist-nationalist state was England. (Switzerland and Sweden did not partake of the general trend. They were the exceptions that prove the rule, for their abstention was largely the result of smallness and institutionalized neutrality.) Until 1939, England remained the last stronghold of Europe's traditional society. England's ruling classes did not share their rule with the bureaucracy and retained in their hands the levers of state. True, the affairs of state, foreign policy, military forces, colonial possessions, were administered by a corps of professional public servants. But these were drawn nearly exclusively from traditional society and, to a large extent, from the oldest estate of traditional society, the aristocracy. Though the stability of traditional society owed much to Britain's strategic position, especially physical isolation from the European continent, its vitality sprang from English political genius. The achievement is summed up by John Morley: "Those nations have the best chance of escaping catastrophe

... who find a way of opening the most liberal career to the aspirations of the present without too rudely breaking with all the traditions of the past."

The revolutions of the Continent failed to attain their ultimate objective; social mobility. English political genius managed to ensure by gradual transformation the "circulation of elites" within the bounds of traditional society. This circulation was not perfect. Great Britain was not a democracy in the sense of American political and social institutions. We have seen, however, that in a democracy the growth of a hierarchy of rank beneath nominal social conformism can bring social mobility as effectively to a halt as did, let us say, the hardening of the feudal-monarchic society in France before the great revolution.

Social equalitarianism and social mobility are not synonyms; they may be mutually exclusive. A perfectly equalitarian society is one in which all its members enjoy perfect horizontal mobility and no vertical mobility whatsoever. English society was not equalitarian. However, it offered considerable latitude to "liberal careers" from comparatively lowly levels to the summits of society. The symbolic prize bestowed upon the successful aspirant was recognition by the monarch. An unending procession of commoners moved across the birthday lists of king or queen into the ascending tiers of honorific letters, knighthoods, baronies, and earldoms. Traditional society renewed itself by generous infusions of blood lacking in pedigree but not in red corpuscles. Measured by the average length of time of titles held in direct descent by the same family, British aristocracy is the youngest in Europe. If it was relatively easy to enter the heraldic gates, it was no more difficult for the noble and enobled to make a discreet exit and to lose themselves in the ways and byways of the nation's work. There was no caste prejudice, as there was on the Continent, against turning an honest penny or engaging in the sweaty work of turning the fallow soil of distant lands into tea and rubber plantations. Primogeniture ensured an ample reserve of younger sons for filling not only the military and administrative posts of the state but also elective offices, positions in business and banking, academic chairs, and a variety of places in the professions—some quite eccentric. The Protestant Conscience may not have ruled the soul of England unchallenged: its sway was extensive enough to remove the social stigma of hard work. Aristocrats turned merchants; brewers turned peers.

One source of renewal was the colonies and, later, the Dominions. There, conditions of work and society approximated those of the United States in the expansive years of the nineteenth century. If in England the working man who had risen to riches and titled eminence was the rare exception and the "circulation of the elites" benefited chiefly the middle classes, in the colonies and the Dominions truly American rags-to-riches careers could be made and were made. Not a few English nobles of Canadian, South African, Australian, and sundry exotic antecedents started their "liberal careers" with the same initial assets which a Rockefeller, a Ford, and a Chrysler pyramided into fortunes: capacity for hard work, ingenuity, daring, and a liberal dash of ruthlessness. Though English traditional society in its Victorian incarnation preserved the aristocratic forms of the eighteenth century it managed to "democratize" their content—a paradoxical achievement worthy of a people that "does not take thought seriously" and bends thought to action. The Victorian ideal of the "gentleman" was, for all its aristocratic connotations, far from exclusive. The status of gentleman implied comportment, education, and compliance with a code of things—things done and things not done—rather than membership in a hereditary caste. It was thus accessible to the scions of the bourgeoisie and, by the route of the bourgeoisie, to the sons of the "lower" orders.

The vigor of English traditional society produced another paradoxical phenomenon, namely, Europe's most vigorous intellectual movement of protest and reform. By the end of the nineteenth century, socialism and social protest had lost, in the countries of the Continent, much of the glamour which, a generation earlier, had attracted the intellectual youths of Europe. In France, Germany, and Italy, socialism and social protest had settled down to the routine chores of party and trade-union politics; the intellectual elite of the Left sent its most brilliant representatives into parliaments and governments. Intellectuals left the study for the field of action. However, gain in power was won at the price of slackening creativity. In France, victory in the Dreyfus case, to which men of letters had contributed so decisively, exhausted the intellectual reserves of the Left. Not until another generation of French creative writers succumbed to the fascination of Communism, after World War I in the springtime of Bolshevik revolution, did the Left recover from the lapse into that mediocrity which, from the 1880's to the beginning of World War I, made French literature of class-consciousness and social protest such tedious reading. In that same period the great names of French, German, and Italian literature and political philosophy were those of men who stood on the Right and, not infrequently, at the extreme Right or maintained a studied detachment from party politics of any kind. Gaetano Mosca, Vilfredo Pareto, Guglielmo Ferrero, Robert Michels, Léon Bourget, André Gide, Thomas Mann, August Strindberg, Knut Hamsun, Gabriele d'Annunzio, Maurice Barrès, Ortega y Gasset, Charles Maurras, Miguel Unamuno, Marcel Proust, Henri Bergson, Benedetto Croce, stood well to the right of center in that period—which was also the period of their highest creativity.

In England, precisely because socialism had not become a political issue it exerted a powerful attraction upon English intellectuals. Whereas the Clemenceaus and Blums were first practicing politicians and then only men of letters, the Fabians fought their foe, traditional society, with the pen and carried their polemics into the halls of learning and onto the stage. There was, on the Continent, no counterpart of the brilliant band of intellectuals who, under the generalship of George Bernard Shaw, L. T. Hobhouse, Graham Wallas, H. G. Wells, J. A. Hobson, Bertrand Russell, and the Webbs, attacked ferociously and wittily the bastions of Victorian and Edwardian society, took apart irreverently the dogmas of liberalism, and called upon the state to make itself "an active instrument for changing social institutions in accordance with the need of the individual." * What distinguished the English Left from the Left in France and Germany was not only its intellectual brilliance and rejection of dogmatism, Marxian orthodoxy included, but also its delightful freedom from the cares of office and thus of political responsibility.

Upon the Continent, the Left had joined many an issue with the Right in the arena of party politics and had, in not a few of these trials of crude force, come out the winner. Even some of its political defeats were programmatic victories. Bismarck created the German welfare state as a weapon against socialism and his generous social legislation paid an underhanded tribute to the growing electoral strength of the German Social Democratic party. In France, the Left had helped to defeat Clericalism and thereafter joined the great procession that led the same contingent of politicians in, out, and always back into ministerial office with monotonous regularity. The Continental Left had learned to wield political power —and had not always resisted the corruption that that experience seems to entail even in the most high-minded and Utopian quarters. The English Left was not exposed to the temptations of office and the moral abrasive of political compromise. It is only after World War I that the Labor party

* J. Rumney, "British Political Thought," *Twentieth Century Political Thought,* J. S. Roucek, ed., N. Y. Philosophical Library, 1946.

became a factor in English politics, and by then many changes had occurred not only in the state of English traditional society but also in the international alignments of Leftist politics. If the rise of the Labor party marked the crisis of English traditional society it also reflected the schism in the Socialist camp: the break between Western socialism of gradualism, moderation, and participation in coalition governments on the one side, and the new orthodoxy of Moscow on the other.

Before World War I, the Fabian intellectuals were the undisputed masters of their house, remote from the "heights of command," snug, and uncontaminated by the unclean things that litter the market place of party politics. The partisan struggle for reform was waged by the great Liberal party and concurrently, within the bosom of English liberalism. And the Liberal party was an integral part of English traditional society. It was also the one remaining authentic heir of the union of Liberalism and Nationalism that was consummated after the Napoleonic Wars and that broke asunder upon the Continent after the ill-starred revolutions in 1848 had failed to reconcile the nations with themselves. Whatever factions vied for influence within the Liberal party, the party remained faithful to its great ideals: political freedom, national freedom, and economic freedom. Its program steadfastly called for universal and equal suffrage, national self-determination, and free trade. The Liberal party was thus the champion of the political ideas that crowned the thought of the eighteenth century. The liberty it upheld against the forces of reaction was the rights of man; its utilitarianism derived from the rationalism of the Enlightenment.

Perhaps no single influence among the host of influences radiating at the beginning of this century into American thought was more decisive than that of English political theory. Bismarck remarked: "The most important fact of the twentieth century will be that the language of both England

and the United States is English." His *aperçu* was a gem of prescience. For England retained one position in her relationship to the United States that proved impregnable to the vicissitudes of shifts in world power and world trade: her position as the United States' interpreter of European thought. Fabian political and economic philosophy, untainted by the ambiguities of practical politics, gained a dominance over American intellectual circles that outlasted the vigor of its progenitors and endured well into the golden years of the New Deal. This remarkable phenomenon of intellectual symbiosis can be attributed in part to the notorious time lag separating analogous social developments in Europe and America, and in part to the boisterous persistence of laissez-faire capitalism in America which supplied the American Left with plain and tempting targets. However, the principal reason for the American intellectual's enthrallment with Fabian and proto-Fabian sirens was that they sang their songs in the English language—and that what the American intellectual came to know about the political and economic thought of the Continent he knew through the mediation of English interpreters. Hence, in America, the Continental spokesmen of the Right, many of whom had passed through the dialectic mills of Socialism and emerged disenchanted, as, for example, Mosca, Pareto, and, later, Ortega y Gasset, were either unknown or without honor. Thus the American intellectual Left and—since by 1933 the American intellectual Right had shrunk to a ragged handful of eccentrics—*the* American intellectual disdained to scrutinize the reverse side of the collectivist medal: the head of the Gorgon, the all-powerful state. It is this circumstance that goes far to explain the fact that the practical alliance of state socialism with militarist nationalism found the American intellectual totally unprepared: this contingency was not covered by the nasty-nice prose of George Bernard Shaw or the elegant analysis of the Fabian and proto-Fabian economists. Not a few of

America's contemporary leading intellectuals have not yet recovered from the shock.

Similarly, American attitudes toward international politics were fatefully influenced by the preconceptions of English liberalism. Woodrow Wilson brought to Versailles not only his abiding faith in the political ideas of the eighteenth century and a Presbyterian conscience but also notions on nationalism of a Gladstonian Liberal. These notions were of unimpeachable validity for Gladstone's England and corresponded with the moral outlook of English traditional society as well as with the concrete purpose of British foreign policy, namely, the maintenance of the balance of power. They were excellent notions, except that, after 1848, they had lost their validity for the continent of Europe. The union of national self-determination and democracy, sealed at Versailles, ensured neither the freedom of nations nor the individual freedom of the nations' citizens, but begot the satellite states, first, of Hitler and then of Stalin, and the thralldom of concentration camps and forced migrations.

The solidarity of English traditional society and the brilliance of the intellectual opposition screened the social and intellectual trends of the European continent from the gaze of America. Upon the European continent, the dialogue between tradition and protest had been drowned by the shouts of the class struggle and the bugles of the barrack yard, and the State had stepped between traditional society and the masses. In England, the Fabians equated the state with capitalist society, and that equation satisfied English realities to the extent that English traditional society had absorbed the new industrial bourgeoisie. English traditional society associated liberally the capitalist entrepreneur with political power. However, this process was one of co-option: admission to participation in rule required the acceptance of terms, and these terms were those of English traditional society.

The characteristics of English society were unique in Europe. To the Fabians, English society was capitalist society, par excellence. This it was patently not, and the Fabian misconception entailed fateful consequences for the intellectual development of the American Left. It never occurred to the Fabians and their eager American pupils that, once the "leisure classes" and the "malefactors of great wealth" had been driven from the citadel of power the democratic ideal of self-government might not prevail and that the oligarchy of bureaucracy might slide into the seats of power vacated by the lords of birth and wealth. Had they but cared to scan the unpleasant vistas opening up upon the European Continent, their childlike faith in the automatic workings of human benevolence, once the political and social status quo had been changed, might have been somewhat dulled and correspondingly their perception of the tricky dynamics of power might have been sharpened. In fact, everywhere in Europe the Marxian juxtaposition of state and capitalism, on one hand, and the exploited masses, on the other, could be discerned already before World War I for what it was: a gross and pernicious oversimplification. In Germany, the state, with its ubiquitous bureaucracy and vast army, was far too powerful to be swayed by the "interests." German business and industry were servants of the state—well-paid ones, to be sure—but servants who "knew their place." In France, the ruling politicians—"la profession parliamentaire"—were leagued with the "interests" and both politicians and "interests" were leagued with the bureaucracy. But the irresponsibility of the parliamentarians, the fluidity of political alignments and the susceptibility of politicians to local and economic pressure groups, helped to entrench the bureaucracy. Centralization and tenure, legacies bequeathed to bureaucracy by monarchy and empire, ensured order and continuity amidst the general disorder of the Third Republic. More important still, in France, the working partnership of politicians, "interests," and bureaucracy had been concluded over the corpse of traditional society. Not only had the problems raised by the Industrial Revolution been left unsolved but the issue of lay education split a society vertically that was already irreconcilably divided on horizontal—economic—lines. Bismarck filched half of the program of the German socialists and turned it into an instrument of the state; he failed in his attempt to divest the Catholic Church of its privileges. The French Radicals tore the schools from the control of the Church and drafted priests as privates into the army; they did not succeed in bettering the lot of the French working man. In both Germany and France the principal beneficiary of the operation was the state.

Neither the Fabians nor the Continental socialists ever grasped the nature of the militarist-nationalist state. Economic determinists, they mistook the class struggle for the one and only struggle which would determine the control of power. Dogmatic pacifists, they mistook capitalist competition and colonialism—"imperialism"—for the principal causes of war. The collapse of the Socialist International at the beginning of World War I and the support given by the Socialist parties to their respective warring governments have been ascribed by socialists to various causes, but never to the most obvious one: socialism's spectacular misreading of the nature of political power. The rank-and-file members of German, French, and Italian trade-union bureaucracy showed a far more realistic appreciation of social dynamics than their intellectual betters when they put the machinery of the labor movement wholeheartedly at the disposal of their respective states, which were merrily engaged in capitalist imperialism's bloodiest war. For nothing is more socialist than is total war. World War I compounded the disintegration of European traditional society—though not quite as the theoreticians of the Left had predicted. World War I unleashed the collectivist revolution that opened the Administrative Age. The makers of that revolution were military and civilian bureaucrats; their instruments were the draft, rationing, censorship, and the printed form of infinite variety. Nowhere did the state, after the fighting had been ended, relinquish all the powers that the populace and its distraught rulers-in-name, princes, or politicians had granted to the military and civilian bureaucracy. Even in England, the Defence of the Realm Act —dismal Dora—remained on the statute books. Upon the Continent, a tight knot of currency regulations and trade and travel restrictions enmeshed the peoples of the victorious and vanquished nations alike. In each country, a host of civil servants recruited to administer patriotically the controls of wartime stayed on to administer, in a more sober spirit, the peacetime system of restrictions. In the newly created states of Eastern Europe, liberated from the yoke of Russian and Austrian rule, national independence did not give rise to sensational changes in the lot of the tillers of the soil and the toilers in factories but to a rapid expansion of national armies and national bureaucracies.

If there is any one discernible trend common to all European countries after World War I it is that of cumulative bureaucratization. While the rate of change of other occupational groups, such as factory labor and professionals, was roughly what it had been before World War I, the contingent of administrative employees had grown at a much faster rate. This, the fundamental law of administrative growth, appeared to operate independently of a country's political complexion. In democratic France, the growth of the administrative apparatus did not lag behind that of fascist Italy, and that of the German Weimar Republic governed by socialists expanded about as fast as that of semifascist Poland; the state bureaucracy of such a model democracy as Czechoslovakia spread as luxuriantly as that of such a moth-eaten monarchy as Romania. Nowhere did the state disband that most bureaucratic and collectivist of all bureaucratic and collectivist institutions: the standing army replenished by compulsory and universal military service. The only exceptions were Germany, forbidden by the peace treaty to have a "popular" army, and Britain whose people thought a large draft army incompatible with liberty and relied for defense on the senior arm of tradition: the Royal Navy. Upon the Continent, the growing power of the state, incarnated in its bureaucracy, was not a socialist theory but a palpable condition that only a theoretical socialist could miss.

World War I was the longest and perhaps most decisive step toward reversing the development set in motion by the Renaissance, namely, the rise of the individual. In the nineteenth century, the failure of traditional society to "humanize" industrialism and the consequent depersonalization of all social relationships, social alienation, and materialism brought on a profound malaise of the European mind. Yet the very injuries inflicted by the corrosive process appeared to call forth latent resources of the spirit. If the nineteenth century was the century of factory slums and sweatshop labor, it was also the century of humanitarianism, philanthropy, social reform, and religious reaffirmation. It was the century of conventions to humanize warfare and to settle international conflict by court procedure. It was, as centuries go, not the most peaceable and not the least bloody, but it was perhaps the most conscious of cruelty to man and beast and most sensitive to the suffering of individual beings as such and not as specimens of economic, racial, or political groups. Though the universal horror at the disaster of the *Titanic* and the loss of a few hundred lives was in part inspired by the new techniques of journalistic sensationalism, it reflected a genuine sensitivity to violence and sudden death that seems to have gone out of fashion in an age calmly adjusted to every conceivable form of mass murder, whether the war of attrition by holiday traffic or the technologically more efficient annihilation of large numbers by atomic blast.

Perhaps the wounds dealt Europe by social alienation and

materialism would have proved fatal even without the culminating calamity of war. Until World War I, Europe fought back. World War I turned the trends toward depersonalization into a system. There are hardly any of the dehumanizing techniques employed in the ensuing peace and second world war that were not developed in World War I: total mobilization of man power and public opinion; concentration camps; bombardment and air bombing of cities; mass expulsion of populations; the conversion of arts and letters into serialized projectiles aimed at the minds of hostile, friendly, neutral, and one's own people; summary repression of dissenting thought; and a radical break with knightly conventions that had been observed heretofore by Christian nations and professional warriors in battle and treatment of defeated enemies.

It is generally overlooked that most of the totalitarian practices of fascism, national socialism, and Soviet communism were, but for some refinements, those in which *all* belligerents had engaged during World War I. The peace treaties of 1919 imposed upon Europe collectivist and statistical principles derived from materialist philosophy and quantifying science. Among these were collective war guilt; national "minorities" and "majorities" as criteria for nationhood; reparations echeloned over the life expectancy of a whole generation; population "exchanges," and similar notions excluding individual and qualitative deviations from the collective norm such as the innocent from the wicked and individual otherness in relation to "minority," "majority," and "nation." In this respect the Russian Bolsheviks merely drove to a logical conclusion propositions that had been universally accepted during World War I and the Peace Conference. Against the collectivity, the individual counted as nothing, and the collectivity was justified in the name of scientifically established principles—to ignore, eject, and liquidate the dissenting individual. Significantly, the first vigorous protest against the summariness of the peace settlement and its inhuman abstractions issued from Europe's last stronghold of traditional society, England. John Maynard Keynes's critique of the peace settlement voiced the revulsion of the liberal spirit of tolerance, compromise, and fair play against the brutalization of war which the peace treaties had institutionalized in the peace. That spirit was the ethos of the English middle classes, the solid base sustaining English society. Though no one exposed more pungently the euphoria of the middle classes than Keynes, he was the very protagonist of their humane ideals, a circumstance that appears to have escaped not a few of his disciples.

Upon the Continent, it was not euphoria that overwhelmed the middle classes, but outright economic and political destruction. The German, Austrian, and Hungarian middle classes never recovered from the inflationary catastrophe that wiped out their savings after World War I. In Poland, Romania, and Yugoslavia, not only inflation but also expropriation of unwanted national "minorities," such as Germans, Austrians, and Hungarians, weakened not only traditional property relationships but the fabric of the entire economic and social system. In Italy and France, inflation took its toll less severely than in Central and Eastern Europe, yet with consequences that, in the fullness of time, were to prove no less disastrous for the Italian and French middle classes and the health of the respective national societies.

Inflation was at once impersonal and depersonalizing. It struck at all persons depending on fixed income, no matter how derived, and reduced them to a common level, creating a new proletariat and thus extending the process of alienation into the very heart of traditional society. It was precisely the middle classes, living on fixed incomes or accumulated savings in the expectancy of the *rentier*'s security and ease, who suffered most directly the depredations of currency devaluation. The savings of the middle classes were the bond of their independence, affording a wide latitude to individual taste and expression in politics, culture, and manners. Among the estates, the middle classes were the least aware of their common status and, in the parlance of the present, the least organized. For middle class and organization are contradictory terms: it was their quest for economic independence and individual freedom that burst the mold of caste and state, guild and autocracy. England's Glorious Revolution and the French revolution of 1789 emancipated the English and French middle classes. The rise of the middle classes in England and France altered the social complexion of all of Europe. Yet the motion imparted from the west of Europe gradually lost momentum as it spread east and south.

In Germany, the middle classes, for all their influence on economic, intellectual, and artistic developments, remained politically feeble. Only after national unification in 1871 did the middle classes assert themselves politically. However, their political power had not been won upon the barricade or the rostrum. It was rather the gift of the Prussian state and the military who had wrought German unity with blood and iron. Imperial Germany endowed its bourgeoisie with privileges and honorific emoluments because it needed its entrepreneurial and professional skills for the expansion of German power. However, there were precincts inaccessible to the middle classes: military and foreign affairs and court society. The German middle classes, on the eve of World War I, had acquired affluence and enviable prestige in the realms of science and the muses; they were about to increase considerably their influence in domestic politics. They had not shaken off a sense of inferiority toward their military masters and the German state which their philosophers had done so much to elevate above the mere mass of loyal subjects. It was this German middle class, so highly competent in its vocations and so psychologically insecure, that was swept into a veritable torrent of inflation. When that torrent had subsided, the economic reserves of the German middle classes had disappeared, for nowhere had the prestige of the state been greater and the middle classes less inclined to doubt its solvency and hence to take evasive measures. The German middle classes never recovered from the traumatic shock. Proletarization was not only economic degradation; it was spiritual annihilation. The German middle classes' response to the inconceivable disaster was to organize themselves and thus to cease to *be,* for the very nature of the European middle classes was nonorganization, i.e. orderly anarchy. The sociological meaning of national socialism was the organization of the German middle classes and hence their liquidation. The German middle classes renounced their status to become functionaries of the Nazi state.

In Germany, the proletarization of the middle classes did not accrue to the power of the "organized, class conscious proletariat." The crisis of German capitalism, inflation, unemployment, and social instability, favoring the emergence of "marginal" men freed of the bonds of traditional morality, resulted in a general degradation of German society as a whole, including the "organized" proletariat. After World War I, German capitalism, creature and servant of the Prussianized German state, had been resuscitated by large foreign loans. It rose from the defeat of 1918 more "co-ordinated" and more centralized than it had ever been. Under the onslaught of the great depression, German capitalism resorted, as it were automatically, to the devices of total war: autarchy and state intervention. The German capitalist, aggressive and authoritarian as he was in his dealings with his workingmen and unorganized competitors, turned to the state for leadership as a matter of course. And it was to the state and not to the trade-union that the German workingman ultimately turned, when industrial "rationalization" and the collapse of Germany's industrial export trade had thrown him out of his job. The German labor movement with its elaborate bureaucratic hierarchy was, for all its "class consciousness" or perhaps just because of it, *petit bourgeois* and conservative. The German unemployed, who drew his dole, went to the movies, attended "mass meetings," and adjusted himself to undernourishment, was no longer a worker and "class conscious proletarian." He, no less than the impoverished member of the middle class, had lost his status. They, the unstable particles of atomized society, became the raw material of political mass movements.

Men reduced to the mere struggle for animal existence, deprived of social meaning, seek instinctively the warmth of the crowd. For man the social being rebels against the horror of isolation. In Germany, the degraded middle classes and the degraded proletariat responded to the most direct and most brutal social attraction, that of the totalitarian ideologies. Nazi and Communist ideologies supplied the myths and symbols that made surrender of human freedom appear to be voluntary submission to the "voice of the blood" and "historic law." In Germany, the "voice of the blood" outshouted the dialectic arguments of the "historic law." But Nazi ideology alone could not claim the conquest of the German people by Hitler. The process of depersonalization had tilled the German earth upon which Hitler was to cast the seed of darkness.

It appears that *particular* ideologies, pre-existing ideas, are of small account in movements leading toward a totalitarian society. What happened in Germany was simply that, while large masses of the German people were struggling for mere existence and vestigial traditional order was dissolving into nothingness, German society survived by simplifying its own structure. Where there had been entrepreneurs and class-conscious workers, aristocracy and clergymen, scientists and artists, individual men and women, there was now one party and one leader. What happened in Germany had been predicted with uncanny vision by Jakob Burckhardt, writing in 1889: "My conception of the *terrible simplificateurs* who will come over our old Europe is not pleasant, and now and then in my imagination I can see these ruffians already in flesh and blood before my eyes."

To the Germany of the twenties and thirties the term massification applies with all its ugly connotations: alienation of the individual from society, disintegration of the traditional classes and values, the kneading of degraded men into the "movement," the capture of power by the one party and the one leader, and the rise of the monolithic state. The forms of power—economic, religious, and political—which traditional society held to be distinct from each other, were fused at the summit of the social pyramid. A few men, nay only one man, knows all, decides all, and does all. National Socialism and Russian Communism must thus be viewed as being both disintegrationist *and* mass ideologies. Their nature is revealed not in their respective "rationalizations" but in their functions: the systematic destruction of organic society and the systematic inhibition of organic social growth. The possibility that traditional society could generate within itself restorative forces, is rejected categorically and "scientifically." In brief, there is but one exit for the individual from the social dilemma: the mass ideology itself.

Once the mass ideology has captured the state and thus assumed the status of state religion its function is to annihilate mental alternatives of life forms apart from itself. Both national socialism and Russian Communism must be viewed as tyrannies in the classic sense, their ideologies as ideologies of tyranny. The structure of the modern collectivist state resembles uncannily that of some city-states of antiquity, such as Corinth and Syracuse, in its growth and main features: there is the same reckless, violent usurpation of social power by a minority rising from the masses, leaning upon them, and flattering them, while at the same time intimidating them. National socialism and Russian Communism also share the most striking feature of all tyrannies: supreme indifference to the social forces that carried them to power.

Perhaps the most dangerous intellectual trap to anyone who seeks to examine clinically German national socialism and Russian Communism is to equate them with each other and to take them as being rooted in the same or, at least, comparable historic and social soils. The economic and social development of Germany in the nineteenth century, the formation of the German state in 1871, the superindustrialization of the German Reich, and the cultural outlook of the German middle classes were phenomena for which not the remotest resemblances can be found in the history of Russia. Rather than seek parallelisms or resemblances, we must view national socialism and Russian Communism as *converging* movements. Russia never formed part of the sphere of Western culture. Up until the Bismarckian unification, Germany was as European as was France, England, and Italy; Germany had always maintained close contact with the Mediterranean region and the entire world of Christendom. The Russian peoples submitted centuries ago to centralized autocracy: Russia remained isolated from the cradle of Western culture and submerged in the orthodoxy of the Eastern rite. It was only at the point of convergence, betrayal of the individual and tyranny, that, in the 1930's, Germany and Russia met. At this point of convergence there was indeed complete assimilation.*

The convergence of national socialism and Russian Communism is manifest in their being tyrannies. There was only one concrete meaning to their ideologies derived from such different premises: to impose and maintain tyranny and dissimulate the fact of tyrannical rule to the ruled.

Once national socialism and Russian Communism—"Stalinism"—are perceived as convergent movements, the resem-

---

* Assimilation is a transformation proceeding from the different to the similar, and transformations are called convergent when they produce an increasing resemblance of the elements they transform. See J. Monnerot, *Sociologie du Communisme*, Paris, Gallimard, 1949.

blance of their respective policies and social structures can no longer be regarded as accidental, and a good deal of ideological chaff can be safely swept out without losing the particular flavor of Nazi myth and Marxian "science." In both Germany and Russia, the economy was fettered by political power and the criteria of profit and loss subordinated to political considerations. In Germany, the state permitted the capitalists to operate for profit but imposed a "four-year plan" upon the industries. Private initiative was tolerated to the extent that it accommodated itself to the directives of the state. Capitalists, executives, and technicians retained their managerial positions but their status resembled increasingly that of the higher functionaries of Soviet economy. The latter drew high salaries and enjoyed privileges that, translated into buying power, approximated the dividends, premiums, and salaries of the German managerial classes. Though the German state left legal titles to property in the keeping of the capitalists, state control of raw materials, foreign trade, currency controls, and state ownership of important industries, banks, transportation, and communication established the effective strategic control by the state of the German economy, misleadingly called "capitalist" and "private." Both in Germany and Russia, the distinction between economics and politics faded into an administrative gray. In both countries the managerial revolution invaded economics and politics long before James Burnham coined the name.* The administrative personnel—the corps of managers—of plant, trade-union, and government was one and the same. Individual managers were assigned to "economic," to "political," and to "military" missions. Functionaries in the true sense, German and Russian administrators administered societies that were organized along functional lines. In traditional society, law, economics and culture were separate and autonomous realms.

* See James Burnham, *The Managerial Revolution*, New York, John Day, 1941.

Now government, economics, religion, art were "managed," and the problems in these respective areas of social interest were reduced to problems in management. Managers are supposed to manage and not question the nature of purpose of control. In Germany and Russia exclusive control of the entire enterprise, totalitarian society, rested with an infinitesimally small group that alone determined its nature and purpose.

Formlessness and personal insecurity are the fundamental characteristics of totalitarian society. Formless mass and intimidation by terror are the preconditions of the totalitarian leadership's rise to power; they are the base of its power. How to reconcile formlessness with organization, terror with loyalty, this is the principal problem of tyranny. That problem was solved in Germany and Russia in virtually the same way: the creation of a hierarchy of rank. Here, too, the phenomenon of convergence is strikingly manifest. The Nazi and Soviet paraphernalia of rank were hardly distinguishable from each other; uniforms, insignia, medals, clubs, official residences, all were minutely graded according to rank. Though these paraphernalia of rank did correspond as a rule to functions and economic status, their significance was social: they denoted class distinctions all the more sharply because they were conferred by a regime that had risen from social disintegration and had been carried to power by the equalitarian aspirations of the masses. Not only did the emoluments and prerequisites of rank ensure the loyalty of the managerial class, rank legitimized the status of the rulers who had captured rule by usurpation. The marshall's uniform is the cloak of legitimacy of the totalitarian leader. Totalitarian society is total rank society; outside its hierarchy of titles, medals, and gold braid there is literally no society: the zone beneath rank is the zone of the "nonparty people" and the concentration camp.

By 1940, this social system had conquered the European continent. Except for Sweden and Switzerland, all the nations of the Continent had fallen under the sway of totalitarian power. Wherever the conquerors left the defeated countries a semblance of independence as, for example, in Norway, France, and Romania, national government was transformed into a replica of the conqueror's. Designations for party, secret police, military formations, and totalitarian elite varied according to the rich nomenclature that is tyranny's principal concession to historical and national sensibilities. In France, storm troops were called "militiamen," a smirking obeisance before the desecrated altar of the Republic. Beneath the signs of Red Star, Swastika, Fasces, Arrow Cross, Red Arrows, and sundry heraldic devices of tyranny, Europe had, at last, found perfect unity—the unity of one vast concentration camp. The proper emblem of the totalitarian international should have been a strand of barbed wire.

Europe's experiences in the years of captivity are untranslatable into the thought images of the American people; for Americans, they are inconceivable. Except for fragmentary reports, the story did not reach America until after the partial liberation of the Continent. Even then, that story had to be pieced together mostly from personal recollections and documents concerning events that had occurred many months, if not years, earlier. Memories had become dulled or suffused by the afterglow of imagination. Some of the principal witnesses were either dead or reluctant or highly partial. Life under totalitarian rule is not attended by the wakeful publicity that radiates into every nook and cranny of American life. Hence the incompleteness of Europe's own account of her fall and captivity. Some of the "facts" are still missing and will probably remain forever buried beneath the rubble of destroyed cities, the sod of nameless graves, and the complicity of silence that is the last refuge of the surviving accomplices of tyranny. More important still, the scale and totality of the terror that held Europe in its grip transcends, for Americans, the range of plausibility.

There are factual data, such as the thousands of light years that separate stars from each other, that are meaningless in terms of human experience. The carefully documented and pictorialized iniquities of Belsen and Auschwitz—and no one knows whether their death and torture chambers represent the true depth of totalitarian ingenuity—lie a million years of darkness beyond the vision of the American public. The trauma of liberated Europe with its elation, vengefulness, and sense of guilt was as inaccessible psychologically to Americans as was the orgy of servility, venality, and self-justification which defeat and occupation unleashed in the homelands of fallen tyrants. That these emotions could not be relived imaginatively by the great mass of the American people, even those who manned the armies of liberation and occupation, attests not to the insensitivity but the poise of American society. If the best of them brought to stricken Europe their compassion but not their understanding, their lack of *Einfühlungsgabe* was due to the fact that extreme situations cannot be understood if they have not been lived. The extremity of Europe's situation was the climax of tendencies without parallels in American society. Thus America's share in, and presence at, the great denouement of Europe's emancipation from one set of tyrants could not but increase the psychological distance between Europe and America. Suffering and humiliation have created a community from which the American people are excluded. In Europe, there was no man or woman to whom tyranny, war, and defeat were experiences derived secondhand. They were *lived* personally and intimately. In America they were not. This was, and still is, the principal difference between America and Europe.

RESTORATION

IN THE first world war the United States intervened late and at a relatively small cost in human lives. Even then, Europe suffered terrible human and material losses. However, World War I began as a war between legitimate governments, each enjoying the support of the great mass of its respective population. The Bolshevik Revolution, despite its implicit threat to the status quo of European society, eased the task of the peacemakers, for a victorious czarist imperialism could but have reopened the issues that had, throughout the nineteenth century, troubled the Concert of the Powers and brought Europe, on several occasions, to the brink of general war. Whatever may be said against the peace treaties, they did not stipulate radical changes in European society. They did not prescribe in the lands of the defeated either wholesale alienation of property, nor mass purges of ruling elites, nor purification of ruling political philosophies. The constitution of the Weimar Republic was deemed a sufficient token of Germany's moral regeneration. What was surprising about Germany was not how deeply she had fallen or how heavy were the fetters of the Versailles Treaty, but how rapidly German goods, German citizens, and German cultural creations returned to international circulation. Britain and France, however heavy had been their sacrifices in war, had won a clear-cut victory. They dominated the League of Nations and held securely their respective positions of world power, all the more securely because Germany, Russia, and Austria-Hungary had been stricken from the lists. Neither in France nor in Britain had the war wrought any seeming changes of social structure. Victory appeared to have strengthened the ruling elites. In Britain, the khaki elections were anything but revolutionary; in France, the premiership of Raymond Poincaré could surely not be construed as a departure from the *juste milieu* of French politics. If the war had spurred American productive capacity, transformed the United States from a debtor to a creditor nation, and introduced American diplomacy into the councils of Europe, these developments were noted with varying emotions by Europeans but were not construed as signifying a radical change in American-European relationships. Americans, on their part, observed with emotions no less mixed the decisive military contribution they had made to the Allied cause, the mounting financial indebtedness of European governments to the United States, and the eager quest for American capital by European business. However, they did not interpret the manifest increase of their stature as implying a corresponding diminishment of British and French power.

After World War I, British and French prestige stood perhaps higher in the United States than it ever stood before, though this by no means signified that Britain and France enjoyed the undivided affection and esteem of the American people. The very nature of Anglo-American and Franco-American tensions—American insistence upon repayment of war loans and Anglo-American disputes about naval ratios prior to the Washington Conference—bespoke a relationship in which Americans, Frenchmen, and Englishmen felt themselves to be each other's equal. If Europeans traveled to America to study production methods or the American scene in general, American intellectuals flocked to Europe to drink at the fountain of Western culture and to partake of what, by common agreement, eluded them in America: joy of living. In brief, Americans still viewed Europe as composed of mighty nations and the seat of a thriving culture. They did not view Europe as a problem. Nor was Europe aware of being a problem. True, there were European "questions": Germany, Austria, and the Balkans. However, the great powers of Europe were disinclined to let any non-European power or combination of powers answer these "questions" for them.

Communism made disquieting gains among the industrial workers and the intellectuals. But Communism was not teamed with military power. The Soviets could hold their own against counterrevolutionaries and half-hearted foreign interventions; they could not challenge the *status quo* established by the peace treaties. In Germany and Hungary, Communists had risen against established governments; they were quickly suppressed. Europe appeared to be returning to a state of uneasy quiescence, somewhat similar to the aftermath of the Napoleonic Wars. The *Decline of the West* registered a minor literary success in England, France, and America; most of the critics disposed of it as an effusion of German pessimism engendered by military defeat. The notion conveyed by the title evoked in the general public, engrossed in more pleasant reading, either no response at all or the tickling sensation of a future doom that might ultimately befall misguided mankind but not one's own generation. The European of the 1920's knew that he had passed through a terrible ordeal; he did not know that an age had ended. Americans shared fully this misconception.

Europe, at the end of World War II, stood bereft of illusions. No Continental nation had contributed materially to the defeat of Germany. Even Britain, her ambivalent status as both a European and a non-European power underscored more than ever before by her world-wide military commitments, was revealed as crucially dependent on her non-European allies and, above all other allies, upon the United States. The British Isles had served as a huge airfield for American air power and a base camp for American invasion armies. In the final phase of the struggle American matériel, air power, and armor had dwarfed the military power of Great

Britain. The rapid deterioration of the British economic position, the crisis of the pound sterling, emancipation of India and Burma, and withdrawal of British forces from Greece dispelled whatever lingering doubt Europe may have entertained concerning the true identity of the victors. The United States and Russia stood revealed as the two incomparable giants, as predicted by De Tocqueville more than a century ago. This revelation was fraught with another and more shocking disclosure: Europe no longer existed as a definable entity. The Oder-Enns line not only halved Germany and Austria, but the entire Continent. The east of Europe was swallowed up by the Asian tyranny that had superseded its European counterpart. Nothing had changed but the devices of totalitarianism and the insignia of its armed guards. The system of mass purges, mass expulsion, and forced labor ground on under a new management. The standardized pattern of peoples' democracies blanketed the lands whence Hitler's SS troops had departed. To Eastern Europe, Allied victory had but one meaning: an exchange of yokes.

While in Eastern Europe the remnants of traditional society disappeared in the maw of Soviet tyranny, Western Europe was free to grope for the broken thread of continuity. The prevailing mood of Western Europe is retro- and introspective. The strength of the Communist parties of France and Italy lies not in the revolutionary temper of the working masses but in the obsession of an ill society with its own ills. Just as a sick man is possessed by his sickness and dwells compulsively upon its symptoms, so the peoples of France and Italy fondle their social ills. Communism in France and Italy is a return to a stubborn dilemma, not the voyage to Utopia. Both France and Italy resumed the dismal discourse between the "two nations" which the bellowing of Hitler and Mussolini had interrupted. There is, indeed, a change, for history cannot be played back like a gramophone record. The topic is the same; the issue is just as irreducible as it was when Mussolini and Hitler encased the sores of society in the plaster cast of their respective police states. But the arguments have lost their zest; the parties to the dispute no longer take the cue of their argumentation from the dispute itself. It is as if the position of the disputants had frozen and the deadlock had been accepted as an integral feature of society. The mass secession of many French and Italian intellectuals from Communism cannot be entirely explained by disgust with Stalinist methods which they had managed to put up with for the better part of their lives. A large number for whom the "light failed" withdrew into pained indifference. They discovered Stalinist skulduggery; however, they did not find the lodestar of a new devotion. The return to the past is blocked by disenchantment; the road into the future is littered by broken hopes.

Europe was old before the calamity of the 1940's; she is now suddenly aware of her age. The withdrawal into despair or fanciful escape is the familiar reflex of intellectual and cultural elites to a historical development that is somewhat misleadingly called restoration—somewhat misleadingly because the past can never be "restored." It was the attempt to reassemble the broken fragments of legitimacy from the wreckage of Revolution and Empire that called forth the effusive and confused protest of the Romantics. The characteristic features of restoration society are clearly apparent in the political physiognomy of postwar France, Italy, and Germany. Given the violence of the storm that passed over Europe, the formal structure, the party alignments, the personnel and the burning issues of the French, Italian, and German restoration, democracies appear to have survived remarkably intact from the age of before-the-flood.

In France, the juncture with the past lies somewhere before the ascendancy of the Popular Front. The parliamentary scene is enlivened by the familiar faces of aged politicians, and ministerial portfolios circulate among the leaders of the coalition parties with customary regularity. The controversy over lay education, begun about 1900, still serves admirably as a diversion from the dispute over irreducible social and economic issues. The programs of the coalition parties are as mutually contradictory as they were in the golden days of Poincaré, Tardieu, and Chautemps, and the coalition cabinets are held together not by internal cohesion but extraneous pressure: it is the enemies of the Republic on the Right and Left that impose on the wobbly center unanimity-in-ideological-compromise. There are changes in political labels, but none in political ideas. Old parties speak through the smooth rhetoric of old men. The Herriots, Reynauds, Daladiers, Auriols, grace the "parliamentary profession," in 1952, as they did in 1932, and the firebrands of proletarian revolution are none other than Duclos, Thorez, and Cachin, ripe in years, who clasped the hand of the bourgeoisie in the Popular Front of the 1930's. To be sure, age took its toll: there are replacements from the rank and file, but the new names are drawn from old barrels. Just as in the time of the Third Republic, the colors appear brighter on the extreme Right where leaders of the resistance and liberation and not a few secessionist intellectuals are banded together under De Gaulle's Cross of Lorraine. But the protest of the Right as well as of Catholic liberalism, though it supplies the bulk of political literature, is not permitted to disturb the traffic of French restoration democracy.

In Italy, the Republic is a fairly faithful replica of the constitutional monarchy which collapsed into the arms of Mussolini. True, the king is gone, but the political alignments and problems resemble closely those of the pre-fascist era of permanent crisis: regional Communist-incited anarchy; now latent, now open peasant rebellion; and the paradoxical Catholic-liberal alliance which ranged the Church and free-thinkers in defense of land-owning aristocracy and industrial bourgeoisie.

In Germany, the shades of the Weimar Republic resumed the verisimilitude of life in the Bonn parliament with its precarious balance between Catholic Center and Social Democratic party and various splinter parties gathering up, beneath innocuous labels, the nationalist opposition to the Republic. At Bonn, too, the dominant politicians are old and youth stands aside from parliamentary politics either in indifference or in defiance. In Germany, too, the intellectuals withdrew into literature and surrendered politics to the politicians. The Bonn republic is confronted by the same problems its predecessor knew, including the sullen resentment of the middle classes, dispossessed by currency devaluation, and haunting fears of nationalist reaction. Its energies are absorbed to an even higher degree than those of its French and Italian sisters by the tasks of material reconstruction and hence cannot be channeled into creative politics. The West German Republic is, as was the Weimar Republic, the child of defeat. Its sponsors, just as those of the Weimar Republic, were not the democratic forces of Germany, but the victors and their armies. Western Germany, unlike France and Italy, is untroubled by a large Communist party and Communist-controlled labor-unions. However, Russian control of Eastern Germany is as powerful a lever on West Germany's politics as would be an indigenous Communist party. The carrot of national unification, dangled by Russia and the Communist government of East Germany before the German people, is as effective as would be the revolutionary stick. If the Weimar Republic was plagued by Communist opposition from within and by the opportunist alliance of Nazis and Communists in parliament, the Bonn republic is troubled by Communist blackmail from without and the collusive intrigues of extreme nationalists and the East German puppet regime.

"NEITHER EAST NOR WEST"

"Poets are a divine race, and often in their strains, by the aid of the Muses and the Graces, they attain the truth of history."
PLATO, *The Laws.*

THE POLITICS and morals of European restoration society are mirrored by its literature. The principal themes of contemporary European creative writing and philosophy are the absurdity of society, the isolation of the individual, and the withdrawal into self. These themes are keyed to either skeptical rejection of all doctrines that invest nature and society with transcendent purpose or to mystical acceptance of man's lot in a world which is coldly indifferent to his fears and yearnings. Though agnostics and believers approach it from opposite ends, they reach the same bleak ground: there is, within the framework of dissolving institutions about them, no way out of the dilemma of man upon this earth other than the forthright acceptance of a situation without issue. Humanly speaking, the world is absurd. But by calling it absurd we affirm a verity which stands apart and above the chaos of the universe and above death, a verity that transforms life into destiny. "The man who thinks creates a little zone of light and order in the cosmic murk." * By accepting his destiny man transcends it. The negative themes, absurdity, withdrawal, isolation, frustration, are thus woven into the affirmation of man's courage and dignity.

The unfolding of this latest phase of Europe's pathetic dis-

* Albert Léon Guérard, "Descartes or the Will to Doubt," *The Pacific Spectator,* Summer, 1951.

illusionment was most clearly discernable at the oldest focal point of European culture, France. The French existentialists exploited most consciously and most brilliantly the possibilities of the "literature of extreme situations." * However, the themes of isolation, absurdity, and violence that are common to the writings of Sartre, Camus, De Beauvoir, Malraux, and Rousset, were developed simultaneously and with surprising similarities by a host of other writers throughout all of Europe. They pervade the entirety of recent European literature, so much so that in writers whose conclusions differ radically, there are striking resemblances in their presentation of certain key situations and problems, even to near identity of style. Carlo Levi's *Christ Stopped at Eboli* and Ignacio Silone's recent play, *And He Hid Himself,* are kin in isolation, absurdity, and violence to the Romanian Gheorghiu's *The Twenty-fifth Hour* and the German Jünger's *Questionnaire,* though these writers appear to stand leagues apart on such issues as democracy, fascism, Communism, and Christianity.

The parallel between the existentialist and the Romantic hero is striking. The latter had reached manhood in the Napoleonic epoch of revolutionary conquest. With the defeat at Waterloo, Europe turned back to the *ancien régime,* and political imagination coagulated in Metternich's celebrated formula for Restoration statesmanship: "propping up of rotten institutions." Similarly, many European intellectuals had pinned their hopes on the Communist revolution and later, on the Liberation. Both were felt to be identical with the grand liquidation of a social order that had been decaying for a long time and had, finally, succumbed to the corruption of tyranny, and hence identical with man's hopes for healing the wounds of estrangement and despair. Both were viewed as the harbingers of a socialist community, though it was not so

* See Albert Votaw, "Literature of Extreme Situations," *Horizon,* (London), September, 1949.

much the political and economic programs of Marxism but rather the revolutionary appeal to self-negation and self-sacrifice that shook many European intellectuals from the perch of aloof cynicism or called them to forsake the vale of despair for the field of political action. A. Rossi ascribed the fascination of Communism for many Frenchmen to the fact that it offered "a welcome refuge from a way of life which, because it makes no demands, seems intolerably tame and enervating"; * and an alternative to a society in which "men tend to divide off into clan like groups. . . . [and], unable to relate [themselves] meaningfully to the broader constituency, the nation, seek and find their community in one of these lesser groupings of which the Communist Party is merely the extreme instance." † It is no accident that not a few existentialist writers embraced Communism as the creed that would reconcile the "groupings" of social alienation with each other —and that Communism captured the intellectual *élan* of the Liberation. For much in the existentialist critique of society could easily be transposed into Marxian terminology, and the Communists were quick to exploit the existentialist rejection of society. But the several European Communist parties cruelly disappointed their intellectual followers, first by the cold-hearted Nazi-Soviet Pact of 1939, and then by wooden-soldier gesturings in obedient response to the shifting line of the Kremlin. The growing anti-intellectualism and philistinism of Soviet "culture," and finally the lurid show windows of Popular Democracy in eastern Europe, converted the intellectual retreat from Communism into a movement resembling a rout.

The wine of Liberation turned into the vinegar of Restoration. The Liberation had been annexed by the Communists who claimed its glory, magnified the military successes of the

* A. Rossi, *A Communist Party in Action,* New Haven, Yale University Press, 1949; p. 215.
† A. Rossi, *op. cit.,* p. 230.

Soviet Union, belittled the share of the Western Allies, and vilified their non-Communist partners in the Resistance. The Communists exploited the turmoil of partisan warfare and summary justice meted out to real and alleged "collaborators." They liquidated their enemies and diverted loot garnered from confiscation to the Party treasury. They imposed levies on frightened "suspects" charged with all kinds of offenses, grave or trivial, during the years of the Occupation. Especially after Allied victory appeared certain, the Resistance had attracted the scum of society. The Liberation disintegrated quickly into an orgy of lawlessness and profiteering and its high purpose of cleansing society of the rot of tyranny turned into a travesty of justice.

The Restoration democracies were thus burdened with the sordid realities bequeathed by tyranny that had despoiled free society. The Liberation turned into a clawing, snarling contest over its scattered assets. Just as the debacle of the French Revolution and the pall of mediocrity and grossness that settled upon Europe after Waterloo choked the hopes of European youth, so, after World War II, the degradation of the Liberation and its myths, and the revelation of the Marxian message as a manual for extortion and mayhem at the orders of the Stalinist bureaucracy, drove the best and the most creative minds of Europe into anguished isolation.

This terrible isolation explains the popularity in Europe today of those writers whose principal characteristic is their disdain, if not their outright hostility, to the most dynamic social forces of their time. The French, German, and Italian Romantics of the 1820s and 1830s were antibourgeois. Some searched for their inspiration in the social and religious wholeness of the Middle Ages, others fled from politics into aesthetical solipsism, and still others threw themselves into the political battle of democracy against the bourgeoisie. They all despised and denounced the grossness and squalor of Restoration society and its principal beneficiaries: the middle class and bureaucracy. The French existentialists and many German and Italian writers linked—consciously or unconsciously—to the existentialist movement are opposed both to the ruling groups of the new Restoration society and to Stalinism. It is significant that Sartre's, Silone's, Koestler's, and Camus' criticisms of Stalinism—i.e., opportunism, anti-intellectualism, and bureaucratic arbitrariness—resemble closely the Romantic attacks on Restoration society.

There are two important affinities between the Romanticism and post-World War II literary protest. Both asserted passionately the worth of man pitted against the absurdity and indifference of contemporary society and both were permeated by a tragic sense of impotence in the face of the political and social realities of their times. Here, however, the parallel ends. The Romantics kept their dreams—the epic of the Revolution, the Napoleonic legend, the promise of an egalitarian republic, and the vision of the springtime of nations. They were, nearly to a man, profoundly religious and attached to nature. Their ideals were identified with a heroic past and projected by their imagination into a future that had the hopes of youth on its side.

By contrast, the European intellectuals who passed through the experience of Communism, turned in disgust from the past that held but a gigantic deception and saw the future blocked by the very real Soviet system, putrid and not at all susceptible to idealization. Caught between the dogmatic materialism of their Marxian schooling and the frigid abstractions of modern science, they were barred from God *and* from nature. If society has denied God, and science has driven him from nature, then there is no point in behaving as if He existed. There is no solace for the modern intellectual. Especially for those influenced by the existentialist emphasis on man's nonaffinity with nature, the beauty and power of nature offer no release from anguish. Nature is indifferent. The modern hero is more lonely than man has ever been.

The literary movement which won a vast following among European youth, contemplating the moral ruins of society and the physical ruin of their lands, wrought impartially by the bombs of Allies and enemies alike, was in America either ignored or decried as an aberration, if not a hoax or vile degeneracy. Its products were lumped under the general classification of "concentration-camp literature." The underlying philosophy was disposed of as Europe's latest bout with nihilism. This verdict is as just as any verdict that men pronounce on the failings of other men whose lot they have not shared, be it in the flesh or in the imagination.

Indeed, the scenes of Malraux's, Sartre's, Koestler's, and Gheorghiu's novels and plays were laid in concentration camps. The frustration and impotence of the modern hero were thus localized in their most typical setting. The hundreds of thousands of Europeans who went through these antichambers to hell and emerged from them alive, still bear the fiery mark. Their unpurged souls still dwell in the concentration-camp universe with its stark as well as its subtle horrors of which the most searing were perhaps the atrocities perpetrated by the prisoners upon one another. The concentration camp was the one genuine social institution created by tyranny. It was the center whence the infection of inhumanity and terror spread over Europe, poisoning all men alike, master as well as slave. All of Europe was pervaded by the dank and acrid stench of the infernal barracks, and the fresh draft of the Liberation did not rid the air of Europe of the clinging, nauseating odor.

Americans did not see, perhaps did not want to see, that men who once were free like themselves had fallen to denouncing and enslaving one another in order to gain the favors of the oppressor; that "collaboration" was not the rare exception but, in one form or another, a matter of degree, and that only a handful of individuals shook off the clammy grip of fear. The speedy revival of European economy obscured the depth of self-debasement which had swallowed, not this or that notorious individual, but whole nations.

Life in a restoration society is not bare of pleasures; people work hard and the arts flourish again against the backdrop of Europe's glorious monuments. But the tyrants have been the victors, at least in the sense that they succeeded in their attempt at subtle demoralization. They revealed the infinite possibilities of man's inhumanity to man. The specter still hovers over Europe, paralyzing men's will and striking fear into their souls.

Thus the somber mood of the European literary scene expresses deep anxieties that grip the peoples. They obsess the masses who have but the haziest notion of the current creations of serious literature that come down to them in the watered-down versions of the movie theater, if they come down at all. Existentialist philosophy is obviously not a popular movement; its key ideas are the common property of millions who have never heard of it. These ideas are anything but esoteric, though their literary formulation perhaps is. Millions, who never saw or read Sartre's play *No Exit,* experienced the frustration and anguish which ravage its hero. Frustration and anguish were the common lot of European man in the age of tyranny and its wars. There was, indeed, no exit.

Europe is surfeited with the horrors of tyranny and war; Europe is weary of the struggle for power yet mourns the power she lost. Europe has become the more conscious of her culture and has talked the more about her culture the more she has become aware of the decline of her power. There is a direct relationship between Europe's growing sensitivity to American cultural encroachment—whether in the form of novels, plays, operas, jazz orchestras, moving pictures, lectures, or America's leading columnists; or in the form of American goods that alter tastes in eating, drinking, housekeeping, and travel—and Europe's growing dependence on the military and economic aid of the United States.

Cultural influence and political, economic, and military power are reciprocals. Greek culture reached its zenith in the era of Athen's commercial and naval hegemony. French drama, philosophy, and architecture attained their greatest splendor in the century that links Louis XIV and Napoleon and brackets the political and military pre-eminence of France. Shakespeare and the Englishmen who had crushed the naval power of Spain were contemporaries; Keats, Shelley, Byron, Thackeray, Dickens, Carlyle, Macaulay, Mill, and Acton stood at the high noon of British power that had vanquished France at Trafalgar. The cultures of France and England were national *and* universal cultures. In the eighteenth century, to be cultivated was to be proficient in the French language and literature, to observe French etiquette, to dwell in houses built in the style of French architecture and filled with French furniture, to belong to the community of the *bel esprit* and the *gentilhomme*—and then only, if at all, to one's own nation. Frederick II of Prussia, who wrote and conversed brilliantly in French and murdered the German language, was the prototype of, and not the exception among, the great of Europe.

The nineteenth century was the century of English manners, English idiosyncrasies, and English literature. The Byronic mood swept Europe, Turgeniev's heroes wore English breeches, and mercurial Italians and Frenchmen affected English phlegm. No democratic revolution was deemed a success that was not crowned by a replica of the English parliamentary system. English novels and plays carried the English twist-of-mind and its very problems to the four corners of the earth. Frenchmen and Hindus, Russians and Hungarians sent their sons to Oxford and Cambridge which Englishmen, in the eighteenth century, had considered miserable educational institutions, far inferior to the universities of the Continent.

Small and weak nations have never had a *national* culture. The great artists, philosophers, and writers of Europe's small countries were European cosmopolites. In the eighteenth and the first half of the nineteenth century, to be German and Italian was to be provincial. Then German and Italian national literature and art were parochial, alive only in the folk song, the folk tale, and mummery. Goethe's life and work were a magnificent search for the universal, transcending the political and social limitations of the Germanies. Some of Germany's and Italy's greatest poets, Goethe included, poured their creative energies into translations of the masterpieces of world literature. It is only after political unification had put an end to the age when Germany and Italy were "mere geographical expressions" and after the status of Great Power had been attained, that the literature and art of Germany and Italy, set in their respective *national* molds, addressed a national message to the universe and contested the popularity of the older "model" cultures, namely the French and the English. Today, to be forcefully Swedish or Swiss or Portuguese is culturally an interesting curiosum; it is of next to no importance as regards the development of Western culture.

Today, the more American a novel or play is felt to be by Europeans, the stronger is its influence upon its European audience. This is not mainly a matter of aesthetic quality or of the relevancy of a particular American problem to Europeans. What Americans think and say about themselves affects Europe. The American writer who despairs of American society, its materialism, its mechanization, and its inhospitality to creative originality despairs of Europe, for American society is the source of the power that keeps Europe alive.

An idea, a mere notion, is conveyed forcefully by the stronger to the weaker; even the best idea loses its vitality in its ascent from the weaker to the stronger. By the time it is assimilated by the stronger society it is either exhausted or has changed its meaning beyond recognition. If the thinker or artist of a small country as, for example, Kierkegaard, Kafka, and Freud, contribute a fundamental or compelling formulation, it is taken up by rich and mighty countries and handed back to the weaker country of origin in an interpretation that its creator might never have thought of. A transformation of this order is now taking place in the case of Goethe: American philosophers and writers invite the German people to contemplate the universalism and "Europeanism" of Goethe as a suitable German approach to the One World of characteristically American features. The European intellectual faces a paradox: the influence of American ideas is vital in the literal sense, for he views Europe's life as depending on what America thinks. Yet, he is not free to appropriate these ideas and transform them in his image, for they have the power to alter the social and economic structure within which he must live, while nothing that Europe thinks can alter the American social and economic structure whence they emanate.

It is here that we grasp the root of a tendency that is growing and ominous: the alienation of the American and European intellectual elites. This estrangement is the result, in part, of differences in the position occupied by these elites in the structure of their respective societies. In part it is due to the power relationships of these societies to each other. The American intellectual elite, during the heyday of the "businessman's civilization," stood on the periphery of American society. Protesting writers and conforming academics shared one distinction: political and social insignificance. In the halls of Congress, in the good clubs, and in the exclusive drawing rooms the American intellectual was either conspicuous by his absence or a prestige item of marginal importance, sponsored by the feminine rather than the masculine half of society. In Europe, the intellectual was as much at home in good society and the world of politics as in literary circles and Bohemia. If American senators and congressmen were businessmen or lawyers trained to corporate law and the intellectual was a rare exception, the European parliamentarian was more often than not a historian, a philosopher, a scientist, a journalist or—a poet. At this moment, there are among the premiers of the most important countries of Europe a professional historian-journalist, and two former university professors; the President of the French Chamber of Deputies is a celebrated historian and biographer, the Vice-president of the German Bundestag a sensitive translator of French poetry, the Foreign Minister of Italy a historian, and one of the leaders of the largest French opposition parties a celebrated novelist and poet. The rosters of English, Italian, and French parliaments list men and women of wide reputations in mathematics, medicine, journalism, art, and letters. By contrast, American legislative assemblies, not to speak of the President's cabinet, reveal a singular dearth of individuals drawn from fields other than business, law, and professional administration.

In America, the intellectual elite is seen to be divided against itself, not merely on the objective issues on which intellectual elites divide the world over but on the question as to what role it should play in American society. The American intellectual and the American writer, unlike their European confreres, do not belong to the same category. The American novelist or playwright, lusty, vigorous, and ruthless, is more often than not an indifferent writer. He says what he has to say and, not infrequently, disappears into mediocrity. He is not the polished craftsman that the European man of letters is; he does not, like André Gide, George Bernard Shaw, and Thomas Mann, supply a coherent and reflective commentary on culture, but bodies forth eruptively and lyrically a highly personal and isolated situation. It was the American imaginative writer who first developed fully the themes of loneliness, violence, and frustration which— another illustration of the phenomenon of convergence—resemble so closely the themes of contemporary existentialist literature in Europe. The American imaginative writer whose production did not command the attention of the "business-man's civilization," expressed the violence of man's solitary revolt against an impervious milieu and against himself. The violence and frustration of the "American" writers, Faulkner, Caldwell, Hemingway, appealed to the European intellectual who, surveying the ravages of World War II, felt similarly abandoned in a historical process which, so they believe, has closed the door to the future. The American writer and European intellectual start from opposite ends: the American rebels against a society that ignores him and is indifferent because of its very bustle and vitality; the European intellectual protests against the indifference of a society that is indifferent because it has no longer the strength to care about its descent into inanition. Both are isolated; but while the American rebels at his situation and transcends it imaginatively into the future, the European mourns the past and protests a future that he is helpless to fashion. The American writer and creative artist stands not only isolated from society but from his fellow intellectuals as well. Jean-Paul Sartre pointed out that, while in France writers and artists shaped social and political developments by their creations, in America one must be an academic specialist in order to deliver a message that exercises measurable influence upon society and politics.* A well-documented book on political economy, Sartre argued, or a punctilious case study on alcoholism or sexual habits, as, for example, the Kinsey Report, have a revolutionary impact on the educated public and, ultimately, through the mass media, upon American society as a whole. American novels and plays may borrow the topic of the academic specialist; they do not "originate" the problem. According to Sartre, no American play or novel ever exerted

* Jean-Paul Sartre, "Défense de la Culture Française par la Culture Européenne," *Politique Etrangère*, Vol. XIV, No. 3, June 1949, p. 236.

by itself and through itself a lasting and profound influence on American social and political development. This criticism is not wholly justified. Sinclair Lewis' *Main Street* and *Babbitt* preceded the Lynds' *Middletown* by some years. The first important investigation of the meat-packing industry was Upton Sinclair's *The Jungle*. And there are many other examples in the past that show Sartre's criticism to be unduly sweeping, although in contemporary America it is increasingly apposite. Conceding the obvious, namely that Sartre, the critic, views the American intellectual scene with a jaundiced eye, unrestrained by Sartre, the philosopher, and Sartre, the dramatist, his observation is apt in so far as it underscores a real and troubling phenomenon: the breakdown in American-European intellectual "communications."

The American academic intellectual may look to Europe for aesthetic satisfaction, cavil at the brutal power of his own native writers, and sample the excellence of European literature and art, though he despises the backwardness of European social and economic institutions. He tells Europe little that the European intellectual wants to know or believes he does not know already. Since his place in American culture is insecure, and since American society views him as an oddity, if not a nuisance, the samplings of his superior aestheticism are lost between the covers of the "small magazines" which no one in America reads except academic intellectuals. On the other hand, the American writer or playwright and his academic counterpart, the respected expert, represent professional specialization that in some respects transcends and in others falls short of the traditional prototype of the European intellectual: the man of letters. The American intellectual makes his living at one or the other of a number of highly specialized crafts, journalism, script writing, literary criticism, academic teaching, etc., and nearly always in the fixed employment of a large and powerful organization. The man of letters, i.e., the independent, free-lance writer or critic, is in

America a vanishing species, because the general trend toward specialization pushes everyone into a narrow groove and, also, because no one can afford to follow this career except with the backing of considerable private means.* In Europe, the man of letters still remains the arbiter of intellectual society and, in such countries as France and Italy, of politics as well—this despite the fact that economic conditions appear far less favorable than in the United States for earning a living in so marginal and so imprecise a trade. The European intellectual, in or out of the great academic institutions, is still a stubborn individualist. In Europe, collective journalism and collective research in the social sciences (and, to some extent, in the pure sciences) are still in their infancy and frowned upon as an American fad, the substitution of a company of well-kept trained seals for individual effort that, however halting, gropes for originality rather than smooth perfection. Indeed, the collective journalism of *Time,* the *New Yorker,* and even of the so-called quality magazines in which individual contributions are carefully packaged to meet "standards" is cut neatly to the intellectual stature of the New Middle Class for which there is as yet no equivalent in European society. Its literary style, clipped, restrained, highly polished yet easily accessible, tolerantly humorous, more angry-in-sorrow than angry, and dead pan with a fleeting smirk or twinkle when the facts of life intrude upon the glossy page, expresses the life style of the New Middle Class with its refinement of small, social differentiations and its emotional reticence. In Europe, the mass media of literature, i.e., "national" magazines, and most "national" newspapers, are vastly inferior to those of the United States. They are trashy, cheaply sensational and, but for such rare exceptions as, for example, the frankly "American" weekly, *Match,* of Paris, badly put together. But everywhere in Europe, the

* See C. Hartley Grattan, "The Trouble with Books Today," *Harper's,* Nov. 1951.

creative life of the intellectual elite is still locked in innumerable small periodicals, their literary style being neither clipped nor restrained. Their style tends to be, no matter what their political and aesthetical convictions, sovereignly anti-middle-brow.

From the American point of vantage, the European intellectual scene is littered by a vast output of uncertain quality and peopled by a host of odd individuals and cliques operating under highly eclectic labels or indulging in the perverse luxury of rejecting all labels. From the European point of view, the American intellectual scene appears as a vast expanse of gloss stretching all the way from the air-conditioned editorial offices of New York to the studios of Hollywood, and the output of America's higher institutions of learning as possessed of that same glossy finish which graces the mass media. Invidious comparisons stack up to this: to the American intellectual, the literary and scholarly product of Europe appears marred by dilettante and flighty generalizations and a sloppiness of execution which betrays lack of teamwork and shoddy technical equipment. To the European intellectual, his American colleagues appear as engaged in a massive, well-lubricated effort issuing in platitudinous irrelevancy or bone-dry pedantry.

The estrangement of the European and American intellectual elites, developing from differences in social status and differences of their respective societies as wholes, has been sharpened by the climactic experiences of Europe in the throes of tyranny and war and, finally, by awareness of fundamental changes in Europe's power situation. If in the United States the political consequences of the estrangement have thus far not been clearly understood, this is, at least partially, due to the fact that American society offers no ready analogy for the position of European intellectual elites in society and politics. If American politics are relatively impervious to the penetration of intellectualism, European politics are highly sensitive to intellectual directives. Existentialism, for example, is a philosophy and a literary and aesthetical school; it also happens to be, though its celebrated exponents do not appear upon the hustings, a political movement. That political movement is directed both against the United States and the Soviet Union. It is, for reasons that can be found in power political and ideological situations, most hostile to the United States.

Existentialism is only one, but perhaps the most typical philosophy of European neutralism. Its central thesis is that neither West nor East, neither the United States nor the Soviet Union can offer Europe a "future." The drawing power, exerted especially upon European youth, of existentialism lies in this political philosophy, rather than in its desperate metaphysics. Sartre expresses a sentiment that is accessible to all European intellectuals, especially those who have trysted with Communism and only reluctantly broken with it, when he writes:

> The political, economic, demographic and military hegemony of a country imposes a cultural relationship for which there is no reciprocity. I would like to examine how imported American values have affected French culture. I am certain that these elements, which are alive and meaningful in America, harm French culture. One may ask: why just American cultural elements and not those imported from Russia? I must reply that, since we must deal with two powerful states and their ideologies, Russian culture poses more complex problems, because its ideology meets us in the cultural elements of our own country . . . America does not know the pessimism [of Europe] that questions nature and social institutions. French rationalism is, fundamentally, pessimism . . . Reason is a struggle against a universal that escapes us everywhere and that we always seek to capture; reason is a

kind of trust in human freedom faced with a nearly hopeless situation. By contrast, American reason is technical, practical, and scientific. It is guided by the effectiveness of its results: it seeks to prove that the universe is rational or that, at least, it can be rationalized. American rationalism is, therefore, optimistic. We know the history of America and know that it warrants optimism. If that optimism, in more or less vulgarized versions, should inundate our culture and determine its future, then we will be led straight into positivism—just as the constructive rationalism of Russia would lead us to an optimistic faith in science and destroy our culture. Then there will be no more problems. Whether we examine American scientism or the faith in science that derives from vulgarized Marxism—in both cases we recognize truth as a given fact: one follows science as a locomotive follows the rails, and need no longer look out for risks, doubts, evil.*

Leaving aside the question as to whether Sartre stated fairly the case of "American optimism" and "scientism" and its kinship to Soviet "faith in science," the above quotation supplies the essence of a European philosophy which vitally concerns European politics and American policy toward Europe: integral neutralism.

Existentialism and its profane offspring, integral neutralism, are far from esoteric poses; they are true expressions of a European mood and expectation, common to millions who have never toyed with philosophy or semantics. The unfolding of the wonders of science, evoked by the powerful wand of American economic plenitude, left Europe both enviously agape and uncomfortable. The nightmare of scientific extermination in concentration camps and by conventional weapons in war now shades into the obsessive reality of poised atomic missiles. The technical achievements of tyranny ap-

* *Ibid.*

peared to elicit the even more efficient devices of mass destruction fashioned by democratic hands. To many Europeans, this
deadly dialectic of scientific progress appeared to warrant
their heretic fear of science.

It was possible, after World War I, to argue that democracy
had won. Today, in Europe, the concentration-camp smell
exudes from the labyrinthian corridors in which men, ostensibly free, line up for innumerable permits, blank forms,
ration books, and the compensations of "social security." The
destruction of democracy is, so it must seem to many Europeans, not simply a matter of evil tyrants enslaving good men,
but a creeping disease that rots even the fighter for freedom.
Even in the west of Europe, victorious or liberated, no one
is rash enough to argue that democracy has won or will win
of a surety. Everywhere the administrative apparatus has
become too big. The agencies of European co-operation, military and economic, so enthusiastically sponsored and financed
by the United States, are merely newer and larger behemoths
piled upon the leviathans of national bureaucracies. These
self-regenerating giants batten on society and sap local initiative and responsibility. America, the America that is represented by troops stationed in Europe and by countless
commissions administering economic and military aid, occupies city blocks of office buildings staffed by cohorts of civilian
and military officials. These issue instructions in an officialese
that blights a variety of languages. America has appeared to
Europe not in the homey guise of the town meeting but in
the shape of a highly rank-and-authority-conscious bureaucracy. That is what Europe sees, and the propaganda handouts
and the messages of American visiting professors in baggy
pants, eulogizing the vitality of grass-roots democracy in
America and its fair promise to all lands, are not entirely
convincing.

In Europe the stock of democracy never having been as
high as in America, has fallen to a new low among peoples

in general and, what is most alarming, even among those social strata that were traditionally associated with the democratic idea and still today adhere to it in theory. European society has become so bureaucratized and subject to extraneous and, therefore, uncontrollable forces that one no longer knows how to assess responsibilities. The result of this development has been the disappearance of those institutions to which Europe has always looked for the guarantee of political freedom: the small, self-governing bodies—what De Tocqueville called, "secondary powers." With them emasculated, the training schools for democratic decision and control disappear. It is in these institutions that European liberalism has always sought the protection against centralized power, be it monarch or mob rule, rather than in "pure" democracy. European liberals, such as De Tocqueville and John Stuart Mill, acknowledged that democracy can lead to the worst despotism unless it is limited by the principles and institutions which, taken as a whole, compose the liberal element of the state. There is some disagreement among European liberals today as to whether the "optimistic" assumptions of American democracy are or are not warranted *in the United States* and as to whether one should or should not discard the "pessimistic" assumptions about democracy *in Europe,* but there is virtual unanimous agreement that American democracy is not a practicable, even if a desirable model for Europe.

The integral neutralists have thus fastened upon two haunting themes of the European dilemma. The power of America nourishes Europe, yet Europe cannot digest the fare, prepared for a different society with its particularly robust constitution. Secondly, the situation of the individual in European society is absurd, if for no other reason than that European polity and its national fragmentations are absurd. The situation of each European country is as absurd as is, in the context of Sartre's analysis, that of France. What Sartre writes about the dangers to French culture faithfully reflects the prevailing mood of the Continent. In the present situation, these dilemmas are no longer specifically French or German or Italian or Belgian or Dutch but exactly the same dilemmas confront each country. Thus the philosophies and literatures of absurdity and frustration suddenly come to life in the concrete historical situation. The slogan "neither the United States nor Russia" expresses a perplexity that resembles uncannily that of the Byzantine people.

The Byzantines, buffeted between the threats of Islam and the encroachments of their Latin and Frankish allies—brethren though they were in Christendom—bethought themselves of their Greek heritage. For the affirmation of that Greek heritage staked a claim to cultural autonomy against the new world of semibarbarous Europe, successor to Rome's western power, as well as against militant Islam, successor to a long line of Asian tyrannies. Islam, by virtue of its kinship to monotheism, proselytized the masses of the outlying territories of the Byzantine Empire encountering little resistance. Islam became the state religion in what we now would call Islamic "satellite states." More important still, the masses of the Byzantine rump empire, before its fall to the armies of the Prophet, viewed the extreme monotheism of Islam as a heresy hardly more pernicious than the suspected polytheist leanings of the Latin Church. "Islam," to paraphrase Sartre's observation, "met Byzantium in Byzantium's own cultural elements."

The spiritual estrangement of Eastern and Western Christendom was climaxed by the military occupation of Byzantium by the armies of feudal Europe. They had come to defend Byzantium and the Holy Land against the infidel and they stayed to carve up Asia Minor and Palestine into Western fiefs. The decline of Byzantine power was brought home to the Byzantine people by the presence of their Western allies rather than by the peripheral pressure of their Asiatic foes. Had "neutralism" not been the popular mood of Byzantium, then the diplomacy of the emperors throughout the long period of the Crusades could not have remained as unswervingly noncommittal as history shows it to have been. The emperors welcomed, housed, and provisioned the Crusaders, since there is little else they could have done about their uninvited, but heavily armed, guests. They did not give military support to the Crusaders, and there is no record of Byzantine manhood flocking to the Crusaders' banners. There is, however, ample recorded evidence that the Byzantine populace ardently hoped that the Crusaders, their mission accomplished or not, would soon return home.

European neutralism is, ideologically speaking, nonpartisan. Its following is drawn from all parties. An individual's professed attitude toward Communism or democracy or fascism does not supply the clue to his stand on neutralism. Some socialists are neutralists, some are not; some Christian Democrats, Catholic as well as Protestant, have proclaimed themselves neutralists, others profess themselves ardent supporters of close United States-European co-operation, military as well as diplomatic. Among the partisans of a United Europe, some view European union as the prerequisite of effective European collaboration *with* the United States *against* the Soviet Union, others advocate European union as a means for securing Europe's independence *from both* the United States and the Soviet Union. Thus the issue of neutralism cuts across party alignments and ideological lines. The question must, therefore, be asked: is not *neutralism the real European issue* and are the political and social ideologies Europeans profess still meaningful *except within the context of the issue of neutralism?*

Merely to ask this question is to acknowledge the crisis in American-European relationships and the cultural rift that the alienation of the Western community has opened. The ancient nations of Europe have awakened to the stark fact of their impotence. The national culture of each *as national culture* is indefensible. Each faces the same choice. No nation can maintain its present social structure except by accepting the economic aid of the United States and thus its cultural writ. The other alternative is to accept the ideology of the class struggle and hence, ultimately the writ of the Soviet Union. If western European nations would seek to maintain the *status quo,* eschewing basic reforms and relying on the economic help of the United States, they would neither preserve the integrity of their national culture nor, for that matter, transform their society in the image of the United States.* For the unique classlessness of the latter and its plenitude of discreetly differentiated status satisfactions lie beyond the technological and economic capabilities of any European country. Moreover, does the unique "classlessness" of the United States, i.e., the new middle-class society, furnish a pattern which Europe can apply to the problem posed by the decomposition of traditional society and the alienation of the masses? In other words, does America still offer Europe an "exit"? Or has the dialogue come to an end and does Europe no longer look to America for an answer? The rise of a centralized civilian and military bureaucracy in America and of a tight hierarchy of rank, swallowing up the traditional liberal society, is a phenomenon in which Europe sees her past, not her future. The "otherdirected man," disciplined agnostic and emotionally inhibited, has presented himself to Europe in many guises. As Europe knew him, he never wore the badge of freedom. The type, however educationally perfectible, functionally efficient, or socially adjustable, is not the one that Western

---

* For a characteristic voice of European defeatism regarding the ability to transform the national society, *except with the help of America* and as the result of developments *in* America, see the statement of a French socialist: *"C'est outre-Atlantique que se livreront désormais les batailles décisives pour la grande transformation sociale, et ce sont elles qui décideront le rhythme des réalisations socialistes en Europe."* Lucien Laurat, *Décadence de l'Europe,* Paris, Spartacus, 1949; p. 83.

culture has acclaimed from the Renaissance to this day as the
incarnation of its human ideal.

Up until the beginning of this century, Europe saw her
future in the United States and searched that future for her
own destiny. Beginning with the 1930's, there took place a
curious reversal in the European attitude toward the United
States. The rise of centralized power and the shrinkage of
local autonomies appeared to trace a path that Europe herself
had trodden. Raoul de Roussy de Sales noted at the beginning
cf World War II, that all that appeared to separate American from European developments was a time lag of about
twenty years.* If that were true, then the case for European
neutralism would be irrefutable and the issue of Western
culture would no longer be in doubt. Then America and
Europe would be doomed to irreparable estrangement and
the fate of Western culture would be sealed. Is there another
alternative? Is the disintegration of Western culture inevitable?

World history is not a succession of happy endings. It is not
proposed here to invent solutions to problems for which there
are no solutions now and for which there were none in the
past. The destiny of man and of peoples is death. The forces
that assail the wholeness of the West are so massive, rise from
sources in the past so remote from this generation, and are
as yet so imperfectly understood, that they cannot be turned
back by a mere flexing of economic, military, and ideological
muscles. They can surely not be defeated by the incantation
of optimistic formulas such as the inevitable victory of
democracy over totalitarianism, of high-standard-of-living
peoples over low-standard-of-living peoples, of a high-class
technology over a somewhat lower-class technology, and of
good over evil men.

We have reviewed the broad trends that have led the

* *The Making of Tomorrow*, New York, Reynal & Hitchcock, 1942.

United States and Europe to a critical point of their mutual relationship. Let us turn to the present situation and examine the concrete political and economic problems that confront us here and now. They are, like all concrete political and economic problems, short range in nature. Not all of these problems appear directly relevant to the broad issue of the survival of Western culture. Some, measured by so broad an issue, seem petty and prosaic. But they are the problems of the present, and the seemingly least important move may engender incalculable and fateful consequences for the future. The past is done. We are the one and only link that joins history to history-to-be-made. Our every gesture affects mankind's destiny—about which we know nothing. The pebble we tread loose may seed the avalanche.

VI
Western Dialectic

WESTERN DIALECTIC

HENRI PIRENNE, the great historian, said: "For a society, there are only two forms of existence: expansion or contraction, and from this all else follows." * In its primitive form, expansion is spatial. However, there is another and more beneficient form of expansion than mere territorial aggrandizement, namely the enlargement of the economic space, of the market of goods and of individual skills. This kind of "expansionism" is nourished by new techniques and new needs and, in turn, gives rise to still newer techniques and newer needs. The spiral feeds upon itself. In an expanding society, the achievements of one man's success widen the range of the opportunities of which others can avail themselves. By contrast, a society must be called a contracting one when its economic space, the market, contracts and hence the opportunities of which men can avail themselves diminish. Needless to say, this condition is not determined by the size of "living space" in the sense in which Hitler manipulated that term. Venice and Holland, each based within a tiny territory, were expanding societies whereas Spain, controlling vast territorial possessions, suffered all the discomforts of contraction long before the Spanish Empire began to shrink geographically. Contraction produces the same effect as the passage of a body of men through a narrowing defile: men push one another and step on one another's feet and the advance of the group as a whole becomes slow and painful.

Europe, as we noted, passed into the stage of contraction

* See Bertrand de Jouvenel, *L'Amérique en Europe*, Paris, Plon, 1948; p. 288.

well before World War I. At the end of World War II, long-standing regressive tendencies turned into a veritable rout, economically as well as geographically. The liquidation of the British and Dutch empires in Asia signalled the end of geographical expansion. The crisis of European trade after World War II, the "raw material shortage," and its twin, the "dollar shortage," marked dramatically the end of economic expansion. Expansion and contraction are not purely objective processes. Business opportunities, for example, are not given as mere statistical facts; they are realized by the ingenuity and spirit of enterprise of the businessman and by the attitude—the receptivity—of the community as a whole. Expansion and contraction are, therefore, to a large measure subjective and political phenomena.

Opportunities diminish wherever psychological and political attitudes harden into set, static patterns and men are impeded by others or by their own state of mind in their efforts to make a place for themselves in society rather than to occupy places that have been made by others. As soon as there is no longer a job for everybody the quest for jobs, specified and limited, turns into a bitter struggle. In that struggle, ideological pretexts can easily be found. Whatever these slogans may be, the real issue in a contracting society, be it a national society or a group of nations, is how to remove somebody from the place which he occupies—the "place in the sun" or merely the place on the workbench—and to occupy that place oneself, because there are no vacant places or because one thinks that there are none. This is the present state of mind of Europe.

The ills of Europe are at least as much psychological as they are objective. Despite the Asian losses, Western Europe after World War II still controlled vast territories overseas, some of which were blessed with frontiers as "open" as those beckoning the pioneers of nineteenth-century America. Despite the wear and tear of war, the technological equipment of Western Europe as a whole is now about as plentiful and as efficient as it was before 1939. American economic aid, in the brief span of about three years, not only closed the gap created by wartime destruction and depreciation but actually helped to raise industrial productivity appreciably above the prewar level. The miracle of European industrial recovery shines forth from virtually every major statistical column: steel, automobiles, railroad equipment, highway construction, building trade and electrical appliances, and, most important of all, employment.*

Yet the political and psychological recuperation of Europe did not keep step with economic recovery. It is this circumstance that is at the root of American doubts about Europe. Europe appears to absorb American economic energies and thrive physically, so to speak, upon the transfusion, yet fails to respond to the treatment by tapping her own sources of political and moral strength. The general impression is thus one of physical recovery and psychological apathy. Europe has not yet regained faith in herself: the staying power of the French and Italian Communist parties despite national economic recovery and vigorous counterpropaganda; the resurgence of fascist parties in Germany and Italy; the indecisive verdict of the British elections of 1951; the mounting evidence pointing to the failure of European unification; the growing strength of nationalism and "neutralism" in Germany; and the growth of nationalist and anti-American sentiment in virtually all countries and among all social strata of Western Europe; all these symptoms concur in the syndrome of contraction psychosis.

For Americans, the issues are plainly drawn: democracy versus Communism, Western freedom against Soviet imperialism. Yet the gaze of Europe seems to stray from these major

---

* See O.E.E.C., *European Recovery Programme, Third Report of the O.E.E.C.*, Paris, 1951, and United Nations Economic Commission for Europe, *European Steel Trends in the Setting of the World Market*, Geneva, Feb., 1951.

issues and to focus instead upon ancient national and class grievances. Viewed from America, the leaky ship of Europe drifts between rocks and whirlpools while the crew engages in a dispute over living quarters and the duration of the watch in the engine room. In American eyes, European particularism, its long and absorbing history notwithstanding, and the ideological stickiness of European internal politics are well nigh incomprehensible. And incomprehensible they would be, were it not for the perplexities of men obsessed by the sense of floating upon a vessel that is not only leaky but also shrinking all the time. Is it not more important to make sure that one keeps one's own place aboard than tend to the course and seaworthiness of the vessel? This parable fits uncannily the behavior of the west-European states who are agreed, in principle, upon the mutual benefits of a customs union, yet dare not surrender their economic sovereignty; who are agreed, in principle, upon the mutual benefits of measures that would co-ordinate their military and diplomatic policies and raise Western Europe to a power status equal to that of the Soviet Empire, yet dare not surrender their political sovereignty; who are agreed, in principle, that man is the measure of society but are not prepared to affront corporate interests, especially their own respective bureaucracies, that interpose themselves between man and opportunity. Europe has geographical and economic room, and room to spare, for all its peoples. Technological developments, especially the latest ones in the realm of nuclear physics and biochemistry, have opened new vistas of unlimited opportunities. When one takes into account the vast combined resources of Europe, in raw materials, technological equipment, and skills, then the current European system of national restrictions upon trade, immigration, and employment promulgated under a host of quasi-patriotic and ideological headings, and the anguished and chronic reliance of a dozen European treasuries upon American financial help, cannot be ascribed to objective conditions. The peoples of Western Europe appear sunk in solipsist contemplation of their own weakness. It is America, calling for concerted effort, that speaks with Europe's true voice.

American policy in Europe, from Marshall Plan to Atlantic Pact, was European and Western in the highest sense. It sought to reverse the paralyzing process of economic contraction and stimulate latent forces of expansion—"help Europe to help herself"—and to furnish military security against aggression from the East. In exchange for this service, the United States insisted upon but one condition: Western Europe was to unite economically and politically. Though this condition was never explicitly set forth as the *quid pro quo* of American contributions—the technical arrangements of European co-operation under the Marshall Plan were limited to the administration of the Plan itself and did not infringe upon the monetary and tariff policies of member states— it was pressed upon Western Europe by countless policy statements and the full weight of American public opinion. The Marshall Plan was America's down payment on Europe's second liberation—and on the promise of its beneficiaries to arrive at an *understanding among themselves*. The United States did not impose its will, though it could undoubtedly have done so in the phase of Europe's extreme dependence on American economic aid. However, the United States steadfastly backed and enthusiastically greeted every step toward European unification—the Brussels Treaty, the Benelux and Franco-Italian customs union negotiations, the European currency clearing agreement, the Council of Europe, the Schuman Plan, and the Pleven proposals for a European army.

The bare bones of American policy in Europe were to persuade the European peoples to do what they should have done a long time ago, for their own good, and what had to be done to save them from barbarian conquest—and themselves. Why has this policy borne such meager fruits? Why is Europe not nearer *political* unification, and perhaps even further away from it, than she was at the beginning of the Marshall Plan? The pathology of the European mind accounts for part of the failure. However, Europe bears only half of the responsibility. The other half rests upon the shoulders of America—or, more justly, the failure of Europe is the joint failure of the principal members of Western culture. Europe is the victim of the West's pursuit of political absolutes, and the United States, throughout the history of its European interventions, has raised the delusion of extreme solutions to the rank of a tutelary myth, presiding over the fortunes of Europe.

The First World War was probably avoidable. It could most certainly have been concluded without the destruction of the European balance of power and thus of European order. Yet the uncompromising application of the principle of national self-determination destroyed the Austro-Hungarian Empire—the Empire "that should have been invented had it not existed"—and created a zone of fragmentation and weakness which could not but arouse the cupidity of the strong. The First World War started over conflicts in the Balkans. The writ of Versailles extended the Balkans into the center of Europe. That extension was not only a political but a moral one.

The fanatical parochialism and political corruption of the tragicomic Balkans crept into the hearts of Europe's oldest nations, once the most stable and the most mundane. That an American President, issuing from the land that succeeded most brilliantly in forging unity from ethnic diversity, and which would be instantly plunged into chaos were "ethnic justice" applied to itself, should have championed dogmatically, in Europe, the principle of "ethnic justice," was the first and ominous manifestation of the new "myth of absolutes." The peace treaties bowed to it in respects other than the right of all nations to flag and frontier; the war-guilt clause and unilateral disarmament were extreme solutions unprecedented in the history of post-Renaissance Europe.

Absolutes call forth absolute reactions. Hitler was the creature of the extreme nationalism that was the true victor in World War I. Both Hitler's Germany and Stalin's Russia were the true beneficiaries of the dogma of national self-determination that delivered into their hands the weak and jealous nation-states of Eastern Europe. It was, therefore, less easy to avoid the Second World War than it was to avoid the first.

If the outbreak of the first was an accident, the outbreak of the second came close to being a necessity in the style of Marxian dialectic. The leading characters of the fighting tyrannies, Germany and Russia, and the intense ideologization of the conflict contributed greatly to the intransigence and extremism of war and peace aims. It is the tragedy of World War II that the one power, the United States, that had suffered least in the fighting and was the least susceptible to ideological infections and could, therefore, have remained emotionally most detached, not only failed to cast its weight upon the side of moderation but proclaimed absolutes, that in their extremity surpassed the World War I dogmas of national self-determination and universal democracy. The Unconditional Surrender formula; the scheme for the de-industrialization of Germany; the ideological purge and re-education programs—to mention only the most outstanding absolutes proclaimed as United States war aims—made certain that reconciliation with defeated opponents would be difficult and that gaping power-political vacuums would attract another hurricane. The 180-degree reversal of official propaganda from the line pursued at the occasion of Russia's attack upon Finland; the incredible panegyrics on Soviet "democracy"; the bland assumption of loyal Soviet co-operation in the postwar order; the disclosure, by installments, of the secret Yalta agreements, particularly those concerning China;

the easy camaraderie and bountiful matériel proffered to Communist partisans in France, Italy, and Yugoslavia; the encouragement given, from France to China, to coalition governments with Communist participation; and finally the manifest indifference toward past Soviet policies and Marxian-Leninist-Stalinist ideology shown, and frequently shown ostentatiously, by the highest American officials—these policies and gestures appeared to commit the United States, in the eyes of its own peoples and of the rest of the world, unreservedly to a course of collaboration with the Soviet Union. The reversal of United States policy, beginning in 1947, found the peoples of Europe psychologically ill prepared, to say the least. Moreover, America's new message was garbled by notes —such as the statements of Henry Wallace and other figures prominent in politics, arts, and sciences—that seemed to belong to the older, Sovietophile melody.

Again, a 180-degree shift was completed. Within three years, a crescendo of official statements revealed the Soviet Union as an imperialist slave state bent upon aggression (which it had always been), and Communism as a world-wide conspiracy. Western Germany had, under the supervision of the Western Allies, adopted a draft constitution which expressly stipulated perpetual nonbelligerency.* The re-education of the German people, vigorously pushed by the United States occupation authorities, had been aimed foremost at purging the German soul of its predilection for martial pomp and lethal instruments. In 1950, the United States Government called for West German contingents in the coalition army of the West and, in 1951, made the admission of Western Germany to full sovereign status virtually contingent upon remilitarization. These radical reversals of high policy and the attendant about face of the mass media, operated

* Article 29b, Basic (Draft) Law. In the Constitution ratified by the *Bundestag*, the categoric "no-war" pledge is watered down: Germany is to abstain from "aggressive war" (Article 26, 1).

with surprising facility, are new milestones on the curvey road of "extreme solutions" pursued by the West. The relative ease with which these "extreme solutions" are first accepted and then rejected reflects an extreme fluidity of values. Instability of public mood and lapse of collective memory are symptoms consistent with the pathology which we called Alienation of the Social Mind. The "extreme solutions," issuing from World War I and henceforth contradicting each other with ever-increasing dogmatic vehemence, are the projections of Social Alienation into world politics. There is no longer a middle ground: the choice is between brutish, bloodstained Germans and fair champions of democracy; between Stalin the Benevolent of Teheran and Yalta and Stalin the Kremlin Despot; between "co-operation" with the Soviet Union and the dismemberment of the Soviet Union according to—of all things!—the principle of national self-determination; between Morgenthau's ruralized Germany and the State Department's resurgent Germany, military and industrial depot of Europe. That these antithetical notions are shuffled at will and upon short notice and with the enthusiastic approval of expert and public opinion does not bespeak collective mental equilibrium.*

* William R. Matthews, the editor and publisher of the *Arizona Daily Star*, Tucson, Arizona, in a letter to the *New York Times* (October 31, 1951), brilliantly and mercilessly took to task the advocates of extreme solutions for "settling" the Russian Question. The letter was particularly addressed to the October 1951 issue of *Collier's*, which was devoted entirely to the Russian Question. Though Matthews did not say so explicitly, it should be noted that some of the advocates of a "war to end wars" against Russia were, during World War II, the most vocal advocates of a Carthaginian Peace for Germany and of cozy Soviet-American co-operation. Excerpts of Matthews' "appeal to moderation" read as follows: "After fighting two world wars within a generation to defend democracy and freedom, with no result other than to see those ideals recede throughout the world, we shall be blind if we do not understand that a third such war, fought for equally unlimited and unattainable objectives, will end in one of the great catastrophes of history....

...Definite themes of thought take form in democracies to create patterns of political conduct. When the articulate publicists of a democracy, by seizing

The irresistible dialectic of "extreme solutions" transformed the European continent (within thirty-five years) into a vast Balkans in which a Russian faction faces an American counterfaction.* This is, in the last analysis, the accomplishment by which Western statecraft in the first half of the twentieth century must be judged. That the United States, as its people felt the hot breath of the conflict which was called the Cold War, came to accept that "accomplishment," the division of Europe into two factions generaled from abroad, as the *ultima ratio* of their foreign policy, reduced the alternative solutions to one: "Who is not for us, is against us, there can be no middle solutions, and whosoever proposes one is, by definition, a partisan of the Soviet Union." If the validity of this conception were not challenged by the concrete conditions of Europe, the fact that it is the exact reciprocal to the fundamental concept of Communism should render it suspect. This concept renounces not only the plenitude of choices that is life, but also the noblest vision of Western culture: variety and autonomy in unity. That vision was

on a national ideal, involving great sentimental appeal, join together in championing a political program, it usually goes into effect.... When what they write and talk about becomes a united theme of agreement action follows....

Much the same pattern was followed in the First and Second World Wars. Freedom and democracy were used to justify our conduct in both instances.... As George Kennan so cleverly explains in his new book, *American Diplomacy, 1900-1950:* "In the name of such principles you fight a war to an end...."

Almost sardonically *Collier's* chose Robert Sherwood, one of the chief publicists of the war theme of the Second World War embodied in the "Four Freedoms," to explain in clear, simple prose how we will become involved next May, 1952, in what becomes the great—and of course glorious—war of "liberation."... The war will last until 1956, but by 1960 we shall still be exercising paternal authority of the great Soviet Union while we help reconstruct what we have destroyed.

The account takes on shocking and frightening proportions because twenty additional articulate publicists join in acclaim of our military prowess and the sanctity of our ideals to assure us that this time we shall be politically as well as militarily, victorious....

Surely it is not out of place to call for moderation...."

* See Raymond Aron, *Le grand schisme,* Paris, 1948.

honored by the Marshall Plan, designed not merely to restore
the individual national economies of Europe but to create
economic unity and thus an "integrated" Europe, that is, in
the dictionary meaning of the word, a complete Europe.
Implicit in that vision was the independence of Europe. The
radical shift of American policy to the mobilization of the
military potential of individual European nations, that of
Germany included, threatened, in the eyes of those who had
most readily accepted the principle of European unification,
both the unity and independence of Europe.

Beginning with the war in Korea, the United States asked
Europe, a Europe that was not united and that had solved
neither the problems of Germany and Spain nor that of its
relationship to the British Commonwealth, to raise armies
and convert to war its separate national economies. It is true
that more insistently than ever American voices admonished
Europe to unite now—and to do politically what the United
States could have compelled Europe to do in 1948 had it not
then limited itself, an unwitting "Marxian," to *economic*
intervention. But the concrete emphasis of American policy
had shifted towards the achievement of an immediate result:
creation of a coalition army.

It is not proposed to examine here the premise that must
be assumed as underlying American policy, namely Soviet
intention to conquer Europe by force of arms—though this
premise may be based on a spectacular misreading of Soviet
strategy together with its philosophical and political rationality. However, it should be clear that—no matter whether
one does or does not accept that premise—a strong Europe is
not one composed of satellites. There is no such thing as
"pure" military security, and the reduction of the European
"problem," as viewed by American foreign policy, to one of
military co-ordination of European resources, empties European integration of the moral content that alone can rouse the
peoples of Europe from their lethargy. "Neutralism" covers a

variety of European attitudes and groups: the Communists in Germany and Western Europe intent upon poisoning the wells of the Western community; nationalists jealous of American power; mellow, introspective culture snobs deploring the very American "gadgets" that they use for their greater comfort; religious and profane quietists—*"quieta non movere"*; profiteers in the black market; and philosophers in black pessimism. There is, however, a "neutralism" that is European in the literal sense and requires no other apology than the profession of European freedom. The argument of this "neutralism" can be summed up as follows:

Only a united Europe is an independent Europe; only an independent Europe is free to join with the United States in the defense of the West; and only a community of free men freely joined together will evoke the moral forces that *can* defend it and make it *worth* defending. Only the common effort toward the political, economic, and cultural independence of Europe can arouse the idealism that will give content to the strivings of this generation. As that effort succeeds in assembling, slowly and laboriously to be sure, the odd and colorful pieces into the larger design of a new community, so the energies of 280 million Western Europeans will fuse into a common will. That common will—the European conscience—is the precondition of Europe's resistance against the tyranny of the East. The hands that hold the weapons will be no stronger than that will. Americans, this argument continues, should see their own best interest in such a united and independent Europe, for the independence of the latter is the prerequisite of co-operation. A Europe that is mere object cannot co-operate. European independence might give rise to American-European disagreements on important issues. An independent Europe would have its own opinions and the power to make them respected—even by the United States. There are things Europe knows that America does not know —Marxism, for example, which is imperfectly understood by

Europeans but not understood at all by most Americans. Honest disagreement would not be damaging to a co-operation that, however divergent the views on the means might be, is based on a profound agreement as to ends. For the United States, the creation of such a united, independent, and powerful Europe involves a calculated risk. For the task can be accomplished only slowly and, in the beginning, cannot be accomplished at all by draining Europe's energies into military preparedness. The military effort cannot exceed a moderate contribution that must not disturb the precarious economic balance restored by the Marshall Plan. The relatively low standard of living of the European masses, the antagonism of the classes, the spiritual unreadiness of the peoples for war, and the dangerous problematics of Germany argue for a system of self-defense that will remain sketchy until the principal problem has been solved: the creation of political unity and new, supranational loyalties. The road is long and arduous. No step can be omitted. One must advance patiently. There is no short cut to safety. Will Western Europe be safer from atomic destruction than it is now when it has hastily assembled thirty or forty or fifty divisions, recruited from its unwilling youth Or would it not serve Europe better were her energies brought to bear first upon the task of organizing her community? Perhaps it is late—perhaps too late—to seek to reverse the fatal trend of the last thirty-five years. The arms of the clock now point to a few minutes before the zero hour. However, "to throw the clock into the face of destiny is no solution." *

It is easy to pick out the flaws in this argument advanced by the Positive Neutralists who seek the junction point of Atlantic co-operation by the route of European unity. First, Americans may ask, will there be time, and, secondly, what is there in Western Europe's recent record that offers encour-

* Eugen Kogon and Walter Dirks, "Europa und die Amerikaner," *Frankfurter Hefte*, Vol. 6, No. 2, February, 1951.

agement as regards the willingness of governments and peoples to honor the ideal of unity by their acts? To which questions the Positive Neutralist replies by posing a counter-question: has America not swung from extreme solution to extreme solution, from urgency to urgency, and has America herself not immensely complicated the task of European unification by the pursuit of absolutes—to be realized instantaneously and to be abandoned at a moment's notice? The dialogue can be spun out indefinitely. It is the dialogue of frustration, a dirge of lost opportunities. Beneath its ephemeral arguments is hidden the West's oldest topic: the twin threat to Western culture of schism and Asiatic tyranny.

Is not the Positive Neutralist speaking with the voice of the West when he avers that society must be made whole, that Europe must save her soul, and that only thus can the challenge of power be met? Is America not speaking with the voice of the West no less authentically when she calls upon Europe to raise her standards against Eastern tyranny and for the arbitrament of power that will secure a world order under law? That Europe and America each hold part of the truth and that the sands are running out because the parts are not being joined together, this is the tragedy of Western estrangement. Europe is bent over the ills of her society and dares not face the challenge of power; America girds herself to do battle for the West and locks the treasure of the great ideals—the devotions of her prime and hopes of Europe—into the vault of her power.

Reduced to the dialectic of American-European relationships the alternatives of Western history are these: an American empire or the Great Republic of the West composed of the United States and a federated Europe affiliated with the British Commonwealth as a separate, yet closely associated member. Though these alternatives allow for considerable latitude as regards organizational detail, they are fixed and mutually exclusive.

Perhaps a historian a hundred years from now will reconstruct the design so haphazardly woven as follows: The United States won its independence by the grace of Franco-British maritime rivalry and the support of France. It imposed its sway over the American continent because Europe, torn by the Napoleonic Wars, was too weak and too divided to defend her trans-Atlantic positions. The United States entered late into two world wars, which she had fomented, and manipulated her Allies and the balance of power so effectively that she emerged from these wars as the strongest power. The Ottoman Empire, Austria-Hungary, and Germany were destroyed. France and Britain were so weakened that they could not preserve the integrity of their respective empires and defend themselves unaided against Russia. The United States assumed their protection and nothing remained to be done but to crush the Soviet Union, reorganize the globe, and establish the reign of the American peace. We know that such a "reconstruction" of history would be a fraud, that the United States had no part in the events leading up to the first world war, would have gladly abstained altogether from participating in both world wars, and assumed her share in the subsequent settlements in the reluctant spirit of an innocent bystander burdened with responsibilities he had not sought. Yet the thesis of a Machiavellian United States, cunningly maneuvering toward the goal of world power across the prostrate bodies of friends and foes, does satisfy at least the human craving for a chain of causation forged by the human will. As it is, it may well be the chain of causation that fetters the will. The United States may come to read into its past the commands of Providence and assume the mantle of Empire ordained by Destiny. Never in history has the temptation been greater—and circumstances may not leave the United States any other choice but to travel the road of Rome. The analogy is striking.

The incorporation of the Greek city-states into the Roman

Empire proceeded at a leisurely pace. More than fifty years elapsed between the first landing of the Roman legions on Greek soil and the destruction of recalcitrant Corinth in 146 B.C., upon which latter event Greece assumed the official status of a Roman province. The Romans, let us recall, were called to Greece by the Greeks themselves, menaced by Macedonian aggression. The Greeks hailed the Romans as liberators. The Roman expeditionary army promptly re-embarked as soon as the Macedonians had been defeated—only to be invited back when the Greeks feared renewed aggression from the north and east and failed to compose their internal quarrels.

The Romans returned reluctantly. For all their admiration of Greek culture, they deemed the Greeks a quarrelsome and decadent people. Moreover, the rich lands of Africa and Asia Minor were far more attractive objectives of Roman expansionism than the eroded hills of Greece. Yet the Romans dutifully came to the aid of the cradle of their civilization, compelled the Greeks to do what they should have done for their own good—and stayed. The Greeks resigned themselves to accepting the evenhanded protectorate of Rome rather than living under their interesting but costly anarchy. The Romans, incidentally, supported conservative against leftist factions in Greek internal affairs.

Americans landed in Europe in order to liberate it from Hitler's Macedonians and departed, except for token forces in Germany and Austria, as soon as the job of liberation had been done. They abandoned, to the surprise of many Europeans, their hard-won bases in Europe and Africa. They were called back by the Europeans themselves to protect Europe against the threats of renewed aggression from the East and its own anarchy.

No people ever created an empire by mere conquest. An empire, to endure, must fill a universal need, the need for an organizing principle acceptable to rulers and ruled alike.

It has been said that the British inherited an empire in a fit of absentmindedness. However inadequate may be this explanation, it does underscore an important characteristic of the British people at the apogee of their power. They built an empire; they did not develop an imperialist ideology.

If the issue of our times is who will create the universal empire, the United States or Russia, then the odds are overwhelmingly on the side of the United States. In the military sphere both the United States and Soviet Russia can boast of great advantages. The United States has an enormous sea and air potential; the Soviets have innumerable divisions. But at the political and economic level the advantages lie overwhelmingly with the United States. The Russian system of planned economy is designed to exploit every dependent country, not to absorb that country into a going system. By contrast, the United States champions ardently the cause of world-wide free trade and pours her wealth into grants and loans to other nations. The United States still is dedicated to the principle of "self-determination"—within broad limits. By adopting the shoddy methods of autarchy, Russia has betrayed her own sense of inferiority. Since she cannot satisfy the demands of other countries economically, she must seek to dominate them politically. The failure of Soviet economic policy is one cause of Yugoslavia's secession. The fact is that while it is fashionable propaganda to talk about Soviet imperialism, the Soviets do not know how to create an empire.

Soviet economic policy is the tacit acknowledgment of Soviet inability to compete with the United States industrially. Measured by the brilliant performance of the United States in the field of industrial technology and applied science, the exertions of the Soviet Union are as unimpressive as Soviet claims to "firsts" are comic. The Soviet's avowed aim is to attain the industrial efficiency of the United States. It is unlikely that the Soviet Union can improve upon its position as a poor second in the race. For the United States has become the intellectual and scientific capital of the world, whereas the Soviet Union is reduced to kidnaping confused French scientists and stray German technicians.

There is hardly a European scientist who will not accept, eagerly and proudly, the invitation extended him by this or that American university, foundation, or learned society to report on his work. The urbanity of American culture and the handsome homage America pays to scientists and artists of all countries, including all kinds of professional and ideological oddities, are in the great tradition of the famed empires of history. American imperialism does not employ mere military force or political coercion. Its weapons are tact, time, generosity, and—an anti-imperialist philosophy. Santayana wrote: "To dominate the world co-operation is better than policy, and empiricism safer than inspiration." * If the American people wish it, the *Imperium Mundi* is theirs.

This, the first alternative, is the alternative of the concentration of power. It is inscribed in the trends rising at the beginning of this century: the falling away, one by one, of the great powers of the nineteenth century, the destruction of the balance of power, and the bipolarization of world politics. As for Europe, the power of the United States would fill the vacuum created by the collapse of an equilibrium that can no longer be maintained by political and social forces generated *within Europe*. The order of Europe would then be enforced by American power; Europe would be a province of the American imperium—just as Greece was a province of the Roman Empire, its most honored province, to be sure. The United States would be a kind master, kinder than Europe's own anarchy, and America would always honor in Europe the guardian of its memories—just as Rome, but for the occasional chastisement of such recalcitrants as frivolous Corinth, dealt kindly with her Grecian wards. As for Russia, the choice would be between defeat and surrender. For the

* George Santayana, *Character and Opinion in the United States*, N. Y. Scribner, 1920; p. 200.

world, its one best hope would be a protracted military stale-
mate and then the acceptance by Russia of the American
writ in order to avoid annihilation, for only thus would mankind be spared a third world war. As for America, trends that
are as yet contested by the forces of traditional society would
gain irresistible momentum. They would transform American society in the image of the great empires of history.

Up until our own times, the dominant features of American society were, we noted, at variance with those of Europe,
especially Continental Europe. American society was not
military-bureaucratic society, its educational precepts were
not those of disciplined uniformity to which, by necessity, a
military-bureaucratic state must bend its youth. The American political ideal was not the centralization of government
which permits the rapid mobilization of national power and
the smooth administration of a universal empire. Centralized
government is hierarchical government. The diffusion of
political power—its checks and balances—must by necessity
yield to the requirements of instant readiness for coping with
military emergencies. The path of history is littered with
charters of liberty torn up by emergencies, alleged or real,
arising out of war and threats of war. Two world wars for
freedom resulted in the recession of the limits of individual
freedom everywhere, the Western democracies included, and
gains here and there in economic and social security have
been rendered spurious by the exactions of national security.
In America, to belittle the effects of permanent emergencies
upon free institutions bespeaks either lack of historical insight or a naïve trust in the nation's sagacity at maintaining
self-restraint in the face of political and economic pressures
that have, in other times and at other places, crushed freedom
and that are, in America, as yet not perfectly understood or
even fully noted. These pressures impinge upon the remotest
or seemingly unimportant areas of social existence as well as
upon the great issues of national politics. That they have

altered, though mostly by subtle indirection rather than bare-faced official authority, the tenor of American life can be gleaned simply by placing side by side the pages of, let us say, the *New York Times* of any day in 1952 and in 1922.

The dilemma of Western freedom is simple: how to preserve liberty at home in the fight for liberty abroad? The tensions of the moment, arising out of the world political situation and sharpened by the overarching threats of atomic and bacteriological annihilation, appear to narrow the choice of alternatives to one: the maximum development of American power so that America can impose her will and order upon mankind at the brink of the abyss. Is there time for solutions that will at best yield results slowly, which are untried, and require a self-restraint in the face of vast opportunities and vast risks unprecedented in the annals of history?

The second alternative is the reintegration of the Western community. It subordinates considerations of political and military strategy to considerations that are essentially moral: the reconciliation of Western society and the restoration of that balance of power which has always been the guarantee of Western freedom. In the context of this alternative, the idea of European unification and the idea of social justice are closely interwoven. Only a European society that is united in common devotion can resist Soviet tyranny. The first step is to reconcile the masses with traditional society. If that step is not taken, the "defense of Western culture" is a hollow slogan. Peoples will not fight for an order that failed so flagrantly to harness the spiritual and material forces of the times to the work, welfare and security of the community. Weapons, even the most modern weapons, cannot defend European nations against the apathy, if not hostility, of great masses of their own people and thus against the most potent ally of the Soviet Union. The might of the Soviet Union is but the shadow cast by the evil genius of the West: the Alienation of the Social Mind. Once the mind of Western society is healed, the Soviet Union stands revealed as a clumsy and backward despotism, as clumsy and backward as all the Asian despotisms which the West has met and defeated.

The world political task is to find the common ground upon which the leading powers of Europe, Great Britain and France, can join hands in the making of European unity. Both Great Britain and France are world powers. Unlike the smaller powers of Western Europe, their national interests and commitments are not confined to Europe, and their attitudes toward other nations, especially toward each other and the United States, are highly sensitive to forces impinging upon their non-European positions. The nucleus of West European solidarity is the West European continent under the leadership of France. For the European consciousness has its roots in the Continent and the call for union does not strike the same responsive chord in the hearts of Englishmen. The ambivalence of Britain and the partition of Europe are the horns of the dilemma impaling the Council of Strasbourg. The problems of Germany and of the readjustment of European trade are inextricably enmeshed with the problem of British participation in European unification. The world political task has to begin with the realization that each of these problems is, within its present context, insoluble.

Great Britain will not surrender her political sovereignty to a supranational authority. Britain's official argument is that joining a European union would mean severing her ties with the Commonwealth and her "special connections" with the United States. Neither the United States nor the Dominions are as conscious of these special relationships as is Britain. Reluctance to tie Britain to the political and social systems of the Continent, unwillingness to meet the economic competition of Continental industries—especially those of Germany— and attachment to the proud and pragmatic diplomacy of the balance of power, are the weightiest reasons shaping British policy. Though these, the most plausible reasons, may not stand up against even weightier strategic and economic reasons, they must be expected to determine British policy for the foreseeable future. The problem is not how rationally to argue Britain into European unification. The task is to create European working institutions that will furnish arguments in the shape of concrete strategic and economic advantages so great as to impel Britain to shelve her objections lest she be immured in the status of an isolated second-rate power. The British problem is not susceptible to theoretical solutions but only to solutions which can be demonstrated empirically. For this is the method of the man of action.

A united Europe halved along the middle is a contradiction in terms. The liberation of Eastern Europe can be achieved now only by turning all of Europe into a battlefield and unleashing civil war. The primary objective of Soviet policy in Europe after World War II was the consolidation of Communist power in Eastern Europe. It was not the conquest of Western Europe. The latter task was left in part to the Communist parties of Western Europe, in part to time and opportunity, namely, the time necessary for the integration of Eastern Europe into the Soviet system and the opportunity arising from capitalist crisis and the consequent enfeeblement of American power. The hold of the Soviets on Eastern Europe cannot now be broken by war and civil war except at the price of the destruction of Eastern *and* Western Europe.

The liberation of Eastern Europe begins with resurgence of West European power. The most powerful threat to Russia's control of Eastern Europe is a dynamic, that is, a free and productive, society in Western Europe. For such a society would exert an irresistible pull upon the peoples of Eastern Europe who have sought for centuries their markets and their cultural and political inspiration in the West and not in Russia. The Western Powers and Russia must ultimately arrive at a negotiated settlement concerning Eastern Europe. The partition of Germany is an intolerable condition; the presence of Russian armies in the heart of Europe is a standing provocation to war. The only alternative to a negotiated settlement is war. How such a war would be fought and what kind of fruits the victor would reap, these questions cannot be answered here. In all likelihood these questions cannot be answered anywhere. The score for the prescience of expert opinion, seeking, before World War II, to gauge the nature of things to come, was remarkably low. However, the logic of the European situation here and now makes it relatively easy to project the condition that must underlie a peaceful settlement with Russia. Such a settlement cannot be made and, once made, cannot be enforced except by creating a united Western Europe strong enough to persuade Russia that she has nothing to gain by war except a Pyrrhic victory.

The military problem is not a military problem at all but a political one. The effectiveness of a European army is dependent on political unity and not the other way around. Without a European spirit and without soldiers who know why and for what they fight, the European army will be the replica of the flabby coalition armies defeated by Napoleon and Hitler. It will not be a *European* army. Once this is recognized the objectives and limits of American power in Europe become instantly apparent. The unity and power of Europe cannot be wrought by the fitful pressures of military emergencies. The House of Europe must be built by patient labors and an unerring sense of process.

The economic task is to remove the barriers that nationalism has raised against the law of least costs through specialization, and thus to create the widest market for industrial manufactures. Only a unified Europe can give full scope to the development of mass production. There is no technical reason why 280 million people cannot create an internal market as rich as that of the United States. At present the average standard of living of Europe's industrial nations, lower by from one-third to four-fifths than that of the United States, reflects the surcharge of high tariffs, insufficiency of domestic buying power, and monopolist restrictions.

The social task is to build the industrial community; to make meaningful and fulfilling the worker's relationship to his work, to his fellow workers, and to the community as a whole; and to restore social mobility. It is upon this task that American and European thoughts converge. The "communalists" are not of one mind as to how the city shall be built, how tall shall be its buildings and how broad its gardens, and where shall lie the boundaries of work and leisure. But across the generations, Frédéric Le Play and Lewis Mumford, Patrick Geddes and Adriano Olivetti, Wilhelm Roepke and Georges Friedmann, Stewart Chase and Elton Mayo, Frenchmen, Englishmen, Italians, Germans, and Americans, non-Marxian and Christian Socialists, conservative entrepreneurs and undogmatic technicians are joined by the bonds of a common recognition: the measure of the machine, as that of all achievements of Western culture, must be man, his freedom, and his faith, lest man and *civitas humana* be destroyed by the machine.

The political task is to recast institutions that no longer suffice to order the economic and social forces of industrial society and leave an ever-widening margin between the formal operations of representative government and the concrete issues of politics. The plant, the trade union, and trade and professional associations are units of political government. In each, it is political power that is at stake though the ostensible reason of their existence is the pursuit of economic interest. So immense have become the political stakes of economic conflict that plant, trade union, and trade association must be recognized for what they are in fact: political bodies. Lest the gap between representative government and the realities of power dangerously widen, leaving a constitutional no man's land, these political bodies must be endowed with the privileges, and made to accept the responsibilities of, representative government. It is precisely by this broadening of the concept of the "political" that the autonomy of economic and professional interests is assured and the power of the state is curbed by corresponding categories of self-government. For the power of the state, in America and Europe, has fed avidly upon that constitutional no man's land left unguarded by responsible and represented citizens.* The political task is to add new pages to the Rights of Man so that these rights retain their force and meaning in industrial society. The political task is to loosen the grip of central power by diffusing power among the largest possible number of efficient units of self-government. The number of *efficient* units would probably be much larger than the now existing units of political (and economic) administration, for the increasing bulk of centralized "management," national, municipal, and business, tends to exceed the optimum size of *efficient* administration.† The political task is one of "building down" rather than vertical integration, of restoring the flexibility of the joints rather than adding muscle, of opposing articulate form to the growth of shapeless gigantism.

The philosophical and ethical task is to establish the relation between fact and value, between reality and truth. The

---

* See Alfred De Grazia's discussion of "pluralism" in his *Public and Republic*, New York, Knopf, 1951; p. 225 *passim*. The argument is as apposite for Europe as it is for the United States.

† See the amendment to the Foreign Aid Law of 1951, proposed by Senator William Benton and adopted by the U. S. Senate, stipulating that American assistance to Europe should be used to "discourage the cartel and monopolistic practices prevailing in European business which result in restricting production ... and encourage where suitable the development and strengthening of free labor union movements in Europe." Though Senator Benton's amendment was criticized on the Senate floor as meddling in European affairs, it represents "meddling" in the best American tradition and a resumption of the historical American-European "dialogue." This is one European question to which the United States *has* an answer which it has earnestly sought to spell out in its own practices. Senator Benton's amendment is, however, incomplete. It should have stipulated that a state-directed economy, i.e., the cartels and monopolies controlled by European governments, should, too, be "discouraged."

rupture of traditional society was "exposed" by the philosophies and psychologies that interpreted the instincts and the unconscious as the real motor of human attitudes and actions. Whatever Nietzsche and Freud knew or thought of Marx, they adopted the same technique of analysis to their theories as Marx had used in historical materialism. For Marx emphasized that human consciousness is distorted and corrupt and deceives itself. The concept of "rationalization" in psychoanalysis corresponds exactly to what Marx and Engels call the "ideological superstructure" and "false consciousness." Marx pointed out that, driven by their class interests, men not only commit isolated mistakes and mystifications but that their whole thinking is false, and that they cannot judge except in accordance with preconceptions determined by the facts of their economic and social conditions. His philosophy of history rests upon the postulate that in a society rent by class interests, rational thought is impossible. Marx's theory was the expression of a society that had lost its belief in itself, and that was driven by its awareness of "the dialectic of everything that comes to pass" and by the antithetical nature of being and consciousness. The technique of unmasking thought and the psychology of exposure, though Marx may be said to have fathered the idea, were "in the air" of the nineteenth century, and Nietzsche and Freud were the intellectual products of the general malaise of bourgeois society rather than of historical materialism. The idea that the self-determination of the mind is a fiction, common to these thinkers and expounded by legions of disciples, brought forth the two major and paradoxical trends which converged in the crisis of our times: first the break with reason consummated politically in the mass ideologies of irrationalism (Lenin and Hitler), and aesthetically in modern art with its denial, or rather violation, of reality; * and secondly, the enthronement

* Arnold Hauser, *The Social History of Art*, New York, Knopf, 1951, pp. 930-31.

of scientific thought as the ultimate authority of human affairs, the notion that human society could be not only analyzed but also ordered scientifically. The belief that society had lost in itself was thus transferred to science. As theory, pure science is concerned with the reduction of diversity to identity. As a practice, scientific research proceeds by simplification. These habits of scientific theory and practice were, to a certain extent, carried over into politics. Wherever a centralized authority undertakes to make plans for an entire society, it is compelled to follow the example of the scientific worker, namely, by arbitrarily simplifying the problem to make it manageable. The procedure of reducing individual peculiarities to a simple norm is justified in the name of science which simplifies complex reality in order to make it comprehensible in general laws. The scientific planner in politics thus views an organized and regimented society whose members exhibit a minimum of deviations from the norm as more scientific and "efficient" than a society of independent and self-governing individuals.*

The havoc which these two notions, irrationalism and scientism, have wrought in the spirit and—through the influence they exerted over political thought—in the body politic of Europe came into the full view of this generation as they contemplated the ruin of cities and institutions. It is not surprising that the search for European unity is paralleled by a search for philosophical "integration," for the wholeness of life, of being and consciousness, of truth and reality.† The search starts from the premise that the scientific picture of the world is inadequate for the simple reason that science

* See Aldous Huxley, *Science, Liberty and Peace*, New York, Harper, 1946; p. 35.

† See attempts at unitary philosophies by Albert Schweitzer in his *Kultur und Ethik*, Munich, Beck, 1925; and *The Decay and Restoration of Society*, London, Black, 1947; and by Lancelot Law Whyte in his *The Next Development in Man*, London, Cresset, 1944 and in his important essay, "Scientific Thought in the Coming Decades," *Horizon*, July, 1944.

does not even profess to deal with experience as a whole, and that however mighty are the daemonic forces—instincts, unconscious, and the ambiguity of all earthy things—that assail the mind, man cannot abdicate the responsibility for his acts to the blind workings of scientific "laws," physiological or psychological or economic—lest he cease to be Man.

The path of the second alternative along which Western society could move toward reconciliation with itself would be closed with considerable finality were Western Europe to transform herself into an arsenal and the forward base of American power. For, in Europe, the spiritual and physical resources for the simultaneous creation of the Good Society *and* a society readied for total war are no longer sufficient. For the latter cannot be organized except by a rigid centralization and regimentation. The idea of economic expansion, as the material condition of individual well-being and thus the subsidence of class antagonism, is incompatible with a regimented austerity which will supply the economic means for the building of a powerful military machine. A united Europe will possess the military power to insure its security and to share with the United States the burden of Western defense the world over. But the ramparts of military power must be raised upon moral and political foundations that are yet to be laid.

These two alternatives, on the one hand the American Empire and its European auxiliaries, and on the other, the West composed of autonomous powers, America, the British Commonwealth, and Europe, have been sketched here uncompromisingly because they involve a fundamental choice of policies and world views. They have been sketched perhaps too uncompromisingly, for approximations are obviously possible on a score of issues. Indeed, the United States, Britain, and Western Europe can be said to "belong" to the Atlantic Community. The common origins and outlook of the peoples of the Atlantic littorals form the basis of the theory of Atlantic Union which has gained an enthusiastic following on both sides of the Atlantic and found respectful hearing in influential political circles. If this proposal for Atlantic Union means the creation of a political structure that will accommodate under one roof all the Western peoples *and* that will allow ample headway for regional interests on the basis of representative institutions, then Atlantic Union is but the political fulfillment of the dream of the Western City. Undoubtedly, the proposal is so meant by its leading exponents. In that form, however, it would not alter substantially the problematics of Western Europe nor relieve the governments and peoples of the Union from making the choice between the two alternative solutions which we have propounded.

It is not certain that the choice still rests with the West and, specifically, with the United States. If World War III is a foregone conclusion because the Soviets have willed it so and if the creation of a military power in Europe *this side* of the limit of tolerance of Europe's social structure will not deter Russian aggression, then alternative II goes up in the smoke of historic might-have-beens and the fate of Europe and of Western culture is sealed. The intense preoccupation with "integration" is itself a danger signal, the red flag on the road into the abyss of dissolution. Perhaps that road is too precipitate and nothing men can now do within a few years or months can halt the momentum of a descent that began a hundred years ago. But as long as the Western schism is not swept into an even deeper rift, opening up under the feet of all mankind, the West is not released from the burden of responsibility. The last page of history is blank; the West must seek to write its own decision. If it does not, other hands will certainly relieve it of the trouble and close the book upon the chapter of Western estrangement.

INDEX